D0437733

WINSTON CHURCHILL
REPORTING

Winston Churchill

Winston
CHURCHILL

REPORTING

Adventures of a
Young War Correspondent

SIMON
READ

DA CAPO PRESS
A Member of the Perseus Books Group

Designed by Cynthia Young
Set in 11.75 point Adobe Garamond Pro by the Perseus Books Group

Cataloging-in-Publication data for this book is available
from the Library of Congress.
ISBN: 978-0-306-82381-7 (hardcopy)
ISBN: 978-0-306-82382-4 (e-book)

Published by Da Capo Press
A Member of the Perseus Books Group
www.dacapopress.com

Da Capo Press books are available at special discounts for bulk purchases
in the U.S. by corporations, institutions, and other organizations.
For more information, please contact the Special Markets Department at the
Perseus Books Group,
2300 Chestnut Street, Suite 200, Philadelphia, PA 19103,
or call (800) 810-4145, ext. 5000, or e-mail special.markets@perseusbooks.com.

10 9 8 7 6 5 4 3 2 1

This one's for Katie, Spencer, and Cameron,

with much love.

To my sons,

I will say the moral of this story is clear:

Don't give up.

Contents

Maps

Author's Note

I can hear the question now: "Why another book about Winston Churchill?" Because Churchill, complex and multifaceted as he was, offers so many angles from which we can explore his life and career. Books about Churchill generally focus on his role as Great Britain's iconic war leader or cover his life in its entirety. The latter tend to paint in broad brushstrokes, if only because there's so much ground to cover. In recent years, however, a number of books have been published focusing on a single aspect of Churchill's long and varied life, whether it be his career as an author (Peter Clarke's *Mr. Churchill's Profession*), his early political life (*Young Titan* by Michael Sheldon), or even his culinary tastes (Cita Stelzer's *Dinner with Churchill*), to name a few.

But the defining image of Churchill is that of unconquerable warlord: the bulldog scowl, the ever-present cigar, the "V" for victory salute, and a legacy of soaring oratory that continues to stir emotions. When most of us think of Churchill, we think of him as the icon immortalized by history—but what forces shaped him into the man he became? He was, after all, sixty-five years old when he ascended to No. 10 Downing Street, with a life behind him not short on accomplishment.

Various Churchill biographers will undoubtedly give various answers. As this book attests, I think his most formative years were those he spent as a war correspondent, between 1895 and 1900. He mastered his command of the language writing articles and books, and experienced the heroics and horrors of combat that forever shaped his complex views of war. And it is war for which Churchill will always be remembered. As a side note, it was during this period that he developed a fondness for whisky and discovered the pleasures of a well-made cigar.

As a former newspaper reporter, I've always been fascinated by Churchill the journalist. The volume in your hands gave me a chance to dive deep into one of the most exciting chapters of an already eventful life—and one that has not yet been the sole topic of a book.

That said, I don't consider this a biography or a work of history—although it contains elements of both. It is, instead, a true tale of adventure featuring Winston Churchill in the starring role. When writing the book, I described it to friends as "Winston Churchill as Indiana Jones." As clichéd as it sounds, I hope you have as much fun reading it as I did writing it.

Cheers.
Simon Read
June 2015

Outside or inside, I will not return
Till my attempt so much be glorified
As to my ample hope was promised
Before I drew this gallant head of war,
And cull'd these fiery spirits from the world,
To outlook conquest and to win renown
Even in the jaws of danger and of death.

— SHAKESPEARE
KING JOHN ACT V, SCENE 2.

History Calling

Winston Churchill pondered the blank sheet of paper, his pen poised, ready to spill his thoughts. He would be blunt; nothing else seemed appropriate. Times of war necessitated hard truths—and this one would no doubt land heavily. A small island, a mere speck on the map, was presently the focal point of a desperate struggle, upon which rested the fate of a fading imperial power. He knew the message he needed to convey, but dipped his pen once more into the ink, debating the best way to start. He began with something easy and scribbled the date at the top of the page: October 4, 1895. The island in question was Cuba, currently rebelling against its Spanish master. Churchill wished to see the war for himself—but first he had to break the news to his mother.

A twenty-year-old subaltern (junior officer) of cavalry in the 4th Queen's Own Hussars, he longed for action. There was certainly none to be had in Hounslow, the borough in West London where the Hussars were barracked. Furthermore, judging from the daily newspapers, all seemed quiet across Great Britain's empire, which encompassed nearly a quarter of the planet. There were occasional skirmishes one might expect when presiding over so much of the world's population, but large-scale campaigns were now a rarity. Not since the Crimean

War, fought from 1853 to 1856 against the Russian Empire, had British soldiers borne arms in a major European conflict. This was good news for most, but peace was not conducive to young Churchill's longing for adventure.

In the course of their daily duties, Churchill and another Hussar subaltern—Reginald Barnes—had discussed the quiet state of global affairs. Both knew if they wished to see action, they would have to search for it. Consulting maps and reading the news, it did not take them long to settle on Cuba. While the British Empire thrived, the same could not be said for Spain's crumbling global dominion. More than 200,000 Spanish troops were on the island, attempting to crush an insurrection by a native populace tired of Madrid's heavy-handed ways. Cuba, with its abundance of fertile soil, was a dominant force in the sugar market. Its cigars were a much sought-after commodity in Europe and America, and its mountains were ripe for the mining of gold and silver. It was no wonder the Spanish—who had nicknamed the island "The Pearl of the Antilles"—sought to maintain control of one of their last colonial possessions.

The two young subalterns pondered the matter at length on the parade ground and over meals in the mess before it was settled: they would venture to Cuba for their first taste of war. Churchill, having been given his rank by Queen Victoria eight months earlier, on February 12, 1895, was eager to experience the thrill of combat. He had ideas about how impressively he might perform in the maelstrom of battle, and wanted to prove himself right. Imbued with the sense of invincibility that is the domain of many young men, he imagined the thrill of bullets missing him by inches, the air reeking of gun smoke, and the searing knowledge that any given minute might be his last.

Cuba would be a dress rehearsal of sorts—one performed with strangers and not his fellow Hussars—to ensure his mettle held under the strain of enemy fire. Perhaps more importantly, Churchill realized that if he wished to follow in his father's footsteps and pursue a political career, he would first have to make a name for himself—and what better way than by impressive performance in conflict?

His lofty ambition, however, was curtailed by the frustrating reality of youth: he lacked the financial means to get to Cuba on his own and so could do nothing without his mother's permission—and pocket-book. He turned back to his letter; knowing full well that Lady Randolph Churchill was no pushover, he decided he would tell her what he planned to do, rather than ask. "My dearest Mamma," he wrote. "I daresay you will find the contents of this letter somewhat startling. The fact is that I have decided to go with a great friend of mine—one of the subalterns in the regiment—to America and the W. Indies."

As he sealed the envelope, he could only imagine her reaction.

CHAPTER 1

In a Hurry

Winston Churchill's enthusiasm for soldiering dated back to his childhood. Perhaps symbolic of someone who spent his life in a hurry, he was reportedly born two months premature, on November 30, 1874, at Blenheim Palace in Oxfordshire. The ancestral home of the Marlboroughs, Blenheim remains an ostentatious monument to the military legacy of John Churchill, the 1st Duke of Marlborough, who defeated the French in the early eighteenth century and subsequently received the estate from a grateful nation. Winston's parents, Lord and Lady Randolph, were visiting Blenheim while workers prepared their fashionable London home at 48 Charles Street, Mayfair, for the baby's expected January arrival. While out one afternoon with a hunting party, the pregnant Jennie Churchill suffered a fall; this, followed by a bumpy carriage ride several days later, forced Winston's early debut. The child arrived at 1:30 in the morning after eight hours of labor. If the opinion of everyone present was to be believed, Randolph Churchill wrote his mother-in-law, the baby was "wonderfully pretty." All things considered, this was one of the kindest things he ever said about this son.

As parents Lord and Lady Randolph left much to be desired. Jennie Churchill, née Jerome, was a dark-haired American beauty and daughter of New York City financier Leonard Jerome, who had been "part proprietor" of the *New York Times* in the paper's early days. After spending her adolescence in Paris, where she attended finishing school, she met her future husband at a yachting regatta in August 1873. They married the following April at the British embassy in Paris. She was twenty; he was twenty-five. A £50,000 dowry (roughly £3 million today) from Jennie's father got the couple off to a good start, but a shared passion for London high society guaranteed a constant strain on their bank account. A similar affliction would hound Winston for much of his life.

While Jennie established herself as one of London's premiere hostesses and tousled the sheets with an impressive number of lovers, Randolph set his sights on high political office. He held the Conservative seat for Woodstock, "the local parliamentary constituency for Blenheim," which he won in the February 1874 general election. He believed he was destined for greatness despite his mercurial temper and vicious tongue. These initially did not impede his political ascent. Under Prime Minister Lord Salisbury, he would serve—if only for a short time—as leader of the House of Commons and chancellor of the exchequer.

With politics and jewel-studded social gatherings being their primary concerns, the Churchills had little time for parenting—even after their second son, Jack, arrived in 1880. Winston nevertheless adored his parents. His mother's radiance and beauty struck him as something celestial, though like a star, she remained distant. He would later describe his father as the defining influence of his early years, but it's difficult to see how this could have been true. Lord Randolph was a cold and distant figure who thought little of his son's prospects and never spared a disparaging word.

Responsibility for Jack and Winston's well-being fell to the family nanny, Elizabeth Everest, hired shortly after Winston's birth. It was in her that Winston confided and found solace in the turmoil of youth. The boys affectionately called her "Woom" or "Womany." She loved and cared for them as if they were her own and in doing so blunted the emotional neglect of their parents. Mrs. Everest hailed from Kent, "the garden of England," and regaled both boys with stories of her home county's beauty, to the point that Winston wished to live there himself. This he would accomplish in November 1922 with the purchase of his beloved Chartwell Manor. Perhaps more important, it was Mrs. Everest who introduced Winston "to the delights of toy soldiers and the romantic world of soldiering." Throughout his life, whether in writing, painting, or politics, Churchill never approached anything half-heartedly—and his toy soldiering proved no exception. His nursery floor became a battlefield, where his army of fifteen hundred lead soldiers refought history's greatest battles. In his first surviving letter, written when he was seven and while spending Christmas at Blenheim, he thanks his parents for "the beautiful . . . Soldiers and Flags and Castle."

His military campaigns, waged in miniature, stimulated a powerful and imaginative mind. The nursery could only contain him for so long. From his earliest days Churchill abhorred mental and physical inaction, prompting him to seek out the "manly pursuits of riding, swimming, shooting, fort-building and catapulting vegetables at passersby." His adventurous spirit nearly got him killed when he was eighteen. Playing war games with his brother and cousin on his aunt's estate, he jumped from a bridge to evade capture, intending to land in one of the nearby fir trees and slide down the trunk to make a daring escape. His aim proved less than accurate, and he plummeted twenty-nine feet to the ground. The resulting impact fractured his thigh and left him bed-ridden for three months.

Devouring books, which he did when not tempting death, seemed more conducive to his physical well-being. He loved tales of adventure and history, seeing in Britain's glorious past high standards by which he would always judge the present. His mind held tight to facts and verse and never let them go. As a thirteen-year-old he could recite, without mistakes, twelve hundred lines of Macaulay's "Lays of Ancient Rome," including these:

> *Then out spake brave Horatius,*
> *The Captain of the Gate:*

"To every man upon this earth
Death cometh soon or late.
And how can man die better
Than facing fearful odds,
For the ashes of his fathers,
And the temples of his gods?"

Despite this mental acuity, he did not distinguish himself as a student. "He has no ambition," wrote the headmaster at St. George's School in Ascot, where Winston's parents sent him at the age of seven. He loathed the place and counted the days until the end of each term. Likewise, the headmaster seemed to think little of his student. "Is a constant trouble to everybody and is always in some scrape or another," notes one report. "He cannot be trusted to behave himself anywhere." Winston nevertheless gained admittance to Harrow, the prestigious public school in northwest London, in April 1888. Founded in 1572 under a royal charter from Elizabeth I, the school counts among its alumni seven British prime ministers, including Churchill, Stanley Baldwin, and Robert Peel, founder of the modern-day police force and the Conservative Party. Although six generations of Churchills had previously attended Eton, Lord Randolph believed the air at Harrow might prove beneficial to his son, who was prone to illness.

Winston quickly dazzled school officials with a blaze of complacency. "His forgetfulness, carelessness, unpunctuality, and irregularity in every way, have really been so serious, that I write to ask you, when he is at home to speak very gravely to him on the subject," the assistant headmaster wrote Jennie three months after the young man's arrival. "[He] is a remarkable boy in many ways, and it would be a thousand pities if such good abilities were made useless by habitual negligence." The young Churchill did not take kindly to the school's emphasis on Greek, mathematics, and Latin, preferring history and English—the latter being a particular strength.

In a prologue to his career as a war correspondent, Churchill demonstrated a flair for writing about military matters in an essay he penned for his English class. A work of fiction, it detailed the British Army's engagement on a Russian battlefield, twenty-five years in the future—July 6, 1914. At Harrow he set out on his military career, joining the Harrow Rifle Corps, which took part in mock battles with competing schools. Here, Churchill displayed a knack for riding and shooting. He also impressed his instructors with his fencing and took a school prize for his swordsmanship. But such skills did not readily impress his father, who foresaw a bleak future for his son. Lord Randolph had initially hoped Winston would attend Oxford and study law. Churchill's performance at Harrow, however, marred by "defiant behavior, fights and disrespect that sometimes led to his own humiliation," did not bode well for a bright academic future. And so, two years after Churchill entered Harrow, Lord Randolph steered his son into the school's army class.

Ironically, Lord Randolph's decision to push Winston into the military partially evolved from a rare moment of father-son bonding. On an occasion when Winston was home during a school break, Lord Randolph paid a visit to his son's playroom and was impressed to see Winston's fifteen hundred toy soldiers arranged on the floor, ready for battle. The level of planning and detail in the colorful formations struck a chord with the father, yet playing with toy soldiers does not mean one is automatically suited for the military. It took Churchill three attempts to pass the entrance exams for the Royal Military College at Sandhurst—but pass he eventually did, in June 1893. Although his scores were insufficient to "qualify him for a future commission in the infantry," they allowed him to enter as a cavalry cadet.

Churchill believed this was a fresh start and sent his father a triumphant letter, but Randolph saw little reason to celebrate. The cavalry, with its horses, riding equipment, and other necessities, cost £200 a year. Winston's failure to make the infantry, in Randolph's mind, only confirmed that his son was destined for failure. To his own mother, Lord Randolph complained that Winston possessed no discernible talent for hard work. The boy seemed to drift through life doing the absolute bare minimum to get by, all the while maintaining a very high opinion of himself. As far as Randolph could tell, his son was sorely lacking in common sense and intelligence.

He did not spare Winston the sting of his disappointment. Putting ink to paper, he penned a blistering denouncement and accused his son of living an insignificant life of wasted opportunities. Members of the cavalry were third-rate soldiers, in Lord Randolph's eyes—meaning, by extension, that Winston was also. In fact, he could hardly understand the young man's sense of accomplishment. Never, Randolph lamented, had he received an exemplary report from any of Winston's teachers. His son's school career was defined by embarrassment and ineptitude. His rage building on the page, Randolph told Winston not to write to him anymore regarding his schooling. What was the point? The boy was incapable of achieving anything worthwhile. He concluded the vicious diatribe with a broadside: "I am certain that if you cannot prevent yourself from leading the idle useless unprofitable life you have had during your schooldays and later months, you will become a mere social wastrel, one of the hundreds of the public school failures, and you will degenerate into a shabby, unhappy & futile existence."

Winston replied with a contrite letter and apologized for being a disappointment. He promised to work hard and make his father proud. At the time Randolph wrote his scathing denouncement, he was frustrated by his own failures. In December 1886, a mere five months after becoming chancellor of the exchequer, he resigned in a fit of pique over a budget disagreement. He wanted to reduce military spending, but the lord of the admiralty and secretary of state for war put up stubborn resistance. Hoping to get his way, Randolph penned a letter to Lord Salisbury, in which he stated, "I do not want to be wrangling and quarreling in the Cabinet, and therefore must request to be allowed to give up my office and retire from the Government." Believing the prime minister would side with his chancellor, Randolph was thrown for a loop when the old man called his bluff and took the missive as a letter of resignation. The move forever left Randolph a pariah among the elite and effectively killed his career. His health did not help matters. A protracted illness—which some accounts claim was syphilis—slowly ate away at him, rendering him physically haggard and mentally frail.

His decline had been evident for some time. In July 1886, when Lord Salisbury had informed Queen Victoria that Randolph would be chancellor of the exchequer, the queen had voiced her misgivings in a journal entry: "He is so mad and odd and also has bad health." Randolph's brutal letter to Winston may have been a by-product of his malady.

Unlike Harrow, Sandhurst seemed to suit Churchill. Tactics and fortification took precedence over Greek and Latin. Learning to dig trenches and construct breastworks, developing an understanding of topography and its impact on battle, and mastering the fine art of setting and detonating explosives enthralled Churchill. He enjoyed learning about recent conflicts, including the American Civil War. On occasion he received invitations to dine with officers at the Staff College, where they taught the mechanics of war, from the makeup of divisions and armies to the maintaining of lines of communication and supply. Such topics were of immense interest to Churchill, but his yearning to learn was tempered by a sadness that knowledge of this kind would only be put to use in mock battles. He cast his mind back a hundred years and imagined marching off to war against Napoleon. How thrilling an experience that must have been! But in the current days of peace and prosperity, progress, and enlightenment, it seemed almost a shame large-scale conflict between great nations was forever a thing of the past.

As at Harrow, Churchill excelled at riding and further improved his skills by taking courses at Knightsbridge Barracks with the Royal Horse Guards. Riding in the saddle was for him one of life's greatest pleasures. He possessed a romantic view of the risks involved, believing that a fatal fall from a horse was a most noble way to die.

Churchill's path appeared to be set. In December 1894 he graduated from Sandhurst with honors, having placed "eighth in a class of 150 cadets." The accomplishment came too late to mean anything to his father. That summer Jennie and Randolph—accompanied by a doctor— had embarked on a trip around the world, hoping it might restore Randolph's health. His condition only deteriorated and prompted the couple to return home early. They were back in London on Christmas Eve, with Randolph in a painful state of rapid decline. He died on

January 24, 1895, aged forty-five. Mourning the loss of his father, but with his ambitions stoked and eager to live up to the man's expectations, Churchill received his commission and joined the 4th Hussars the following month.

The regiment, dating back to 1685, had fought against Napoleon and seen action in the first Anglo-Afghan War and other far-flung corners of the empire. As the 4th Light Dragoons, it took part in the legendary "Charge of the Light Brigade" at the Battle of Balaclava. Despite its gloried history, life for the regiment was quiet at the time Churchill joined it. He spent his days taking part in riding drills and pondering ways to finance the high lifestyle the regiment expected of its officers. His annual pay was £150—some £500 shy of what he needed to furnish his own quarters and purchase the required "one charger, three polo ponies, and two hunter-jumpers."

His quest for funds was coupled with his desire for action. Perhaps one could support the other. The army divided the year into seven months of summer training and five months of winter leave, with officers "receiving a solid block of two and a half months' uninterrupted repose." Churchill's acquisition of polo ponies and the other accoutrements of an officer's life had depleted what meager funds he had. What he sought during his first winter leave was an exploit that would pad his bank account. And so he wished to go to Cuba to report on the conflict there.

His mother was taken aback—as Churchill expected—by her son's decision, especially as it would fall on her to finance the whole thing. Churchill guessed the adventure would cost no more than £90, travel expenses included. He did not yet possess his brilliant command of the English language—at least where Jennie was concerned. She was not entirely thrilled at the prospect of her son heading off to a war zone. She reminded him that he and Jack were the only two people she had left in this world and chided him for his presumption: rather than telling her he was going, it would have been more appropriate to ask if he could. Certainly it would have been polite to consult her the moment the idea dawned on him. Nevertheless, she understood his desire for new adventures and promised not to interfere with his "little plans." It was just as well, for Churchill would have gone with or without his mother's blessing. Maybe, she wrote, "experience of life will in time teach you that tact is a very essential ingredient in all things." Churchill and tact would, for the most part, always remain strangers.

A few strings had to be pulled. Young British officers did not normally hop on boats and head to war zones of their choosing—but not all young officers were Churchills. The name brought with it connections that could make things happen. The British ambassador to Madrid, Sir Henry Drummond Wolff, was—as luck would have it—a family friend. Wolff and Lord Randolph had in 1883 founded the Primrose League, an organization tasked with spreading Conservative principles throughout Great Britain. Wolff arranged for the Spanish minister of war to write a letter of introduction on Churchill's behalf to Marshal Martinez Campos, the captain-general of the Spanish Army in Cuba. Appealing to the commander in chief of the British Army, Churchill received the blessing of the War Office. The head of the Intelligence Department at the War Office provided maps and other useful information on Cuba. By October 21, 1895, everything was set, but the matter of compensation remained unresolved. Churchill hoped to make a profit from his expedition.

He contacted Thomas Heath Joyce, editor of the *Daily Graphic* in London, and secured a contract for five dispatches from the front lines for twenty-five guineas. This would be Churchill's first foray into journalism and introduce him to a lifelong love. Writing to his mother, he promised to bring home a vast quantity of fine Havana cigars, which he hoped to store in her London cellar at 35 Great Cumberland Place.

On November 2 Churchill and his fellow Hussar subaltern, Reginald Barnes, set sail on the Cunard Royal Mail steamship *Etruria*. It was Churchill's first transatlantic voyage, at the end of which awaited adventure and—he hoped—his first steps into the public limelight.

CHAPTER 2

Havana via New York

C alm seas carried the ship that first day, but they turned violent thereafter. Waves pummeled the *Etruria* and soaked the deck. This nearly proved too much for Churchill and Barnes, but though they came close, they were spared the indignity of joining other passengers bent over the railings. Despite their severe queasiness, the two young officers never missed a meal in the ship's saloon. They could be proud of being among the sturdy few, for no more than a handful of nauseated passengers ever braved the evening dinner service. Miserable weather and culinary courage aside, the transatlantic voyage proved uneventful—too much so for Churchill's liking. He played the occasional game of bezique, but proved unlucky at cards. Fortunately the games were played for modest stakes. Always in search of stimulating conversation, he found his fellow travelers—although pleasant to be around—an utter bore. "There is to be a concert on board tonight at which all the stupid people among the passengers intend to perform," he wrote his mother, "and the stupider ones to applaud."

Churchill found little in the nautical experience to enjoy. It remained a mystery to him why anyone would subject himself to such mind-numbing tedium. The young man, who as a statesman and war leader would later take great pleasure in sailing on British ships of war, could not fathom ever wanting to travel by sea again. The journey took seven interminable days, by the end of which Churchill was all but ready to leap overboard. New York, its buildings taking shape through the heavy gray mist on the morning of Saturday, November 9, was a grand vision to behold.

Hosting Churchill and Barnes in the big city was William Bourke Cockran, a Democratic New York State representative and renowned political orator. Cockran knew the Churchill family through a past romantic entanglement with Jennie. Prior to her son's departure, Jennie had written to Cockran, asking him to look after Winston. In a testament to Lady Randolph's charm, Cockran kindly obliged. He put the two young men up in his penthouse on the corner of Fifth Avenue and Fifty-Eighth Street and exposed them to New York's high society.

That first night, Cockran hosted a lavish dinner party for his guests. On the list of those invited were a dozen members of the state judiciary, all of whom Churchill found worthy of his attention. One guest, a Supreme Court judge, invited Churchill and Barnes over drinks to visit his courtroom and view American jurisprudence in action. The case in question was the murder trial of David F. Hannigan, who had shot and killed one Solomon Mann. Mann had seduced Hannigan's sister, got her pregnant, then made her seek an abortion, resulting in medical complications and the sister's eventual death. The tawdry details of the case made it a media sensation.

The two young officers accepted the invitation. In the meantime, there was much for Churchill and Barnes to see and do. On their first full day in town, they took a tugboat tour of New York harbor and visited the headquarters of the Atlantic Military District. An early dinner was scheduled with the Vanderbilts for five that evening, and it did not disappoint. Their hosts treated the two young subalterns like royalty, spoiling them with drink and food and offering them guest memberships to some of the swankiest clubs in town.

Churchill and Barnes initially planned to stay in New York for three days, but decided to extend their visit to six. The American way of life enthralled and fascinated Churchill. New York proved to be a world unto itself, unlike anything Churchill had yet experienced. London may have been the world's capital at that time, but New York hummed with its own unique energy. Churchill noted the trains clattering on the elevated rails, the ferries cutting back and forth across the harbor, and the cable cars with their clanging bells. It was a loud, wondrous extravaganza of organized chaos and innovation. That both the upper and lower classes could indulge, side-by-side, in the convenience of such amenities struck the Victorian Churchill as remarkable. This was a fine example of American enterprise. Men of vision and business had built the city's transportation system with the end goal of making a fortune.

Churchill—eager to strike it rich on his own behalf—admired this entrepreneurial verve, but he found American currency distasteful. He thought the paper dollar an abomination and felt strange using one to pay his way across the Brooklyn Bridge. It lacked the heft and class of a pound sterling. He could not fathom how a country brimming with youthful vitality could have such a cheap and unseemly form of currency. He thought it reflected poorly on the government and could only surmise that the nation's sharpest minds were in business and not politics—though Cockran proved the exception. The two men often stayed up late discussing everything from government to Cockran's enthusiasm for yachting.

On Wednesday, November 12, 1895, the two British officers found themselves in a New York City courtroom with a front-row seat to the Hannigan murder trial. The experience perfectly crystallized Churchill's opinion of America. Neither the judge nor the lawyers wore the robes and powdered wigs of their English counterparts. It was a glaring lack of tradition that spoke to a certain simplicity. Americans were a straightforward people, uninterested in pomp and history. They adopted a utilitarian view of life and had little time for ceremony. In Churchill's mind, there was nothing romantic about America, but he admired its bare-bones approach to things.

What he did not admire was West Point, which he visited the following day. Far from being impressed by the American military academy, Churchill thought it a travesty. Rules prohibited the cadets, in their early twenties, from smoking or possessing money. Not until they completed their first two years of training were they granted a paltry two-month leave. It seemed that school boys in England enjoyed a greater degree of freedom. It puzzled Churchill that young men would submit to such restrictions. Could someone who so willingly surrendered his freedom, he wondered, be expected to fight for the liberty of others?

There were other adventures to be had in the great metropolis. The city's fire commissioner, at Cockran's request, arranged for Churchill and Barnes to tour several fire stations. At one the sudden, loud jangling of an alarm bell threw the place into a fit of frantic action. Horses were harnessed and hitched to the fire wagon, while men—some not even fully dressed—zipped down the fire pole, leapt atop the wagon, and raced off to fight the blaze. The enthralling performance lasted no more than a few seconds, so well rehearsed were the players. It was a mesmerizing feat, a great display of energy and vigor, emblematic of Americans in general. Everyone seemed to be in a hurry to get somewhere or accomplish something—sentiments Churchill could fully appreciate. But in their rush, Americans could often be uncouth. They reminded Churchill of a rambunctious minor who, having no respect for authority, throws food at the dinner table or talks out of turn. The initial reaction might be one of shock or disgust, but the child's youthful exuberance and joyful disregard of the consequences are somehow entertaining—perhaps even enviable. Churchill thought the United States a fun but wild child among nations, one with little time for the traditions and stuffy reserve of the Old World. The country displayed, if anything, self-confidence in blazing its own path.

On the evening of Friday, November 15, Churchill dined with his cousin Sunny, the 9th Duke of Marlborough, who had married the American railroad heiress Consuelo Vanderbilt nine days earlier. The *New York Times* covered the event in great depth and declared the ceremony at St. Thomas's Church on West 53rd Street to be "without exception, the most magnificent ever celebrated in this country." Churchill enjoyed Sunny's company and the lavish hospitality of the Vanderbilts, but he cared little for American journalism. It was, in his estimation, entertainment for the lower classes, catering to gossip, innuendo, and hyperbole, with little regard for the truth. So accustomed had Americans become to reading such tripe, that even the upper echelons of society mistook it for a quality product. Nevertheless, the city and its people made a lasting impression on Churchill, instilling in him a love for America that would never diminish. And in William Bourke Cockran, Churchill found the closest thing he would ever have to a mentor: a man who resembled his father in terms of success and power, but who recognized a kindred spirit in Churchill's intellectual curiosity and treated him as an equal. The two men forged a lasting friendship, but the time had come to leave New York for Key West and venture on to Cuba.

Thanks to Cockran, Churchill and Barnes made the thirty-six-hour journey by train in the comfort of a private stateroom. Although Churchill found the food barely edible, he was thankful not to endure the long trek in a cramped carriage with the traveling masses. Upon reaching Key West they boarded the steamer *Olivette* for the ninety-mile crossing to Cuba. The journey proved more pleasurable than the torturous Atlantic voyage from England. The waters remained calm and the onboard company did not bore him, while the prospect of adventure lent the crossing an air of exhilarating expectancy.

Churchill and Barnes arrived in Havana on November 20, 1895. A storm in the early morning hours disturbed Churchill's sleep, the rain slashing at his cabin window. He made his way up to the deck when the weather cleared and watched the dark outline of Cuba take form on the horizon. As the ship finally steamed into Havana's outer harbor, Churchill saw—high atop a cliff—the imposing Morro Castle, guarding the entrance to Havana Bay. On the voyage over he had learned that the compound, once a fort, was now a prison and place of execution. One story he heard detailed the fate of a poor Spanish lieutenant, who during the previous May had commanded fifty troops. One morning, while he and his men were enjoying breakfast at a local café, they were taken prisoner by a gang of rebels. They were soon released, but not before being stripped of all their weapons. Spanish military authorities promptly arrested the lieutenant, hauled him before a court martial, and sentenced him to death for dereliction of duty. He was killed by a firing squad in the castle's courtyard.

Once on shore Churchill and Barnes established themselves—if only for the night—in the Gran Hotel Inglaterra, planning to leave for the front the next morning. Conditions in Havana were better than Churchill expected. During the crossing from Key West, rumors on the boat had suggested the city was a cesspool of disease and rife with rebellion. Yellow fever was supposedly ravaging the populace, an assertion that proved untrue. In fact as far as Churchill could tell, everything appeared normal. Other than a vigorous search for concealed weapons in his baggage when he disembarked and a close inspection of his passport, he encountered no signs of a rebellion. People came and went, performing any number of mundane tasks that carry one through the day. Everything appeared to be business as usual. The dearth of insurrection coverage in the local newspapers, however, did strike Churchill as odd. He was told that government censors, who preferred to keep citizens in the dark, edited the papers. While Spanish officials excelled at concealing news of war and any progress made by the rebels, the Cuban insurgents exaggerated their gains, no matter how minuscule, resulting in an environment completely devoid of the truth.

Churchill and Barnes would soon begin discovering the facts for themselves. On that first night they met with Alexander Gollan, consul general for Cuba, who assured them all necessary arrangements for the ensuing adventure had been made. They returned to their hotel, which overlooked Havana's bustling central piazza, and puffed their way through several cigars. Although the brand of cigar they smoked remains a mystery, the Cuban-made Romeo & Julieta would become one of Churchill's personal favorites. As he smoked, savoring the slow burn of the tobacco, he considered the adventure before him.

In later years, writing for a public still recovering from the horrors of trench warfare, Churchill admitted that some might "not understand the delicious and tremulous sensations" he felt at the prospect of combat. The technological advancements in weaponry that would render the Western Front an abattoir two decades later were still a faint glimmer in some dark imagination. For Churchill, the Cuban expedition was his chance to start building a public platform. Although a military man, he did not plan on making a career of the army. He wished to pursue politics but needed to establish his credentials and character. Reporting from a war zone would certainly get his name out there.

Early on the morning of November 21 he and Barnes set off for the central town of Santa Clara, where Marshal Martinez Campos—sent by Madrid to subdue the rebellion—maintained his headquarters staff. They traveled twelve hours by rail, through the towns of Matanzas and Cienfuegos. The journey was not without risk, as rebels routinely tossed dynamite at passing trains. Spanish soldiers patrolled the route and rode the rails, but the insurgents remained a brazen threat. As Churchill gazed out his carriage window at the passing jungle, he cursed himself for not bringing a camera. The stations along the way resembled small forts. Some were simple stockades made of lumber, others a sturdier construction made of stone—but all had a garrison of up to twenty men. A concrete blockhouse guarded passage across every bridge, for the rebels were efficient at sabotage. It was not uncommon for them to hack away the support timbers of a bridge, causing considerable destruction when a train crossed the expanse.

Churchill learned one favorite tactic employed by the rebels involved loosening rails on the track and tying a thick wire around the unfastened length of railway. When a train passed over the compromised stretch, the rebels would yank the wire and pull the track out from underneath the train, often causing a derailment. When Churchill's train reached the station of Santa Domingo, the passengers learned that insurgents had cut the line several miles ahead, sending a train off the tracks and seriously injuring fifteen of its passengers. An armored car was added to Churchill's train for extra protection. Fortunately—though perhaps not for Churchill—the journey passed without incident.

He and Barnes arrived at Santa Clara early that evening and were met with a warm welcome by Marshal Campos. Campos had successfully quelled a rebellion in Cuba in 1867 and returned to his native Spain, where he reaped the political benefits and became prime

Map 1: Churchill in Cuba

minister. He had also served as his country's minister of war before the latest Cuban rebellion drew him once more to the lush island. Campos placed his guests in the care of a young lieutenant who spoke very good English. The lieutenant told Churchill and Barnes their best chance of seeing any action lay in joining a patrol column. Unfortunately the local commander, General Juarez Valdez, had set off with a column that morning for the town of Sancti Spiritus, some forty miles away. Churchill, desperate to be in the thick of things, suggested they leave immediately to catch up with the patrol. The young lieutenant shook his head. They would get no more than a few miles into the jungle before meeting an unpleasant end. Churchill was incredulous. Where, he wanted to know, were the enemy? The lieutenant smirked and said they were everywhere, explaining that the nearest enemy outposts were no more than half a mile outside the town. If challenged by a sentry in the jungle, one's survival very much depended on the answer given, either "Spain" or "Free Cuba." The problem seemed to be that it was not always clear who had issued the challenge. Discerning a friend's voice from that of a foe, noted Churchill, often involved "a process of deduction Sherlock Holmes might envy."

But hope was not completely lost. After discussing the possible risks, the men decided to travel by train to the town of Cienfuegos and catch a steamer to the port of Tunas, on the island's eastern shore. From there another train—this one heavily guarded by armed escorts and fortifications along the track—would take them to Sancti Spiritus. The route totaled 150 miles but would allow Churchill and Barnes to reach the town one full day before Valdez and his men emerged from the nearly impenetrable jungle.

The men arrived in Tunas late that night only to learn rebels had cut all communications between the port and Sancti Spiritus, blown up a portion of the railroad tracks between the two towns, and ambushed a train. They would have to wait for the line to be repaired the following morning before setting off for their final destination. They checked into the local hotel, "an establishment more homely than pretentious," and waited for daybreak. For Churchill, the delay must have been agonizing. It was not merely the prospect of seeing combat up close that excited him, but the opportunity it presented to try his hand at serious journalism. His first dispatch covered his arrival in Cuba; the second would detail the journey from Tunas to Sancti Spiritus.

Churchill and Barnes boarded a train at first light. The thirty-mile route, they learned, was considered the most dangerous stretch of track on the island. Churchill couldn't help but notice that the sides of the carriages were reinforced with steel boiler plates. Armed soldiers and men of the Guardia Civil—the Spanish military police—occupied every compartment. The railway itself hugged the mountains, firmly held by the rebels, and passed through thick jungle that offered no more than a few yards of visibility. More than two dozen small forts lined the route, which was patrolled by some twelve hundred Spanish troops. An eager Churchill and Barnes took their seats. The train traveled at a sluggish ten miles an hour and made prolonged stops at every station, where the commander of the nearest fort had to confirm that it was safe to proceed down the next stretch of the line.

Only a week before, the rebels had overtaken one of the railroad fortifications. General Máximo Gómez, the Cuban military commander, led the assault and positioned a number of his men on a hill five hundred yards from their objective. His troops opened fire to distract the Spanish defenders, who failed to notice enemy forces charging the fort from both sides. While the fort's garrison, which numbered no more than fifty, fought desperately, another wave of rebels hit the fort in a frontal assault and battered down its main entrance.

Churchill and Barnes arrived in Sancti Spíritus and were dismayed by what they saw. The town was a dismal slum overwhelmed by filth and disease. Twelve people had recently died of smallpox, while another eleven had succumbed to yellow fever. The slow onset of winter and the cooling temperatures, however, were helping to bring the dual epidemics under control. The poorest citizens and the soldiers stationed in the town seemed to be suffering the worst of it. Beyond the town, in the jungles and mountains, lurked some twenty thousand rebels. If a small group of Spaniards dared venture more than a mile beyond the tree line, they would likely vanish and never be heard from again. Safety lay strictly in numbers. Only a lengthy column of infantry and cavalry bristling with firepower could expect to make it through the jungle—but they were not immune to attack.

One might think that Churchill, a diehard imperialist, would have little respect for those rebelling against their European masters, but initially this was not the case. He admired the rebels' cunning. They did not wear any formal uniform, only a badge, allowing them to move about virtually with impunity and conceal themselves among the normal citizenry. They could spy in the open without fear of capture. Local villagers loyal to the rebellion served as an informal intelligence network, reporting anything they saw or heard that might assist the fight for independence. The Spanish were at a consequent disadvantage despite their might. The rebels kept tabs on every Spanish general and knew the state and disposition of all Spanish forces.

Decamping in wretched Sancti Spiritus, Churchill found himself surrounded by the enemy. The circumstances presented a grand predicament for an eager war correspondent. Roughly three thousand Spanish troops arrived in the town the day after Churchill. They came in from the jungle, armed with double bandoliers and sweating under oversized panama hats. They looked surprisingly fit—in Churchill's opinion—considering the length of their march and the terrain they had to conquer. He and Barnes sought out their commanding officer, General Valdez, and made their introductions. Valdez was more than happy to have two British officers join his infantry column. He viewed their presence as a symbolic gesture of Britain's support. Churchill, through an interpreter, thanked the general for his kind words, saying he believed the ensuing adventure would prove to be "awfully jolly." The general appreciated the young man's enthusiasm and said they would be departing at first light. He explained that the purpose of his mission was a two-week march through enemy territory to capture and kill rebels, and to check on towns still garrisoned by Spanish troops to ensure all was well. Conditions in Sancti Spiritus were such that he wished to move his men out as quickly as possible. After dining with Valdez, Churchill and Barnes retired for the night.

Before going to bed, Churchill penned a letter to his mother. He was, he wrote, thrilled to be leaving Sancti Spiritus—and its dual plagues of grime and contagion—with his health intact. How unfortunate it would be to have traveled all this way only to fall victim to disease.

CHAPTER 3

Churchill Under Fire

I t was still dark when Churchill woke up and ventured outside. In the predawn gloom, he could see the silhouettes of Valdez and his men as they bustled about preparing for their departure, checking weapons and fastening saddlebags. Churchill and Barnes, following their example, unholstered their revolvers and inspected the cylinders, ensuring that a round occupied every chamber. As a correspondent Churchill could not actively engage the enemy, but he could defend himself if need be. He looked beyond the town to the dark shapes of the nearby mountains. He felt no fear, only exhilaration, and desperately hoped for some kind of action. What young soldier wouldn't? In the saddle, Churchill could not think of one fellow Hussar back home who wouldn't surrender a month's salary for such an adventure.

The column of six hundred infantry and three hundred cavalry set off beneath a brightening sky. The air, even at this early hour, felt uncomfortably heavy and settled on the skin like warm, wet gauze; the jungle—thick and damp—soon encroached on the men from all sides. Having heard the stories of enemy outposts so close to town, Churchill rode in a state of constant expectation, waiting for gunfire to shatter the tropical idyll at any moment. Trudging along on his horse, he took mental notes of everything for his next *Graphic* column. "I find the chief difficulty of writing these letters," he reported, "is that where material is plentiful opportunity is scarce, so that when one has much to write of one has usually but little time to write it in, and conversely." On this occasion, however, he need not have worried, for his passage through the jungle proved extraordinarily uneventful. Churchill emerged disappointed from the overgrowth into open country, without so much as a glimpse of the enemy. It was nine in the morning. An order came down the line to dismount for breakfast.

While some men cooked meals, others busied themselves tying hammocks between the trees in a nearby copse. Once the morning's ration of coffee was downed, a large bottle of rum cocktail made the rounds. Churchill, never one to pass up a drink, indulged and discovered that he enjoyed the sweet libation. He observed the soldiers around him as he drank. They had passed through eight miles of jungle—their backs bent beneath rolled canvas blankets; pots, pans and other cooking utensils; canteens; and nearly two hundred rounds of ball ammunition—and still had another eighteen miles to go before reaching that day's objective.

He could not help but be impressed by Spanish fortitude. The morning's march had been nothing short of grueling, made all the more strenuous by the relentless heat and unforgiving terrain, but no more than a few men had fallen out of line. Although the average Spanish soldier was in his midtwenties, many looked older, with scruffy facial hair and their skin turning leathery from constant exposure to the tropical sun. Presently the soldiers, having finished their rum, checked and cleaned their Remington and Mauser rifles. The humid conditions and the fording of rivers meant the upkeep of weapons remained a constant priority. When they finished, the men retired to their hammocks for their morning siesta and encouraged their British compatriots to do the same.

For two soldiers in Her Majesty's Army, stopping midmarch for a nap was an alien concept, but the Spanish and Cuban cultures were to leave an indelible mark on Churchill. It was here that he developed his lifelong passion for cigars and an appreciation for the well-timed nap. During the First World War, when he served as lord of the admiralty, Churchill claimed that by taking an hour-long nap after lunch, he could extend his workday by two hours. Now he clambered into a hammock in the shade of a tall tree and quickly dozed off. The men slept until two o'clock and afterward were on the march within an hour. The remainder of the day passed without incident. At dawn on the second day the column set off for a place labeled Iguara on Churchill's map.

As the men tramped through the heat and jungle, a Spanish soldier told Churchill their destination was wholly dependent on food convoys from Sancti Spiritus. Insurgents, the soldier claimed, had Iguara completely surrounded. Such knowledge made the approach to the town all the more exciting. The men followed a narrow, winding track that could hardly be called a road. In some places it ran along the edge of a creek; in others it veered upward to a broad, grassy ridge before dropping back down again. It was not ideal for transport or traveling. It often passed through large areas of swampy ground that forced the men to take wide detours, sometimes through thick vegetation. The route, with its many bends and obstacles, made conducting any meaningful reconnaissance impossible. The column marched single file, the horses struggling with the terrain. The going proved slow and dangerous, for the landscape favored the enemy. Jungle and valleys offered countless places to hide. If the rebels attacked, the road would be too narrow for the column to fan out and muster an adequate defense. All the men could do was keep marching forward.

Upon arriving at Iguara, Churchill discovered it was not a town, but a smattering of houses and barns numbering no more than five. Here Valdez's column reprovisioned the Spanish garrison with enough supplies to last them the next two months. The column stayed in town for just one night before moving out early the next morning. Until now Churchill had harbored a certain respect for the Cuban rebels—an unprofessional army of untrained civilians, fighting a major European power for their independence. But the more he spoke with his Spanish cohorts, the more his attitude changed. The Spaniards viewed the conflict as a matter of national integrity. Losing the island—a cherished possession—would be a major blow to Spanish prestige. It surprised

Churchill that the Spanish viewed their colonial possessions the same way the British viewed theirs. It had never occurred to him that other nations attached a similar value to their imperial holdings.

Although the rebels remained elusive, evidence of their activities was not hard to find. Houses burned to the ground, incinerated sugar fields, and smoldering campfires betrayed the rebels' movements. As the troops pressed on with their mission, it became evident they were under regular surveillance. A lone horseman would occasionally appear on a high ridge or materialize at the edge of a jungle clearing before quickly retreating from view. On the third day of marching, Spanish troops attacked members of a Cuban reconnaissance party spotted in some nearby brush. For several frantic minutes the jungle echoed with gunfire as rounds tore bark from trees and thinned the rebels' hiding place of cover. When it was over, one Spanish soldier and several Cubans lay dead. It was hardly a battle, nor was it the experience for which Churchill had traveled so far—but he remained hopeful.

On the afternoon of November 29 the column reached the town of Arroyo Blanco. It was larger than Iguara, consisting of twenty single-story homes, which, Churchill noted, were "destitute of floors." The town—although not much in terms of appearance—was of strategic importance to the Spanish because of its nearby heliograph station, a signaling device in which a moveable mirror was employed to flash Morse code messages to headquarters in Santa Clara using reflected sunlight. Churchill learned upon arrival that the enemy had attacked the town two days earlier. The local garrison of two hundred Spaniards had fought off the assault and in the process reportedly killed twenty insurgents.

The day they arrived, news reached Arroyo Blanco that Maximo Gomez and some four thousand of his men were camped several miles to the east. The Spanish decided to give chase early the next morning. Churchill was told the rebels had a very limited supply of ammunition and supposedly went into battle with no more than three rounds allocated to each man. What ammunition they did have was of little use, as the Cubans were considered lousy shots. Only at close range, the Spanish told Churchill, could a Cuban hit a target. This also allowed them to slash and stab with their machetes. It was, Churchill reported, Cuba's weapon of choice. The machete was an indispensable tool for cutting sugar cane, chopping wood, clearing brush, and just about every other kind of work that called for hacking and slicing. In times of war its short, wide blade made it a lethal implement. The Cubans, having honed their skills through nearly constant use, made deadly swordsmen. In close-quarter action a machete could easily sever a limb or cut a rifle in half with one powerful strike.

That afternoon Churchill and Barnes joined a patrol to reconnoiter the heliograph. The small party skirted the enemy outposts in the jungle and climbed a hill beyond Arroyo Blanco, up to the station. Because the journey took longer than anticipated, the sun had retired beyond the tree line and left them in darkness before they made it back to town. The return trek, through nearly two miles of rebel-infested jungle, excited Churchill. His only escort was six lightly armed officers from the Spanish military police. Should the rebels attack, he and his party would be hopelessly outgunned. Their ponies moved slowly through the nearly impenetrable growth. On several occasions a pony would lose its footing on the uneven ground and dispatch its rider to the earth with a thud. The overhead canopy of trees blocked the sky from view. Churchill strained to see more than a few feet in either direction, but the night was complete. As they carefully picked their way down the invisible trail, he wondered why the rebels had not yet attacked. This did not, in his opinion, speak well of their initiative and daring. Nevertheless, it was a relief to reach the town in one piece.

Churchill had arrived in Cuba with preconceived notions of war. Nourished on the history of campaigns by Wellington, Napoleon, and his own illustrious ancestor, the 1st Duke of Marlborough, Churchill envisioned large armies on the field of battle, their banners unfurling in the wind, marching headlong into the fray. The Cuban campaign was a corruption of that romantic view. Here, there would be no great clash of forces. When the enemy attacked, it did so quickly, materializing out of the undergrowth and striking fast before dissolving once more into the jungle. Churchill saw no way for the Spanish to win such a conflict.

Spain was a country of limited financial resources, yet it had deployed a quarter million men to this distant land.

Despite Spain's fading power, its army marched into the Cuban jungle expecting a quick victory. Most soldiers thought it would all be over come springtime—an outcome Churchill considered highly unlikely. The rebels were masters of the terrain and employed it well to their own tactical advantage. The Spanish Army was a relic of the old European style of war, unaccustomed to the hit-and-run attacks favored by the Cubans. In some cases the rebels were darting back into the brush with smoking rifles before the Spanish had any clear concept of what was happening. If the enemy continued employing such methods, Churchill opined in one *Graphic* column, he failed to see how the Spanish could ever emerge victorious.

The voicing of such opinions would not go unnoticed in London.

The following day, November 30, 1895, Winston Churchill turned twenty-one. As had become routine, he awoke before dawn and prepared to move out with the column, which numbered roughly seventeen hundred men, organized into the artillery and two squadrons of cavalry. The day before, Valdez had dispatched two battalions with provisions to resupply Spanish garrisons throughout the area. The men who remained behind would catch up to the enemy and, it was hoped, force them into a decisive confrontation.

A serpentine mist swirled about the men and horses as they moved out at five that morning. The mist began to rise and grow more opaque as they entered the jungle. They were not far out of town when, with a loud, whip-like crack, gunfire erupted near the end of the column. Churchill swung around in his saddle and searched for the telltale puffs of smoke from long-bore rifles, but the mist concealed the enemy's position. Although eager for action, Churchill and Barnes were not foolhardy; neither wished to be shot, regardless of the bragging rights that might attend the ordeal. The fighting raged seven hundred feet or so down the line, a fact that brought Churchill some measure of false comfort. The column continued moving, leaving its attackers behind, and soon passed into open country. The mist began to thin and revealed an inhospitable route of bogs, creeks, and dead grass.

A faint path, almost overgrown with brush, wound its way through the swampy terrain. Officers at the front of the column drew their machetes and began attacking the vegetation. The column made slow but steady progress and stumbled at midday across what appeared to be a vacated rebel camp hidden in the woods. Piles of charred wood remained where bivouac fires had once burned near now-empty shelters made of palm leaves. Flattened grass and snapped branches betrayed the enemy's path of escape, and the column set off in pursuit. They reached the town of Lagitas at five o'clock—if a place comprised of one barn could be called a town. Around the solitary structure, Churchill saw smoldering campfires and half-eaten tins of food. A conversation with the farmer who called the place home confirmed the rebels had departed not long before the Spanish arrived.

Valdez gave the order for his troops to dismount and establish camp for the night. As Churchill and the others climbed down from their horses, someone shouted in alarm and pointed to a nearby field. Twenty-five rebels, who had been watching the so-called town, had broken cover and were retreating to the nearby woods. A contingent of Spanish troops gave chase, but the Cubans vanished into the trees some four hundred yards away. Later that night, to prevent a surprise attack, four infantry companies were placed on guard duty between Lagitas and the woods. Now it was time to eat.

Churchill sat down to his meal, struck by his surroundings as he ate. The moon—full in the sky—bathed the tops of the palm trees in silver light but failed to reach the jungle floor. Several fires burning along the jungle's edge fared no better in penetrating the blackness. An enemy patrol, if it were quiet enough, could easily maneuver within striking distance without being detected—yet Churchill, taken by the night's beauty, gave little thought to such things. The glow of the moon, the flickering of the fires, and the gentle rushing sound of a nearby river lent the scene a mystical quality and rendered war an alien concept.

The cat-and-mouse game continued early the next morning, when the column vacated Lagitas before sunrise. No sooner had the Spanish commenced marching than the tree line of nearby jungle roared to life with gunfire. The thick vegetation and morning mist camouflaged the enemy and thwarted Spanish attempts to fight back. For ten minutes bullets flew, slamming into trees, tearing up earth and dirt, but missing their intended targets. Then the commotion ended just as suddenly as it had begun, as the rebels retired once more into the jungle's depths.

All the while, the column pushed forward and soon found itself battling its way through thick vines and creepers and low-hanging branches heavy with leaves larger than a man's hand. Churchill, surveying the dense vegetation, realized the enemy could easily sneak up on them, with devastating effect. The infantry took the lead position, while the cavalry secured the rear. The soldiers in the front, their uniforms soaked and blackened with sweat, hacked away at twisting, entangled branches and forged a path for the horses. At eleven o'clock the men came to a clearing no more than a couple of hundred yards across. It was here they decided to breakfast. Churchill was biting into a bony chicken when enemy fire battered the clearing. One round, missing Churchill's head by no more than a foot, struck a nearby horse. The Spaniards returned a salvo and advanced on the enemy's perceived position just beyond the clearing. When the infantrymen reached the spot, all they found were spent shell casings and trampled undergrowth.

The experience awakened Churchill to the real dangers of his adventure. Until now the risk of death or injury to him had seemed remote. He approached the wounded horse, a dripping red hole between its ribs where the slug had struck home. It hung its head in obvious agony as a soldier removed its saddle and bridle. The horse was promptly put out of its misery. The episode gave Churchill pause. This journey may at first have been a game in his youthful eyes, but child's play it was not.

Valdez ordered his men to immediately saddle up and move out. Once more the men reentered the brush. Churchill, not for the first time, marveled at the colors of the jungle—the deep greens and the vibrant hues of alien plants—and the massive palm trees that towered overhead. They marched for another four hours, at one point wading across a river, before coming to a place marked on their maps as Las Grullas. It was not a town—nor could it even be called a village—its

sole feature being a rundown cabin. It was here they decided to camp
for the night. Although the sun was beginning its rapid descent, the
heat remained oppressive. The men had sweated through their uniforms, which clung uncomfortably to their damp skin. Churchill got
off his horse and reconnoitered the immediate area. It was bordered on
three sides by the river and offered no adequate cover against enemy
fire. Ideally, one would not want to stay here long—but as this was
their only option, the men made the best of their situation. Making the
best of it in this case meant going for a swim.

The cool rush of the river proved impossible to resist after the jungle's sweltering embrace. Churchill and Barnes peeled off their soiled
clothes and convinced two officers to join them for a dip. Naked, they
jumped in and happily washed away the day's grime. The river, blue
and clear, lent the setting an idyllic quality. After this brief respite,
Churchill and his companions emerged from the water and began
to dress on the riverbank. A rifle thundered somewhere nearby, followed quickly by another, and forced the men—still only partially
dressed—to duck for cover. A sentry upstream from Churchill's position crouched behind a fallen tree and fired at the insurgents, who
could be seen advancing through the jungle, fleeting glimpses of their
figures between the trees. They were no more than two hundred yards
away when one of the officers who had swum with Churchill ran off,
half-dressed, to muster reinforcements; he returned with fifty soldiers.

"Of course," wrote Churchill in his dispatch, "they had their rifles—in this war no soldier ever goes a yard without his weapon—and
these men doubled up in high delight and gave the rebels a volley from
their Mausers, which checked the enemy's advance." Churchill and
the others ran back to their camp and found a fierce battle raging less
than a mile away. The thunderous boom of the enemy's Remington
rifles overpowered the "shrill rattle" of the Spanish armaments, but
that counted for little. The hot exchange continued for roughly thirty
minutes, until the rebels called it quits and quickly vanished into the
brush with their dead and wounded.

They returned at eleven o'clock that night. Churchill was sleeping
in the solitary thatched hut that made up Las Grullas. One round tore

through the shack's straw roof; another struck an orderly standing outside the door. Churchill's first impulse was to throw himself on the floor—but as no one else made a similar move, he forced himself to stay put. He did find a measure of comfort in the rotund Spanish officer lying in the hammock between him and the cabin wall. Surely a bullet would strike this unfortunate—yet conveniently large—individual before Churchill.

The orderly proved to be the evening's sole casualty. After raking the camp with several fierce volleys, the rebels melted once more into the ether. The men awoke from fitful sleep the following morning to find the clearing choked with mist. The enemy, they knew, might be mere yards away. They packed what few belongings they had and mounted their horses for another long day's march. Crossing the river proved slow going, as the cavalry had to wait for the infantry to wade across first. As the men negotiated the currents, they again came under wild and erratic fire. The soldiers, laughing and mimicking the sound of gunshots, took it all with good humor, which greatly impressed Churchill. Yet the gunfire killed several men in the river and a few in their saddles. The general leading the column's spearhead, having spotted the enemy in the brush, directed the fire of his troops accordingly. The rebels quickly fell back in a fighting retreat. For the next two hours, from six to eight, insurgents harried the Spanish troops and repeatedly sent men scrambling for cover. The march, noted Churchill, was "very lively for everybody."

The Spaniards continued despite the maelstrom and soon came across a clearing. On the opposite side, the enemy sat in wait. As General Valdez surveyed the landscape, Churchill made note of what he saw: a wide grass incline a mile in length, bordered by stunted trees on one side and a wire fence on the other. Beyond the trees and fence stretched fields of waist-high grass. A large cluster of palm trees grew halfway up the incline, which disappeared at the top into thick jungle. In moments, the setting would be the scene of battle. Valdez ordered two companies to advance up either side of the clearing—the cavalry on the right and the infantry on the left—while the artillery took the center ground. Valdez and a battalion of troops brought up the rear behind the artillery.

The Spanish cleared three hundred yards of ground before the Cubans responded. Churchill saw clouds of gun smoke rise above the rebel-occupied crest-line. A second later the clatter of their rifles drifted down to where he sat watching the engagement. The Spanish did not break stride. Soon gun smoke socked in both ends of the battlefield as one violent exchange followed another. General Valdez, dressed in white and gold lace, astride a gray horse, made a conspicuous target. Consequently, reported Churchill, casualties on the general's staff were "out of all proportion to those of the rest of the force." This was Churchill's first true battle, an exhilarating experience. "There was a sound in the air," he wrote in his war dispatch, "sometimes like a sigh, sometimes like a whistle, and at other times like the buzz of an offended hornet."

The Spanish continued their advance toward the enemy line, the ruckus of their Mausers overpowering all other noise. Churchill, sitting astride his horse with members of the general's staff, watched the Cuban forces loose cohesion and fall back to the woods behind them. The rebel fire soon ceased altogether, as the Spanish seized the high ground. Valdez ordered his troops not to give chase, owing to the density of the forest and the fact the Spaniards only had a day's worth of provisions left. Churchill found the whole thing anticlimactic—and truth be told, pointless. The Spanish had merely seized a hill that, as far as Churchill could tell, lacked any strategic value whatsoever.

The Battle of La Reforma—as it would become known—was hardly a resounding Spanish victory, for they allowed the rebels to get away. "It seems a strange and unaccountable thing that a force, after making such vigorous marches, showing such energy in finding the enemy, and displaying such steadiness in attacking them, should deliberately sacrifice all that these efforts had gained," Churchill reported. Here was a glimpse of the aggressive nature that would define Churchill as war leader, always pushing his generals to be on the offensive and show the enemy no quarter.

The Spanish pulled back and set off marching for the town of La Jicotea. The journey took the better part of a sweltering day, and not until four o'clock that afternoon did the haggard troops reach their destination. Unlike some of the places Churchill had stayed in recent days, La Jicotea was actually a town—albeit a small one consisting of only one street. Here at last was a place with proper houses and beds. They were met by the town's Spanish administrator, who treated Valdez and his staff—along with Churchill and Barnes—to a feast of sausages and guava jelly. Tankards of English cider helped wash it down. Churchill, always a man of vast appetite, demolished the meal and then set off to explore the town's only street. It presented a delightful scene.

Fifteen hundred Spanish troops sat around several large bonfires and celebrated the day's end beneath a sky awash in stars. Some stirred pots of food; others cleaned their rifles—but all spoke in cheerful tones despite having marched through twenty-one miles of jungle. "They were," Churchill noted, "fine infantry."

Churchill enjoyed the comfort of a proper bed that night, his Cuban adventure all but over. At daybreak he and Barnes set off with General Valdez and his staff for the town of Ciego d'Avilar, some fifteen miles away. They rode small ponies, which carried them along at a jaunty trot. In two hours they reached the town, "surrounded by palisades, with frequent stone flanking towers." Here the small party had lunch before boarding a train to the coast, where they caught a gunboat to Tunas. Churchill and Barnes bid farewell to their hosts, grateful for their kindness and hospitality. From Tunas they made their way to Havana and returned once more to the Gran Hotel Inglaterra on the night of December 5. After an adventurous two weeks chasing the Spanish through the fetid jungle, it was a relief to be ensconced once again in more civilized surroundings. A stack of letters from Churchill's mother awaited him when he checked in.

Sitting at the small desk in his room beneath a gray cloud of cigar smoke, he penned a letter to Jennie to say he was safe and happy. His trek through the jungle had dulled, if only slightly, the sheen of war. He realized, having had several close calls, that running off to a combat zone in search of adventure might have been reckless—but it would hardly change his behavior going forward. He still considered the experience an enjoyable one. On December 10 he and Barnes left Cuba for the United States aboard a steamer out of Havana harbor. He had done what he set out to do, having proved his mettle on the battlefield. Not only had he held firm in the face of enemy fire, he had found the experience enthralling. In his pocket he carried a souvenir from the front line: "a rough insurgent bullet" retrieved after it fatally struck a Spanish soldier.

Churchill's dispatches for the *Daily Graphic* in London ran on December 13, 17, 24, and 27, 1895, under the headline "The Insurrection in Cuba." It had been his intention to pen his last column while watching Cuba fade from view where the sky meets the sea—a romantic notion quickly scrapped by seasickness. Not until he reached Tampa Bay on December 14 did he put his final thoughts to paper, which appeared in print on January 13, 1896. Although his sympathy for the Spanish diminished his regard for the rebels as fighting men, he appreciated the legitimacy of their cause.

Crippling taxes levied by Spain milked the island for all it was worth, he noted, leaving businesses with little money to develop and expand. Spaniards made up the Cuban government and went about their day-to-day jobs for the betterment of their native land. For these reasons, Churchill could sympathize with the rebellion, but not with those who fought it. Under such conditions, he opined, one would assume that all who were in fighting shape would eagerly take up arms against Madrid. This was not the case. He had spoken with many peasants who regaled him with tales of their bravery in combat but who, very obviously, had never fired a shot in anger. Churchill could not respect anyone who failed to back his words with action.

The men doing the actual fighting, however, proved to be no better. They enjoyed playing the role of the daring patriot willing to sacrifice life and limb for their home, but very few of them—from what Churchill had witnessed—displayed true audacity on the battlefield. If they would only wage one hard battle against the Spanish, going all out instead of employing their usual hit-and-run tactics, perhaps another foreign power—primarily the United States—would take note and lend validation to their struggle.

As things stood, Churchill viewed the rebels as thugs. Setting fire to farmland, shooting from the cover of thick jungle, attacking enemy soldiers as they slept, and derailing trains, risking injury to innocent people, were not the acts of noble warriors. They were the work of brigands and unseemly actions upon which to establish a free nation.

Despite his criticisms of both sides, Churchill nevertheless believed the island had a bright future. He imagined a peaceful and wealthy Cuba operating under a government made up of its own people and doing business on the world stage. From its cigars and sugar, to its talented cricket players, the country had much to offer. Surely there were better days ahead.

Winston Churchill and Reginald Barnes arrived back in New York City by mid-December. Having survived their Cuban "baptism of fire," they decided the occasion called for a meal in the grand style and went to the Hotel Savoy shortly after nine in the evening. Told they were too late for supper, they retreated to the hospitality of Bourke Cockran's Fifth Avenue penthouse, the Bolkenhayn. The two Englishmen, reported the *New York World,* spent most of their remaining time in the city "trying to learn the name of the house in which they were domiciled, and consequently had very little time for sight-seeing." Because of Churchill's family lineage, the local newspapers took an interest in his recent exploits. In Cockran's opulent sitting room, Churchill held court with the city's reporters, charming them with his eloquence and wit. "Of course the war isn't like a European war," he said, "but there was a great deal that interested us. The most remarkable fact seems to be that two armies will shoot at each other for hours and no one will get hit. I believe that statisticians say that in a battle it takes 2,000 bullets to kill a man. When the calculations are arranged, I think it will be found that in the Cuban war it took 2,000 bullets to miss each individual combatant."

Some newspapers editorialized against Churchill's trip, claiming he and Barnes were sent to Cuba by the British government to show the

Spaniards "how to whip the secessionists." Matters were not helped by the Spanish government's decision to award the two young men the *Rioja Cruz* (Red Cross), a military decoration for gallantry—one that Churchill and Barnes happily accepted but were prohibited to wear by the British War Office. At least one paper, the *New York World*, dismissed any political intrigue as "nonsense." "Churchill is not yet twenty-one years old," it reported incorrectly, "and knows only the amount of strategy necessary for the duties of a second lieutenant. He and Barnes went on the trip actuated only by youthful enthusiasm."

"What about the alleged political significance of your trip?" asked one reporter.

"Rot!" replied Churchill, who—in the words of a reporter —"fiercely denied that he intended to write a book."

As for the conflict's outcome, Churchill predicted Cuba would be granted its own parliament but remain a Spanish colony. The Spaniards, he said, were not adept at the guerrilla tactics favored by the rebels, but they were the better combatants. What the rebels lacked in courage, they made up for in speed and maneuverability. It was Churchill's belief that if Campos could rid certain key towns of insurgents, the rebellion would collapse by spring—but the odds of such a thing happening were far from favorable. For Campos, Churchill had nothing but high praise and said that without him, Cuba would descend into mass slaughter and total anarchy.

On the morning Churchill and Barnes left New York, they arrived at the Cunard dock with only five minutes to spare before the *Etruria* set sail. A crowd of reporters waited near the ship's gangway, hoping for one last comment. Churchill, being the center of attention, was in his element. He believed the fighting in Cuba would prove to be the island's ruin and hoped the United States would intercede to help broker a peace. The imperialist in him, however, did not want Spain to surrender its colonial possession. Churchill, notes one biographer, was incapable of imagining colonies as sovereign states.

At last it was time to board the steamer for the long voyage home. He returned to England with a generous supply of guava jelly for his mother and no shortage of cigars. *Daily Graphic* editor Thomas Heath

Joyce was most pleased with Churchill's work and told the budding journalist the articles made excellent copy. The stories reveal a great flare for descriptive writing but suffer, as a result of the relatively light fighting, from a dearth of action. Although having experienced combat, Churchill was spared the full ferocity of war.

His adventures abroad did not please everyone. The idea of a young army officer gallivanting off to some foreign war that had nothing to do with queen or country made some in the British press raise an eyebrow. "Mr. Churchill was supposed to have gone to the West Indies for a holiday," the *Newcastle Leader* complained on December 7. "Spending a holiday fighting other people's battles is a rather extraordinary process even for a Churchill." Sir Henry Drummond Wolff, the British ambassador in Madrid, having read Churchill's dispatches, cringed to see in ink criticism of the Spanish government in Havana and made no secret of his displeasure.

Churchill soon put Sir Henry's concerns to rest with an article he wrote for the *Saturday Review* on February 15, 1896, in which he cast the Cuban rebels as outright villains. If they won, he warned, "revolutions would be periodic, property insecure, equity unknown." The *Saturday Review* piece seemed to put things right. After circulating the article "in the proper quarters," Drummond informed Churchill the story had "created much enthusiasm." Several months later, in a letter to his mother, Churchill expressed regret over the article. In an attempt to curry favor with the Spanish, he had been overly harsh about the insurgents. The episode proved to be a lesson in objective journalism.

CHAPTER 4

Letters and Books

Winston Churchill may have been a second lieutenant in the 4th Hussars, but he felt little compulsion to go where they went. Early in 1896 the War Office alerted the regiment to a pending nine-year deployment to India, where, as far as Churchill could ascertain, nothing of any significance was happening. The regiment began preparations that spring for their September departure. Churchill was allowed to live at his mother's house in Great Cumberland Place and venture at his pleasure to the barracks at Hounslow. It was a good time to be in London. The British capital buzzed with celebratory fervor as it prepared for Queen Victoria's Diamond Jubilee. Churchill enjoyed the festivities, spending evenings and weekends socializing under the glittering candelabra of royal estates and in the city's finest salons.

His pending deployment, however, cast an unfortunate shadow over the frivolity. Had orders declared that he be sent to an active war zone, he would have responded with great enthusiasm, but sitting around and doing nothing under the sweltering Indian sun held little appeal. Churchill, never one to do anything he didn't want to do, began scheming. He was, after all, an experienced war correspondent.

Another paper would surely be happy to send him someplace where bullets were flying.

It did not take long to find such a locale. In March 1896 a Muslim replaced the Christian governor of Crete, sending the island's Christians into armed revolt. Churchill approached the *Daily Chronicle* and offered to be their Cretan correspondent if the paper covered travel costs. The *Chronicle's* proprietor turned him down. If, however, Churchill ventured to Crete at his own expense, the paper would happily publish five articles at "ten guineas a letter." Churchill craved the experience but had no way of getting there unless the paper footed the bill. He was not one to be easily discouraged and searched for another opportunity. Stories of brewing discontent and open conflict saturated the newspapers.

In South Africa British forces found themselves wrangling with a native uprising in Matabeleland. Churchill decided he wanted to go there, but no paper would finance the excursion. He imagined the army asserting the will of the empire against hordes of charging Ndebele warriors. The battlefield called, but he could not answer. Without the backing of a newspaper, he instead faced the miserable prospect of banishment to India. He placed the burden on Jennie to pull some strings in his favor. This was Churchill at his best and worst: desperate for action and burning with ambition, but almost sulking at the prospect of not having his way. He wrote his mother a wordy lament, saying that if he did not get to South Africa he would regret for the rest of his life missing out on the experience. With her connections to people of wealth and influence, how could she not make things happen? Surely there must be someone who, in honor of Lord Randolph's memory, would grant the son what he desired most. He urged his mother to do whatever she could to ensure his passage to Matabeleland. It would be nothing short of a crime if he did not go. There was no point urging patience, he wrote. Men as young as—or even younger than—he were on the front line. He could not tolerate doing nothing when so much action was happening on distant shores. If she loved him, she would do her utmost.

Jennie did what she could to grant Churchill his wish, appealing to the highest authorities in the War Office on her son's behalf. She received a reply from Secretary of State for War Sir Henry Charles Keith Lansdowne, who said there was nothing he could do. Churchill had already skipped out on his regiment once to brave gunfire in Cuba. If he did not ship to India with the Hussars, it would surely set tongues wagging. All avenues proved to be dead ends. Churchill, much to his chagrin, was destined for the subcontinent. On September 11, 1896, at Southampton, he boarded with his regiment the SS *Britannia*, a troop transport carrying twelve hundred men, for the nearly month-long voyage to Bombay. Seven days out, between Malta and Alexandria, he decided the voyage was much to his liking. In stark contrast to the Atlantic crossing, on which he had spent frigid days crippled by nausea, he enjoyed the glass-like surface of the Mediterranean, with its mild winds and gentle sun. The journey passed with all the urgency of a pleasure cruise.

He spent his afternoons playing chess and passed the evening hours listening to the ship's string band. The food, which he found satisfactory, didn't hurt, either. At night the other men on board opted to sleep on deck beneath the stars, leaving Churchill alone in the cabin—another thing he found agreeable. The *Britannia* soon reached the Suez Canal, gateway to the Red Sea. The steamer made its passage at night, guided by the light of the moon and searchlights along the canal's banks. Churchill stood on deck, awestruck by the canal's massive scope and the ingenuity of its construction.

The ship might as well have sailed into a blast furnace. By day temperatures soared to 140 degrees in the sun and 110 degrees in the shade—but games of piquet and chess kept Churchill distracted. He became a formidable chess player over the course of the voyage and made it to the semifinal of an onboard tournament. By September 30, after twenty days at sea, the ship was one day shy of Bombay. Churchill craved a change of scenery. At three in the afternoon the following day the boat reached its destination. Men crowded the decks and gazed upon an exotic scene of lush, swaying palms and ancient architecture, of fishing boats cutting through white-tipped surf and dock workers unloading that day's catch. After the isolation of a long sea voyage, everything seemed alive and frantic. Disembarkation, the men were told, would begin at eight that evening once the heat of the day began to subside. Officers, however, were given permission to go ashore early and do some exploring. Churchill and several other men summoned one of the small skiffs that bobbed alongside the *Britannia*. It took fifteen minutes for the boat to reach the slippery quayside of the Sassoon dock. As Churchill scrambled out of the boat, he slipped and dislocated his shoulder. The injury would plague him for the rest of his life. At the time there was little he could do except utter a few choice words in anger and soldier on.

At eight o'clock on the evening of Thursday, October 1, the *Britannia* pulled up alongside the Sassoon dock's quay, and the real work began. Churchill and the other officers helped with disembarkation and the unloading of luggage. From Bombay the Hussars traveled by rail to a rest camp in Poona, where they spent their second night roasting in tents. At daybreak a number of locals entered the camp seeking jobs as caretakers to the officers. Churchill hired a servant to handle the needs of a gentleman officer abroad. One could live like royalty here. It was paradise for anyone who cared to be served hand and foot. The dressing boy maintained one's wardrobe, the groom cared for the horses, and the butler tracked and managed one's bills, all for a meager wage and the occasional pat on the back.

On October 3 members of Churchill's regiment took part in an impromptu steeplechase. The racing ground was of miserable quality, pockmarked with holes, strewn with boulders, and littered with dead or dying vegetation. People of a certain class in England would not even have considered walking on it, let alone mounting a horse and charging full throttle across it in the name of fun. A crowd of locals gathered to watch the proceedings. Churchill cast a critical eye on the lot, particularly the women, whom he found to be "nasty—vulgar creatures all looking as if they thought themselves great beauties." After three days in Poona, the Hussars continued the long trek to Bangalore.

Reveille drew the men from their tents before sunrise. At ten past five that morning, October 6, they boarded a train for the journey to their final destination. It was not a pleasant experience. Sweating bodies crammed side-by-side on uncomfortable wooden benches rendered the air increasingly fetid as the hours endlessly dragged. In the shade the temperature never dropped below triple digits, meaning the rest camps along the way offered little relief. It took four torturous days to reach Bangalore. At least the city was worth the misery of getting there. At three thousand feet above sea level, the temperatures were relatively mild. Although the days could be scorching, the cooler mornings and evenings offered blessed relief. Churchill and two other officers were installed in a pink-and-white stucco bungalow surrounded by a large garden. Whereas he initially had dreaded the idea of posting to India, his surroundings now imbued him with the hope that all would not be so bad.

And why not? Churchill and his two roommates each had their own butlers to wait on them and maintain the stables. Each man had a valet, assisted by a second dressing boy, and for every horse there was a groom. Churchill had three bedrooms to himself, which he adorned with pictures of his mother to remind him of home. There were a few necessities he required. He compiled a list and asked Jennie to send him a card table for hands of piquet, a French card game for two players; books, regardless of topic or author; a dozen or so shirts and any cummerbunds he had left behind; a collection of sporting cartoons from *Vanity Fair*; and his bike, for peddling about the camp.

And then he asked for a few things to help him pursue his latest hobby:

> 1 small collecting box
> 2 large collecting boxes
> 5 setting boards assorted
> 1 net
> 1 box pins
> 1 killing tin

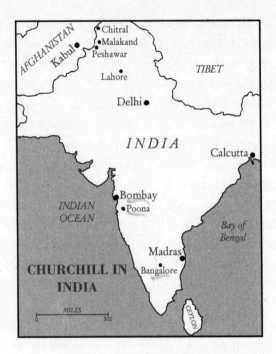

Map 2: Churchill in India

A brilliant assortment of butterflies, some the likes of which he had never seen in England, fluttered about his garden. Always needing something to occupy his time and mind, he thought collecting a display case of specimens might prove a worthwhile pursuit.

When he wasn't stalking the garden with a giant butterfly net, his great passion was polo: "the serious purpose of life." He played polo three times a week and displayed a natural talent for the game despite his injured shoulder, which forced him to ride with his right arm strapped to his side in a leather harness. Each morning, before dawn, the men got up for six o'clock parade and an hour and a half of riding, drilling, and maneuvers. Afterward they returned to their respective bungalows for a hot bath before gathering for breakfast. Attending to the stables was the next order of business, then it was back to the bungalow—usually well before noon—to avoid the midday spike in temperature. Because the heat remained so oppressive and the camp was so spread out, soldiers thought nothing of trotting about the place on horseback to get from one point to another. Lunch was at half past one and was consumed in the blistering heat. Afterward many retired to their quarters and slept until five. "Now the station begins to live again," Churchill wrote. "It is the hour of polo."

Polo is not a game for the faint of heart. The risk of serious injury, even death, for horse and rider runs high. Churchill lived for the game; it appealed to his assertive nature and adventurous spirit. Heavy mallets swinging, galloping beasts hurtling toward one another—the sport is gladiatorial and physically punishing. It kept the men in shape and sharpened their riding skills. They played until sunset, then retreated to their quarters—bruised and battered—for a hot bath. They then convened at half past eight for dinner, downed their meals, and listened with a well-deserved drink to idle conversation and the efforts of the regimental band. Smoking and games of whist occupied the remainder of the evening until the "all to bed" sounded between 10:30 and 11:00. Considering all he had done to excuse himself from the regiment's deployment to India, Churchill found—quite unexpectedly—that life was not so unbearable. He voiced as much in a letter to his brother, Jack, and encouraged him to visit. One could not imagine how different India was in contrast to the United States. Here the natives were a servile lot and cheap to employ. One would be hard pressed to find such subservience in a typical American. Housing was also surprisingly inexpensive. With little money, a British officer could live a rich life—something not likely to happen in New York.

When not engaged in polo matches or his military duties, Churchill kept himself busy reading, writing, and hunting butterflies. He soon amassed such a collection that the officers with whom he shared his quarters complained the dead specimens gave the place an unsettling atmosphere. Nevertheless, Churchill still thought it a pleasant abode. He had put much effort into the furnishings and the hanging of pictures. Oriental rugs covered the floors, and new curtains kept the sun at bay. One would be unlikely, Churchill thought, to find a nicer bungalow in camp.

Despite these relative comforts, his butterfly collection, and the thrill of polo, Churchill yearned for more mental stimulation. Mail call at camp was a source of great excitement. He always hoped for a letter from home with news of the real world. In Bangalore he felt far removed from civilization and at times lonely. The men in his regiment were fine, but his fellow Hussars failed to meet his high standards of conversation. It is perhaps for this reason that, as Churchill's twenty-second birthday approached in November 1896, he decided to make up for his squandered opportunities at school.

He focused on history, philosophy, and economics, devoting up to five hours a day to reading. He sometimes tackled four books simultaneously to keep his interest piqued, slogging his way through all eight volumes of Gibbon's *Decline and Fall of the Roman Empire* and Lord Macaulay's five-volume *The History of England*. He soon moved on to *Plato's Republic,* Darwin's *Origin of the Species,* and a myriad other titles. Churchill had always been a voracious reader, but now he read to satisfy his intellectual curiosity. Bartlett's *Familiar Quotations* became a personal favorite. He believed studying the quotations of educated men imparted wisdom, and they inspired him to seek out the full works composed by such enlightened minds. The list of desired titles grew day by day. He sent his mother a steady stream of letters requesting more books, among them Adam Smith's *Wealth of Nations* and Henry Hallam's *Constitutional History of England.*

The more he learned, the more he questioned—particularly in matters of religion. Morning and evening prayers had been part of the curriculum at Harrow, in addition to three services every Sunday. He had attended church once a week during the holidays with his family, accepting all he read in the Bible and heard from the pulpit. Now he wondered why. Christianity, it seemed to him, was merely a disciplinary tool aimed at ensuring that people lived by a certain standard. Weren't all religions basically the same thing? If so, why did they matter—who was to say one was more important than the others?

Churchill delved into several books, including William Winwood Reade's controversial *The Martyrdom of Man*, that called into question all he had been raised to believe. Reade's book was a secular history of the Western world, essentially arguing that religion imprisoned free thought. Reade's work, and others like it, resulted in Churchill's rejection of traditional Christian beliefs. He instead decided to believe in whatever he wanted to believe—and if that meant a higher power at times of great peril, so be it. In the years ahead he had no problem saying a prayer before exposing himself to enemy fire, nor did he feel self-conscious uttering a word of thanks whenever he emerged unscathed from a battle. Nevertheless, he thought there was little good to be found in too much religion, arguing that it bred fanaticism, which in turn could lead "to murder, mutiny, or rebellion."

Although he primarily focused on works of nonfiction, Churchill made a point of reading Rudyard Kipling's volume of poetry, *The Seven Seas*, released in October 1896. He was not impressed and, in a sharply astute letter to Jack, elaborated on the finite skills of authors:

> Few writers stand the test of success. Rider Haggard—Weyman—Boldrewood are all losing or have already lost their prowess. What happens is this. An author toils away & has many failures. Rejected contributions—books which the publisher's [*sic*] won't publish accumulate. Money does not. One day he writes a book which makes him famous: *King Solomon's Mines*, *A Gentleman of France* or *Robbery Under Arms*. His name now is on every one's lips—his books are clamored for by the public. Out come all the old inferior productions from their receptacles, and his financial fortune is made. Few authors are rich men.

Churchill took a brief sabbatical from his books in November, when his regimental polo team traveled to Secunderabad—some seven hundred miles from Bangalore—for the Golconda Cup tournament. Being stuck in a train for twenty-four hours offered little prospect of enjoyment, but it seemed to Churchill journeys of such length were the norm out here. And so another day was lost to the cramped and stagnant confines of an overheated railway carriage.

The regiment played well and, after a series of bruising matches, won the tournament. The Hussars left the field with a silver trophy and the distinction of being the first English regiment to win a championship tournament after being in India for less than a month. Local newspapers, Churchill boasted, made quite a fuss of the victory. While at Secunderabad he met the lovely Pamela Plowden, seven months his senior and daughter of a local British colonial official. She was, Churchill informed his mother, the most stunning woman he had ever laid eyes on. He hoped to take her on an elephant ride through the city of Hyderabad, seeing as the locals did not take kindly to Europeans strolling their streets and often expressed their disapproval with a well-aimed glob of spit.

But not even the prospect of love could prevent the slow rot of boredom from settling in. India was quickly losing its luster. The food, drink, and social activities fell well below the standard one would expect in England, while his fellow officers showed no interest in learning about the country and were content chatting only about horses. And so the months began to drag. It became increasingly difficult, as Churchill sat at his writing desk, to pen letters of any substance. He had put on paper all he thought to be worthwhile and again found himself longing for a change of pace and scenery. It appeared he would soon get his wish.

As the blistering summer season approached, a number of officers were told they could take three months' leave to England beginning in April. Many men passed up the opportunity, as India remained a grand novelty. Churchill, on the other hand, couldn't get away fast enough. His mother urged him to reconsider. Lord Randolph, upon his death, had not left a large fortune. Churchill relied on his mother for every financial need, including any trips he made from India to England. In a letter dated March 18, 1897, Jennie said although she would love to have him back home, the exorbitant cost of the trip and the short leave time did not justify the travel expense. It was time Churchill gave greater consideration to his finances—or lack thereof. She could not talk him into doing anything he didn't want to, but warned him that, should he return, every creditor in England would pounce on him like a starved beast. Churchill would not be swayed and told his mother he hoped she would receive him with a warm and enthusiastic welcome. He did not anticipate arriving home until June 1, just in time for the derby at Epsom. His plans called for sailing to Bombay and traveling from there to England via Paris. Whatever sort of welcome lay in store, he was desperate by April to be on his way. India now failed to charm in every conceivable way. The sun beat down without mercy, the dead and barren landscape offered nothing to the eye, and the poverty and filth in Bangalore were sickening to behold. Books and butterflies were no longer a panacea.

War, as always, continued to stir his passions. There were dark rumblings in Southeast Europe, where Greece and Turkey were disputing the status of Crete. The Greek majority on the island, then a Turkish province, wanted a union with Greece. Churchill followed the drama in the newspapers and saw another chance for adventure. In mid-April the two belligerents went to war. Churchill could not have been happier. He wrote his mother to let her know England was off his travel itinerary. As he already had approved leave, he proposed traveling to the war zone and reporting on the conflict. He asked his mother to approach the London newspapers on his behalf. He wanted £10 to £15 an article and if necessary could provide simple illustrations. He would not go if she objected, he wrote with a lack of conviction, before laying on the guilt and reminding her that Cuba had been a risk worth taking. Here was the possibility of an even greater experience—no doubt Jennie, yet again, would do all she could to facilitate his wishes. Once all the necessary arrangements had been made, he instructed, she could send his press credentials to Brindisi, on Italy's Adriatic coast, where he'd be stopping en route to the front.

Churchill set off before receiving his mother's reply. He boarded the steamer *Ganges* on May 8 and sailed out of Bombay for the Yemeni seaport of Aden. The voyage was hot and miserable. He changed boats at Aden and sailed for Italy, anxious to reach his ultimate destination. With Britain backing the Turks, Churchill feared the war would end before he again set foot on land. His fears were justified. On board the SS *Caledonia*, he received the disheartening news that the conflict had come to an end. His great scheme thwarted, he decided to spend a few days in Rome and then Paris before returning to England, where he still hoped to attend the derby at Epsom.

CHAPTER 5

The Theater of War

By 1897 the British and Russian empires had clashed twice over Afghanistan. The Russians had been slowly extending their reach into central Asia. The British—with the Union Jack planted firmly in India—feared the Russians might use Afghanistan as a staging area to invade "the jewel of the British Empire." In a preemptive strike, Britain invaded Afghanistan in 1838 and installed a puppet regime, which collapsed when the British vacated the country in 1842. The Russians stirred the dying embers in 1878 when they sent a diplomatic mission to Kabul. The British again stormed Afghanistan shortly thereafter and engaged in a two-year conflict, in which total victory eluded both sides. The British then established a buffer zone between Afghanistan and British India, the 1,640-mile-long Durand Line, to deter any Russian designs on the Raj.

Native to this region, colonial India's North-West Frontier, were Pashtun tribesmen, the fiercely independent ancestors of today's Taliban. "Every influence, every motive, that provokes the spirit of murder among men, impels these mountaineers to deeds of treachery and violence," Churchill would later write. "The strong aboriginal propensity to kill, inherent in all human beings, has in these valleys been preserved in unexampled strength and vigor."

The warrior tribes on the British side of the demarcation line did not take kindly to an imperial force laying claim to their land. A Pashtun fakir named Saidulla, known among the British as the "Mad Mullah," stoked the collective agitation of the region's tribes into open rebellion. "He was," notes one contemporary account, "giving out that he had been inspired to preach a 'Jihad' or Holy War against the unbelievers." As he made his way through the Swat Valley, preaching his message and stoking the fire, his followers grew rapidly in number, attracted by the promise of riches in this life and the attainment of paradise in the afterworld.

The combative zeal of the Mullah and his followers reached its flashpoint on the evening of Monday, July 26, 1897, when thousands of tribesmen swarmed down the Swat Valley "in a storm of fanaticism" and hurled themselves against British forts at Malakand and Chakdara. Soldiers scrambled in the dark, their rifles at the ready. "The troops hastened to their posts," recalled one battle participant, "and they had hardly occupied these before the first shots rang out which heralded the onslaught, which continued night and day, with but slight intermission, for the next five days." The British ultimately prevailed, inflicting two thousand casualties on the enemy at a cost of 206 men. London, however, had no intention of leaving the matter at that and sent forth a punitive expedition to end the native rebellion.

The Malakand Field Force comprised roughly twelve hundred men, "mostly Indian army troops," and was commanded by the aptly named General Sir Bindon Blood. A descendant of Colonel Thomas Blood, who had gained notoriety for stealing the crown jewels during the reign of King Charles II, Sir Bindon was a soldier of vast experience, having so far seen action in the Zulu Wars of 1879 and the Afghan War the following year. In 1895, when twelve thousand tribesmen lay siege to the British fort at Chitral, Blood had served as chief staff officer on the relief force sent from Peshawar. An imperial army of fifteen thousand had checked the onslaught, suffering only sixty-nine casualties to the two thousand natives killed or wounded. The tribesmen had retreated back to their mountain redoubts and, for the most part, had remained there until this most recent uprising.

Blood and Winston Churchill first crossed paths in 1896 during a soiree at the home of Winston's aunt, Duchess Lily. Enthralled by Blood's tales of adventure, Churchill made Blood promise that should he lead another expedition on the Indian frontier, he would find a role for the young Hussar. If Blood forgot the promise, Churchill certainly did not. He was enjoying an afternoon of warm weather at Goodwood racecourse and the unfamiliar sensation of having money in his pocket, courtesy of a winning streak, when he heard talk in the crowd of Blood's expedition. Churchill, never one to delay, immediately sent the general a telegram reminding him of his promise. Not waiting for Blood's response, he cut his leave three weeks short and made arrangements for his hasty return to India. He would leave London by train for Brindisi, where he planned to catch a mail boat for the arduous journey back east. Before departing from Victoria Station, Churchill dined at the Marlborough Club with Lord William Beresford, Duchess Lily's husband and, as it so happened, a friend of Blood's. Promising to put in a good word with the general, Beresford introduced Churchill to several gentlemen smoking nearby. By way of introduction, he told them Churchill was setting off that night to cover the war on the frontier. The club members, elder gentlemen all, nodded their approval. "Heading to the front, are you?" one of them asked around his cigar. "I hope so," Churchill replied.

Few people would ever hope to serve on a battlefront, but there was nothing typical about Churchill. Battle was a worthy alternative to boredom, which to Churchill was the greatest sin. With his eye on a political future, the young soldier had the spotlight very much in mind. With any luck he would enjoy his fair share of adventure and finally establish a name for himself. He left the club in high spirits and caught his train with only minutes to spare. In Brindisi he secured passage on the mail boat SS *Rome* and boarded with his nerves on edge, for he had yet to receive word from Blood. He began to wonder whether he had cut his leave short for a worthless pursuit.

By August 7 the boat was in the Red Sea. Standing on deck—blinking the sweat from his eyes—Churchill gazed out at the water, amazed that it didn't turn to steam. Every breath weighed heavily on his lungs regardless of the hour. The air in the dining saloon at night was thick with heat, the smell of subpar food, and the stench of perspiring bodies. But Churchill's mental anxiety proved greater than any physical discomfort. When the *Rome* docked at Aden, he could scarcely contain himself as the steward distributed the mail. Churchill watched with growing dismay as the steward called name after name and the stack of mail slowly diminished. With the letters all handed out and none being for him, he was doomed to return once more to Bangalore. Back in his pink bungalow by the middle of August, he dwelled on his lost opportunity.

The general had obviously reneged on his promise—but why? Churchill, not wanting to believe Blood would mislead him on purpose, theorized that someone higher up at the War Office must have disapproved. Although he still hoped a summons might arrive at his door, the reality of the situation grew increasingly stark with each passing day. It all seemed so pointless, sitting here in his pink stucco house with nothing of consequence to do. It was, he thought, symbolic of his army career. He could not thrive in such an environment and realized a life in the military would only mean disappointment. Boredom once again assailed him on all fronts. In his rush to get back to India, he had left in London a considerable number of books—as well as his dog, Peas.

Churchill passed the time working on a project he had started on the voyage from Britain. He "had a liking for words and for the feel of words fitting and falling into their places like pennies in a slot." His command of the language and his power of description were already evident in the dispatches he had filed from Cuba. Wanting to put his talents to the ultimate test, he had decided to write a novel.

The story, a political thriller, takes place in the imaginary Mediterranean republic of Laurania. He gave it the working title *Affairs of State* but eventually settled on *Savrola*. Churchill channeled himself into the title character, the verbally gifted ruler of a burgeoning political party opposed to Laurania's dictatorial President Molara. "'Vehement, high, and daring,' was his cast of mind," Churchill writes of his on-page alter ego. "The life he lived was the only one he could ever live; he must go on to the end. The end comes early to such men, whose spirits are so wrought that they know rest only in action, contentment only in danger, and in confusion find their only peace." The plot thickens when Molara's wife, the beautiful Lucile, falls in love with Savrola. Intrigue and chaos ensue, and Savrola eventually overthrows the despot. Churchill had up to this point written eighty manuscript pages and thought it the greatest thing he had yet put to paper. This would prove to be his only work of fiction.

Despite his enthusiasm for the project, he remained bitter about Blood's flagrant slight. He wrote his mother to say he was disgusted at the general—a state of mind not helped by Blood's lack of response to Churchill's numerous wires. Things changed, however, on August 22, when a telegram arrived from Blood, who was in the Upper Swat Valley and preparing for his expedition.

The general struck a contrite tone, explaining that he had first had to fill vacancies on his personal staff before attending to the business at hand. If Churchill still wished to join the expedition, Blood said the only way possible would be to do so as a press correspondent. Army headquarters in Calcutta handled all appointments to the Malakand Field Force—with the exception of Blood's personal staff—and it was not prone to cronyism. Should Churchill secure a credential from a respectable paper, however, the general felt confident he could make a case for having a journalist tag along.

An ecstatic Churchill, after a lot of heavy-handed persuasion, convinced his superiors to grant him a month's leave and set off on August 28 for the North-West Frontier. He would soon experience the full realities of war. The Malakand Field Force was operating out of the cantonment of Nowshera, today located in the Khyber Pakhtunkhwa Province of Pakistan, but at the time of Churchill's adventure "situated on the India side of the Cabul River."

"How far is it to Nowshera?" Churchill asked the ticket clerk at the Bangalore train station.

"Two thousand and twenty-seven miles," the clerk replied nonchalantly.

Churchill, momentarily stunned, blinked the sweat from his eyes. He realized the immensity of India had completely escaped him. It had merely been a possession on the map, a jewel in the glittering mosaic of Britain's empire. It was both impressive and intimidating—almost comical in its absurdity, a testament to Britain's greatness and the supremacy of English blood, the idea that a small island nation could preside over a distant dominion so massive in size.

The journey by train would take five days in the usual sweltering heat. With no other option available to him, Churchill purchased a ticket for the epic northward trek and resigned himself to a long, hot haul. He naturally traveled in what comfort was available, booking a compartment for himself. The carriage, with its leather-padded walls and windows shuttered against the glaring sun, was kept somewhat cool by a wheel of wet straw one had to crank by hand for a modicum of breeze. Churchill, who never traveled light, brought with him what books he could scrounge up. Nevertheless, the journey was an ordeal. He spent five days in his compartment, reading by lamplight with the blinds and jalousies shut tight against the outside world. Occasionally he braved the sun to view the passing landscape. The train cut its way through vast desert before the cracked, arid ground surrendered to the green, rolling vistas of the Central Provinces. The land again turned barren as the train approached the foothills of the Himalayas. The endless rattling of the carriage, the cloying heat, and the smell of unpleasant food grated on his nerves. *Savrola*—with five chapters written so far—was locked away in a drawer. The grand sweep of the North-West Frontier and the conflict ahead dominated Churchill's thoughts. His novel would have to wait.

He knew the inherent danger in this constant pursuit of action, but saw it as the only way to build his political credibility. However, there was another factor at play. Tempting fate on the battlefield was a gamble, and he enjoyed the game. The prospect of death did not faze him. One did not stop playing cards because he feared a bad hand; such risk made the game worth playing. Compensation for his time didn't hurt, either. It was up to Jennie to find a paper willing to contract Churchill as its correspondent. He had already arranged to write three hundred words a day for an Indian newspaper, the *Pioneer*, but he needed the backing of a London publication to accompany Blood as a journalist.

He only hoped his mother came through before he reached Nowshera. He could not present himself at the general's headquarters with his only press credential being that of a third-rate rag in Allahabad. His adventure would come to an end before it even began, disappointing not only Churchill but the *Pioneer*'s eager editor.

He was desperate to be part of the expedition, not just for the thrill but for what it represented: the avenging of a grievous wrong. British prestige was at stake. To his brother, Jack, he stressed his belief in the British cause. "It is impossible for the British Government to be content with repelling an injury," he wrote. "It must be avenged." In the first week of September, after five sweat-soaked days, he reached Nowshera, having stopped along the way at Rawalpindi, where preparations for war were clearly evident.

At the railway station, soldiers and provisions crowded the platform, while long transport trains hauling supplies to the front continuously steamed in and out. The sight of one such train amused Churchill. Among the cars it pulled was an open-roofed carriage holding half a dozen camels. As Churchill stared, a soldier on the platform told him the animals were tied down at the knees to prevent them moving about. Nevertheless, their long necks still rose high above the sides of the car. On rare occasions, the soldier said, they sometimes managed to free themselves from their restraints and stand fully upright. The presence of numerous tunnels along the route generally meant a scene of horror when the train pulled into the Rawalpindi station with headless camels among its cargo.

From Nowshera, Churchill still had fifty miles of parched wasteland to cross before reaching Blood's men at the Malakand Pass. He caught a tonga—an uncomfortable cart jostled along by a team of ponies—for the final seven-hour leg of his journey. He rode past creaking wagons hauling war supplies and men preparing to head for the front. A group of armed Sikhs, barking and yelling commands, pulled and prodded a long line of shackled prisoners. The tonga driver explained they were known troublemakers being taken away until things in the region had calmed down. Churchill wiped the sweat from his brow and the dust from his eyes. On either side of the primitive roadway, clouds of flies

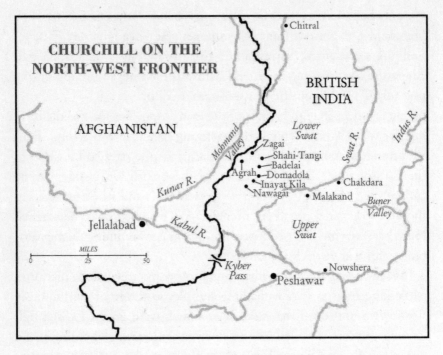

Map 3: Churchill on the North-West Frontier

hung thick and heavy over the rotting corpses of horses and oxen, their throats apparently sliced by long blades.

In the more civilized environs of London, Jennie busied herself approaching the various newspapers on her son's behalf. She struck out with the *Times* but secured interest from the *Daily Telegraph*. What the paper wanted, proprietor Edward Lawson responded, were hard-hitting letters that painted in words the savagery of the region and the fierceness of the struggle. Jennie assured him Churchill could provide what he wanted. By the time Churchill arrived at the Malakand Camp, his body covered in dust and grime and sore from many days of travel, he had the necessary credentials to accompany Blood into battle. He surveyed his new surroundings. The ground was a nightmare of sharp rock, dry scrub, and various deformities that made it difficult for men and horses alike. The surrounding hills were little better, smothered in boulders and tree stumps, but offered more amenable ground for pitching one's canvas shelter. All up the slopes soldiers had raised their tents on wooden platforms built into the hillside.

He presented himself at the camp's staff office and learned that Blood was away on an expedition against the Bunerwals, a fierce Pashtun tribe, who occupied a not-too-distant valley. Awaiting Blood's return, Churchill settled into his new surroundings. He was given a place in the staff mess and a tent to stow his belongings. While waiting for Blood to return, he passed his time writing letters and his first dispatch for the *Telegraph*, dated September 3, in which he detailed the long journey from Bangalore to his present location. "Rumors run through the camp of movements here and marches there, all ultimately pointing to a move against the Mohamands," he wrote. "It should be remembered that this powerful tribe deliberately made an unprovoked attack on a British post and, without cause or warning, committed a violation of the Imperial territory. I rejoice to be able to end this letter with the news that such audacity is no longer to remain unchastised, and that movements are now contemplated which indicate the adoption of a policy agreeable to expert opinion and suited to the dignity of the Empire." The policy in question would prove to be brute force.

Churchill prepared for the campaign. Even in the middle of nowhere, there were high standards to maintain. Protocol required he purchase two good horses, hire a military groom, and buy certain accoutrements for his martial wardrobe. But where could he find such things out here? Much to Churchill's good luck—but their misfortune—several men had recently been killed in action. Adhering to the region's military customs, the bodies were stripped of all useful items prior to burial. With the funerals over and the graves filled in, the possessions were auctioned off to those with a more immediate need. Churchill found the whole thing quite morbid. Staring at various items of clothing—jackets, boots, and shirts—alongside cooking utensils and sidearms laid out in the dirt for perusal and sale, he couldn't help but think it was slightly degrading to the deceased. There was, however, an economical logic to it all no matter how off-putting, and it allowed Churchill to acquire the necessary clothing and equipment for the campaign.

The heat proved an ordeal, with the mercury riding far north of 100 degrees. Refreshments in the camp were limited to tea, warm water, or whisky. Churchill's favorite libation was champagne, though he also enjoyed wines—both red and white. The smoky taste of whisky had never been to his liking. Whisky in those days was considered a rough-and-tumble drink, something to be sipped while out on a hunt, but not enjoyed in polite company. The civilized classes enjoyed brandy with a splash of soda, but that was another world away. Forced to choose between tea and tepid water, Churchill went with the only sensible option: whisky. Compelled by harsh conditions, he soon found the stuff tolerable. Repeated tastings, and there were many, soon bred a deep appreciation. At Malakand whisky became Churchill's drink of choice. It proved to be no fleeting infatuation, but an abiding love that spanned the decades and saw Churchill through to the very end.

Fully equipped for the desert and with enough whisky to keep him happy, Churchill awaited Sir Bindon's return. The general, victorious in his campaign against the Bunerwals, rode into camp five days later. Churchill emerged from his tent, struck by the vision before him. Blood, astride his steed, cut an imposing figure against the mountain-ous backdrop. When Churchill had last seen Blood, at his aunt's dinner party in England, the general had seemed more a dapper country gentleman than anything else. Here, on the wild and savage frontier, Blood bristled with absolute power. The general's standard-bearer stood nearby as if adding emphasis to the man's importance. Blood welcomed Churchill to the expedition and explained their mission in simple terms: avenge British honor and teach the Pashtuns a lesson they would not soon forget. The warrior tribes held the advantage in the rugged mountains and deep valleys they called home. They had fortified the valleys with mud-built strongholds and lookout towers with slits in the walls for rifles, allowing them to lay down heavy fire without exposing themselves. In the mountains and hills they enjoyed the advantage of their elevated position. And regardless of geography, the Pashtuns were a fierce and fearless people "trained by constant war."

Nothing about the coming action suggested easy victory. On the night of September 5 Churchill, a whisky in hand and cigar clamped in

his jaw, wrote a final letter to his mother before marching into "an unknown country with an uncounted & improved enemy." He implied
that he might be dead by the time she read his words—but such were
the risks he took pleasure in chasing. He urged Jennie not to worry and
told her to keep an open mind, that she should take comfort in knowing he was following his own path. On a more practical note, in regard
to his *Daily Telegraph* dispatches, there was the matter of whether he
should take credit for his work or remain anonymous. Naturally he
wanted his name on each piece. Wasn't the point of this exercise to
build his public profile? Anonymity would do nothing to help him
establish his political credentials. Regardless of the credit, he expected
to be paid at least £10 per dispatch. As it transpired, the *Telegraph*
would run fifteen dispatches by Churchill at £5 an article ("about £300
today") and credit him as "A Young Officer." This was Jennie's doing.
After consulting friends in London, she thought it best that her son's
name be omitted, lest he be considered a glory hound.

On the afternoon of Monday, September 6, Blood and his men
mounted their charges and left the Malakand camp. The hooves of the
horses kicked up clouds of yellow dust as they traversed a rough road
dominated by steep, rocky slopes and dangerous drop-offs. Over the
course of four miles the road slowly descended to the "fertile plain" of
the Lower Swat Valley. Venturing even this meager distance from camp
was not without risk. "In spite of the shortness of the way, and of the
cowed and humble attitudes of the natives in this valley, the regulations
as to traversing it are strict," Churchill reported. "Individuals must be
accompanied by an escort. Whenever possible they will arrange to go
in couples, and in every case arms must be carried. Isolated incidents
of fanaticism have to be guarded against, and it is only through the
precautions observed that no accident has so far occurred." Churchill
listened intently as an officer, who had recently seen action against the
tribesmen, contrasted the now-quiet nature of the surrounding landscape with the bloody chaos that had embroiled the scenery just prior
to Churchill's arrival. Enemy snipers had wreaked havoc on the British, taking shots from their concealed positions on the high, rugged
embankments.

The officer pointed out random patches of dirt where one soldier or another had died by enemy fire or blade. And there, in the near distance, was where the British had finally charged the enemy and chased them into the hills. Churchill eyed the rock and sand for signs of past battles but saw nothing. The men passed the remains of a mud fort—really nothing more than a simple, square construction. Large, jagged holes disfigured the walls of the crude structure. It was here, the officer said, that a number of British soldiers had taken up position to fire on the enemy. "The tribesmen cut through the walls and got in," the officer said. "The soldiers ran frantically from one hole to another, trying to stem the flood—but it was useless. They didn't have a chance."

Blood's main objective that first day on the move was the fort at Chakdara, which guarded a swinging rope bridge across the River Swat. It lay ten miles from the Malakand camp, a considerable distance when traveling through enemy territory. The fort sat on a rocky knoll surrounded by hills that looked down on the compound, making it vulnerable to attack. As night crept up the valley, sentries made the rounds and lit lanterns, casting everything in pallid, watery light. Churchill watched the men go about their duties and pondered the mysterious enemy that lay in wait. The Malakand Field Force faced a number of tribes, including the Swatis, Bunerwals, and Mohmands—all well-versed in war. They showed no fear in battle and embraced death. Rarely did they take a defensive position, choosing instead to charge British and Indian troops in bloody close-quarter clashes. Once committed to the attack, they did not retreat; only a well-aimed shot could stop one in his tracks. Even in hand-to-hand combat they cared not for their own safety, thrusting and slashing wildly with their swords, hell-bent on killing their opponents.

The tribesmen, Churchill reported, showed a keen grasp of tactics in their use of the landscape. They were masters at utilizing the natural setting as camouflage and attacked seemingly from out of nowhere. If such admirable skill could be considered a virtue, it was, Churchill wrote, their only one:

Successful murder—whether by open force or treachery—is the surest road to distinction among them. . . . Their principal article of commerce is their women—wives and daughters—who are exchanged for rifles. This degradation of mind is unrelieved by a single elevated sentiment. Their religion is the most miserable fanaticism, in which cruelty, credulity and immorality are equally represented. . . . It is impossible to imagine a lower type of being or a more dreadful state of barbarism.

Such barbarians were immune to the voice of reason, for "in a land of fanatics common sense does not exist." Churchill closed the dispatch with an appeal to the patriotism of his readers. He imagined them back home, browsing the paper at breakfast or after dinner in their parlors, surrounded by the comforts of civilized life. They were the overseers of a vast domain, the greatest empire in history, a source of immeasurable pride. What would they think upon reading that "savages" were killed for acts of violence against British possessions? Churchill believed he knew the answer. They would say, "with firmness and without reserve, 'So perish all who do the like again.'"

Blood's march resumed the following day. The landscape offered little to please the eye. Churchill found it stark and depressing, weighted by the history of countless barbaric acts, but every desolate mile brought him that much closer to the action he craved. The long marching days were an exercise in tedium and discomfort. Even for British troops accustomed to India's searing climate, the heat proved challenging. They marched in heavy pith helmets, the wide brims shielding their eyes and skin from the glaring sun. The uniforms were made of loose-fitting khaki, but the padded spine protectors the men wore added little in the way of comfort. Marching alongside Indian troops, who did not feel the heat so acutely, the British did not complain.

"The dominant race," Churchill reported in the *Telegraph*, "resent the slightest suggestion of inferiority." Blood's men covered eight to fourteen miles a day; the ranks, although tired, remained "cheery and good-humored" at the prospect of thrashing the enemy. At the end of each grueling day the British soldiers appeared "strained and weary," though none offered any complaint. This, in Churchill's opinion, was the stuff upon which empires were built. The next day would see more of the same: making slow progress through narrow canyons and up steep, rocky hills, traversing treacherous mountain passes, all the while keeping one's guard up against an ambush. At night the men would set up camp, their silhouettes by firelight an enticing target for the Pashtuns monitoring from the bluffs above. Sniper fire routinely pierced the nocturnal silence, so much so that Churchill and the others came to expect such attacks after sunset. They proved more a nuisance, however, than a serious threat. Finally, in the second week of September Blood's force reached Nàwagai, gateway to Mohmand country. Churchill dashed off a quick note to his mother to let her know all was well. He had yet to encounter the enemy, but expected to do so any day. Conditions were generally miserable, but he found the whole experience exhilarating. He was too exhausted to write anything more, but enclosed another two dispatches for the *Telegraph*.

On September 13 Blood invited Churchill to join him on a reconnaissance mission to survey a nearby mountain pass. Churchill readily accepted but was disappointed when the enemy failed to make an appearance. Riding through a village with Blood's intelligence officer, a man named Stanton, Churchill saw a dozen tribesmen, all armed with rifles, milling about. They glared at the British officers as the two men rode past. Incensed by this apparent show of disrespect, Stanton demanded the natives stand up and salute. The tribesmen refused, prompting Churchill to shift uncomfortably in his saddle. Stanton barked his order again. The natives held his gaze and slowly got to their feet. Churchill, unsure of their intentions, dropped his hand to his sidearm. The tribesmen stood still, their rifles within easy reach, and for one excruciating moment seemed to ponder their options. Their decision made, they slowly raised their arms in salute and sat back down. Satisfied, Stanton snapped the reins of his horse and went on his way. The confrontation, Churchill thought, was a strange one.

That evening, back at camp, as Blood and his staff dined in the mess tent, the tribesmen commenced their nightly sniping. One round tore through the canvas walls and buzzed over the heads of those at the table. Blood's servant, busy dishing up food, hardly flinched and carried on his duties without missing a beat. In a letter to Reginald Barnes the following day, Churchill said British troops considered the Pashtuns' nocturnal sniping to be poor sportsmanship. Things, he wrote, would soon be escalating. In the next few days Blood's men would start burning villages and killing anyone who resisted. Churchill realized the barbarity of such actions, but to his mind cruelty was necessary to avenge British honor. Besides, this was not a civilized land for civilized people. He had seen things that would forever stay with him. On one occasion, at Malakand, he had watched several Sikhs pick up a wounded man and shove him into an incinerator, the flames melting skin off bone as the screams slowly faded. No one made a fuss about it. Law was meaningless out here.

On the morning of September 15, as Churchill ate breakfast with Blood's staff, an Indian officer from the force's 2nd Brigade arrived, breathless, on horseback to say the brigade's camp, twelve miles away, had come under heavy fire during the night. Three British officers and twelve Indian soldiers were dead, and nearly a hundred horses had been wounded. Enraged, Blood ordered the brigade—commanded by Brigadier General P. D. Jeffreys—to march the length of the ten-mile-long Mohmand Valley and avenge their losses.

Blood turned to Churchill and said he should leave immediately and join Jeffreys if he wished to see action. Churchill excused himself from the table and rushed to his tent. He rummaged through his trunk and picked out some fresh khakis, along with the more vital necessities of chocolate, a toothbrush, and a waterproof blanket. He wrapped his few possessions in a saddle pack and then left to catch up with the Indian officer and his escorts, who were already on their way back to the 2nd Brigade's camp. For the first six miles they cut a winding course through a network of steep ravines that rendered Churchill and his travel companions easy targets from the bluffs above. The men "picked their way with care and caution" through the narrow passes, all the while scanning the rocky slopes for any movement. Here and there the soldiers spotted several tribesmen monitoring their progress, but just as quickly the men seemed to fade into the landscape. At one point

Churchill noticed "native beds" discarded along the rocky path. From the apparent bloodstains, it appeared the tribesmen had suffered their own casualties in the previous night's action and carried their wounded here before abandoning the beds and transferring their casualties to the backs of horses or oxen.

Churchill's party soon emerged from the dangerous canyons onto the broad plains of Nàwagai. They scanned the horizon for signs of the 2nd Brigade and saw, on a distant plateau, a long, khaki-colored line of men and horses making its way into the Watelai Valley to set up a new base of operations. Clouds of dust marked their progress. Churchill and his escorts rode quickly to catch up and take safety in larger numbers. Upon reaching the plateau, Churchill could see the valley spread out beneath him. In the near distance the glare of burning villages blotted the landscape. Great plumes of smoke curled skyward, a startling black against the deep blue. As Churchill surveyed the scene, the small raiding party responsible for the fires returned to camp. Churchill could not help but notice thick smears of blood on their cavalry lances. They seemed well-pleased with their recent efforts.

If Churchill feared he had missed all the action, he need not have worried. As the men, their faces blackened by dirt and smeared with blood, dismounted from their horses, they spoke in upbeat tones of the recent battle. "How many?" someone shouted. "Twenty-one," replied a soldier, "but they are still game. There'll be another attack tonight."

Churchill looked around the newly established camp and saw evidence of the previous night's ordeal. Bullet holes scarred most of the tents; the cries and groans of the wounded drifted from the field hospital. The men looked exhausted, their eyes red from lack of sleep, their faces drawn tight by the stress of combat. "You were lucky to be out of it last night," a soldier told Churchill in passing, "but there's plenty more coming." Hardly words of grim warning to Churchill; this was what he longed to hear. All around the camp men prepared for battle. Soldiers busied themselves stacking bags of flour around the hospital to shield it from enemy fire. Others worked on constructing a defensive wall about three and a half feet high that stretched along the camp's perimeter. A good number of men tackled the hard earth with picks and shovels to dig holes in which they could sleep that night, as tents offered scant protection. Despite these necessary precautions and their evident weariness, the men were confident. They voiced admiration for the bravery and combat skills of their adversaries and discussed the previous night's attack—how bullets had peppered the camp in a seemingly endless volley, how the soldiers had maintained their calm, and how the medics had braved the onslaught to carry the wounded away—like men discussing a well-played polo match.

As the sun sank in a vibrant splash of blood red, word reached the camp through some local "friendlies" that the Pashtuns were tired and would not be attacking that night. The news did little to put the men at ease. Under the black vault of sky, soldiers went about their nightly ritual of lighting fires and prepping dinner. Shortly after ten o'clock, from a high ridge to the north, came the crack of rifle fire. The Pashtuns may have been too tired to launch an all-out assault, but they had no intention of granting the British a reprieve. Bullets churned up dust and rock as soldiers scurried about the camp, extinguishing fires and collapsing tents to spare them further damage. Under the cover of darkness, they retreated to the holes they had dug in the ground.

The firing continued unabated for several hours but caused no injuries. The report of rifles and the noises of the camp came together in a strange symphony. In his dugout Churchill heard the rounds ricocheting off earth and rock, sentries yelling orders, mules and horses neighing and stomping their hooves, and soldiers calling back and forth to one another. Some men, accustomed to such ruckus and exhausted by recent excursions, slept through it all. It was, Churchill considered, a good moment to be alive. He felt a surge of exhilaration, aware that only the present mattered. The past and future weren't worth considering. The situation was strangely liberating in its own way, as it set one free from all other cares.

He listened to the commotion until the shooting subsided around two o'clock. He remained in his shelter and stared at the indifferent stars above until sleep finally overcame him.

Churchill woke to reveille at 5:30 that morning, the air still refreshingly cool. He emerged from his hole in the ground, stretched his aching body, and watched as the camp came to life with daybreak a pale ribbon on the horizon. On this day—Thursday, September 16— the 2nd Brigade would embark on its mission of vengeance. To ensure the Mohmand Valley in its entirety was at the brigade's receiving end, General Jeffreys split his force into three columns. One would set ablaze the village of Domadola on the valley's eastern edge. The column to which Churchill was attached would march up the middle and attack the villages of Badelai and Shahi-Tangi. The third column would destroy villages along the valley's western wall. A number of men would stay behind to protect the camp, while another force would make up a survey party. This left twelve hundred men to carry out the main attacks. At six o'clock they mounted their charges, formed their columns, and rode off under the fluttering colors of the Union Jack.

It did not take long for Churchill's column to stumble across the enemy. After an hour's ride, "long lines" of tribesmen dressed in blue and white gowns could be seen on a hill to the north between Badelai and Shahi-Tangi. Each appeared to hold a rifle upright at his side. They at first paid little heed to the soldiers fanning out on the plain below, but as the Anglo-Sikh force closed in on the villages, they began to descend the hills.

The cavalry of the 11th Bengal Lancers charged ahead and by 7:30 was within firing distance. The men, Churchill among them, dismounted and ran forward a hundred yards before opening fire with their rifles. Clouds of dust and splintered rock rose from the hillside. The tribesmen responded in kind from their elevated position. Churchill could see puffs of gun smoke drift up from behind boulders and squat stone huts, giving him some indication of where to shoot. The two sides exchanged volleys for the better part of an hour, gun smoke wafting gray and heavy across the rugged landscape. The tribesmen scurried among boulders, trees, and the dilapidated stones of a hillside cemetery, never relenting in their barrage. Despite the ferocity of the exchange, neither side inflicted much damage on the other. The tribesmen soon withdrew up the hill and faded from view.

Much like the Spanish in Cuba, the British were up against a guerrilla force. This was not a campaign in the traditional sense, as Churchill's readers in London might have expected. There were no large-scale armies or thousands of cavalrymen charging defended positions with swords drawn. Even the thunderous cannonade of heavy artillery was noticeably absent, but this did not make the campaign any less dangerous. The British faced a worthy adversary—"savages," in Churchill's words, "impelled by fanaticism"—fueled by the strongest of motivations: to expel an invader from their homeland.

Seventy-five men were ordered to secure the hill, while the remainder of the column—Churchill included—was ordered to advance on Shahi-Tangi, which sat atop the highest point of a steep spur comprised of three hillocks, each one higher than the other. Rows of tall Indian corn and a sharp climb appeared to be the only obstacles in the line of advance. A few enemy snipers remained behind some rocks and trees and fired steadily on the troops scrambling up the sharp incline. "Well-aimed volleys," however, forced the tribesmen from their places of cover and sent them up to higher elevations. Moving up the spur proved tough going, as loose rock and gravel, the steep angle, and the retreating fire of the natives hampered their progress, but by eleven o'clock they reached the village. Anticipating a strong defense, the men were surprised to find the place strangely quiet. Not a single tribesman materialized in the hills above or among the earthen huts. The soldiers, eager to avenge the attack on their camp, could only express surprise at the enemy's timid nature. This fell short of the savagery and fearlessness that defined the tribal warrior.

The British entered the village and set the small, primitive dwellings ablaze. The flames quickly took hold and sent thick, black smoke curling skyward. Churchill sat on a rock to mop his brow. The sun, high overhead, baked everything below. Churchill took a deep swig of water from his flask and, through his field glasses, surveyed the desert plain beneath the spur. Immediately something struck him as odd. The 2nd Brigade appeared to have vanished; nowhere could he see a soldier, horse, or any other remnant of the attack force. What he saw were scattered villages built of mud and stone and a snaking network of irrigation ditches dug into the hard earth. Here and there were islands of vegetation, like oases in the desert, lending a splash of green to the colorless vista. The great valley, it seemed, had swallowed men, horses, and cannons. Feeling very isolated, Churchill looked around the burning village and realized just how small his raiding party was: five British officers, including himself, and eighty-five Sikhs. He found the vulnerability of their party strangely exciting. "Like most young fools I was looking for trouble," he recalled later, "and only hoped that something exciting would happen. It did!" While Churchill pondered this somewhat precarious position, a captain from the vanished army appeared. It was apparently still down there but obscured from view by the spur upon which Churchill sat. A withdrawal had been ordered, the captain said. Churchill and his party were to stay put and safeguard the rear flank.

The men hung about the village for ten minutes, waiting for additional orders, and then the full might of the enemy broke upon them. The silent, barren hillside above the village writhed with sudden activity. From behind rocks and trees countless figures seemed to spring from the earth, screaming and waving swords. An army of Pashtuns thundered into battle beneath brightly colored banners and opened fire with their Martini-Henry rifles. The Sikhs in Churchill's party fired frantically to stem the oncoming wave, which quickly closed to almost spitting distance.

Armed only with a revolver, Churchill borrowed the rifle of the Sikh next to him and took aim. Finding something to shoot at did not prove to be a problem. He burned through ammunition as the Sikh handed him one cartridge after another. The air buzzed with bullets and reeked of gun smoke. The clatter of guns and the yelling of men were almost deafening. And still the tribesmen advanced. Churchill finally had the fight he wanted. He and his party began falling back from the village and worked their way down the spur in a fighting retreat. Several Pashtuns emerged from the cover of some nearby rocks and fired at close range. One soldier near Churchill collapsed with a ragged hole in his chest and bled into the ground. Another lay nearby, screaming in the dirt. One bullet sliced the air near Churchill's head and hit the British officer behind him. He turned in time to see the man spinning, the round having removed a good portion of the officer's face, including his right eye. One did not leave a fallen comrade behind, especially on the North-West Frontier, for the tribesmen did not take prisoners. A slow and miserable death inflicted by sword and spear was the fate of any poor wretch who, in battle, fell into Pashtun hands.

The men still standing dragged and carried the screaming wounded, ignoring their agonized protests. Churchill wondered how any of them would survive the ordeal. Looking down the spur, he saw no evidence of reinforcements. Two Sikhs were helping Churchill carry a wounded man when one of them took a round through the leg. The Sikh refused all help and insisted on making his own way despite the gaping wound. He crawled, hopped, and stumbled, but managed to get away. The same could not be said for the company adjutant, a man of considerable bulk, who had just taken a bullet. Four soldiers were struggling to support the man's weight and move him down the spur to safety. A dozen screaming Pashtuns emerged from a cluster of nearby huts. One by one the soldiers panicked and fled, leaving the adjutant to collapse in the dirt. The men who ran, Churchill later wrote an acquaintance, were "utterly out of hand." One of the tribesmen—tall and lean, wearing what looked like grimy white bed sheets—lunged forward with his sword and slashed the adjutant four times. Enraged, Churchill acted. Overwhelmed by a strong and sudden bloodlust, he went deaf and blind to the chaos around him and focused only on this one "savage." He felt the reassuring weight of his cavalry sword at his side—the blade sharpened to a lethal point—and rushed forward, his hand on the sword's hilt. The tribesman, standing over the prostrate and bloody form of the adjutant, saw Churchill approach and hurled a rock at him. At twenty yards Churchill opted for lead over steel and drew his revolver. He took as careful aim as circumstances allowed and squeezed off three rounds. The tribesman quickly disappeared behind a rock.

Churchill, not bothering to see if his bullets had found their mark, turned and ran. The adjutant was dead, and the area was swarming with tribesmen. Bullets kicked up dust at Churchill's feet. Everywhere was the din and carnage of battle: the clatter of rifles, the frenzied screams of the enemy, and the bloodied and mutilated remains of fallen soldiers. Startled, Churchill realized he was caught in the maelstrom alone. All he saw around him were angry Pashtun faces. Somehow, he'd been left behind.

He ran as fast as he could and was relieved to see a number of Sikh soldiers on the next hillock down. He rejoined their ranks and snatched a rifle and some ammunition from a nearby corpse. The men were in danger of being surrounded. Churchill fired rapidly, without the benefit of aiming, while also helping to drag a wounded man down the hill toward the safety of the plain. It was a grueling endeavor that left him gasping for breath and trembling with exhaustion. There was no cohesion, no set battle plan; the men simply fought to survive. They fired in all directions to stave off encirclement. Some who fell to enemy rounds could not be recovered and were surrendered to a grisly fate. Thirteen men, some wounded—others, fortunately, dead—were sliced, stabbed, and disemboweled. Eight other men, suffering wounds of various degrees, were spared such slaughter and carried to safety.

The men continued to fall back under heavy fire on ground that offered minimal cover. Churchill glanced over his shoulder and saw the bottom of the hill fast approaching, where those who had already made it down were regrouping. At last he reached level ground. Around him his fellow soldiers—exhausted, bleeding, but still in the game— rapidly fixed their bayonets and waited for someone to sound the charge. When the shriek of the bugle rose above the noise, they surged forward, venting their fury in a barbaric roar, all the while gaining momentum on the upward slope. The two opposing forces clashed but were not entangled for long. The tribesmen broke off the engagement to gain the advantage of higher ground—but as they withdrew, Sikh marksmen inflicted a bloody toll. Then, as suddenly as the melee had begun, it was over.

The Anglo-Indian force had reclaimed the spur by five that evening and retrieved the hacked-up remains of the adjutant and other fallen comrades. Daylight soon began to fade. Storm clouds rolled in with the darkness, bringing rain and thunder, washing clean the blood and gore from the ground. The day had taken a toll. Churchill could now claim to be a true veteran of war, but if he had gone into combat with any romantic notions, the brutality he witnessed had swept such sentiments aside. His clothes were splattered with the blood of the wounded he had helped carry down the spur. The men returned to the camp from which they had set out that morning. Anticipating an attack, "the camp had been reduced to half its size" for easier defense.

Everywhere Churchill looked, crumpled tents lay in discarded heaps to deprive snipers of easy targets. Horses and mules, corralled together in a distant corner, seemed content to stay put. The rain gradually stopped, but the remaining clouds blotted out the moon and stars, rendering everything pitch black. It was impossible to tell who was who—but as the men got their bearings in the dark, it soon became evident that Jeffreys and his party—"two companies and the battery"—had not made it back. The sudden sound of gunfire somewhere beyond the camp's borders underscored this disturbing realization. A search party was quickly organized to retrieve the lost men, but the order was rescinded. The impenetrable night, the hostile terrain, a lurking enemy, and men worn ragged by combat did not bode well for success. Nothing could be done until daybreak.

The men, exhausted, slept in mud and filth. What few tents remained standing housed the wounded. Their pitiful cries in the dead of night and unceasing rain stabbed at the heart of every man. The surgeons did what they could with morphine injections and bandages to ease the suffering, but their efforts only went so far.

Reveille sounded a half hour before sunrise. General Jeffreys and his men were still missing. At first light a single squadron of Bengal Lancers set off on a search-and-rescue operation. Churchill tagged along. They had no idea where the general and his men might be, but they had heard their guns throughout the night and moved in the direction of the firing. Three miles out of camp they spotted the shattered ruins of a village, where they found Jeffreys and what remained of his column. The corpses of men and mules littered the village. Some of Jeffreys's men busied themselves burying the bodies of dead tribesmen. Nearby, in a roofless hut, sixteen wounded soldiers lay groaning in the dirt.

Churchill, recording the scene for his next dispatch, noted "their faces, drawn by pain and anxiety, looked ghastly in the pale light of the early morning." Jeffreys, his tunic drenched in blood, nursed a nasty head wound. He said they had taken shelter in the village when it became clear they would not be returning to camp by nightfall. Tribesmen had pounced on them immediately. Jeffreys and his detachment were forced to seek cover behind the dead and fought a desperate defense well into the night.

The men were escorted back to camp, the wounded wheeled back on dollies. The injured were tended to and the dead were buried. It was naturally a grim affair, made even more so by the lack of military pomp. A shortage of Union Jacks meant old blankets were used to cover the thirty-six bodies. There was no gun salute, as it was feared rifle fire might disturb the wounded. The bodies were placed in unmarked graves to protect the burial spot from desecration. Solemn words were spoken, prayers uttered.

Later that day Churchill put his thoughts on paper. Although living the adventure he had wished for so long, he found it a shockingly dirty business. War was a strange game, bringing fame and honor to some, the thrill of adventure and the priceless gift of experience, while it robbed others of everything they had. Staring at freshly dug graves that would soon be lost to time and memory, the majesty and glory of war struck Churchill as nothing more than the "unsubstantiated fabrics of a dream."

CHAPTER 6

Once More Unto the Breach

On September 18, 1897, Churchill and the men of the 2nd Brigade were back in action. Jeffreys, still in fighting shape despite his wound, received orders from Sir Bindon Blood via heliograph to march into the Mohmand Valley and "vigorously continue operations against the Mohmands." Jeffreys had no intention this time of dividing his force. They left camp at first light for the village of Domadola, guarded at its entrance by a fort and watchtower made of mud. Rocky hills and fields of maize and barley dominated the surrounding landscape. Churchill pulled out his field glasses and surveyed the scene as the brigade approached the cluster of huts. Behind the village, snow-capped mountains soared five thousand feet into a perfect sky. Churchill could see armed tribesmen gathering in the foothills overlooking the village to survey the British and Indian troops approaching on foot and horseback. Rifle fire from a distant ridge drew both sides into battle. An artillery battery of four cannons supporting the 2nd Brigade's advance began shelling the bluffs above the village, sending up roiling clouds of dust and rock. Tribesmen not pulverized by the heavy fire abandoned their positions for the safety of higher elevations.

Shortly after 8:30 the lead infantry seized the fortress and watch-tower. Sappers followed close behind and wired the structures to blow. With the push of a plunger, the earthen fortifications went up in large columns of flame and blood-red dirt. The thunderous detonation echoed off the mountains and battered the foothills before subsiding to a mere ringing in the ears. Sniper fire erupted from a nearby spur as the men, moving through drifting smoke and burning embers, entered the village.

A return volley killed one marksman. Churchill climbed the hill to investigate. He found the man, his body riddled with bullets, draped against a stone near a shallow pool, his face a glistening wreckage of torn flesh and shattered bone. Blood blossomed across the front of the dead man's dirty blue linen robe. The sight sickened Churchill, and he turned quickly to leave. In the village below, sappers went from hut to hut and rigged each one for destruction. Simply applying flame to the buildings would do no good. The roofs were flat and would not burn adequately unless a hole was punched through them first to allow the intake of air—something the explosives would accomplish. By eleven-thirty that morning, pillars of flame marked where the village once stood.

Jeffreys ordered the 2nd Brigade to withdraw, prompting the tribes-men in the hills to push forward with a new attack. They came crashing down the slopes in a frenzied wave of flapping gowns and banners, blazing rifles, and gleaming swords. Jeffreys's men, however, main-tained their cohesion. Troops in front formed a firing line and shot into the oncoming rush of tribesmen. When their rifles were emp-tied, they fell back to reload and allowed a new line to move forward and maintain fire. All the while, officers roared commands over the head-splitting din, directing the well-orchestrated maneuver. The result proved devastating. Tribesmen fell in heaps, their chaotic charge mak-ing them easy fodder for the retreating brigade.

Inflicting a heavy toll on the enemy was the dumdum bullet, pro-duced just outside Calcutta at the British Army's Dum Dum Arsenal. The bullet's cupro-nickel jacket did not cover its rounded nose, which allowed it to expand on impact and inflict a larger wound. Despite nearly four hours of relentless enemy fire, British casualties were light, with only two killed and six wounded.

The brigade returned to camp, pleased with its performance. The tribesmen had suffered heavy casualties, though it proved impossible to put a number on the fallen. While other men discussed the day's events, Churchill busied himself completing three dispatches for the *Telegraph*, in which he detailed his recent escapades. He put them in a letter to his mother the following day, September 19, and told her writing such long pieces exhausted him mentally and physically. He said blood stains still covered his clothing, but his desire for action remained unabated. On one recent excursion, he had stayed in the saddle, trotting along the firing line, while other men sought cover. Such behavior, he confessed, might be foolish, but he was here to establish a reputation—and one did not do that lying face down in the dirt. He voiced the pragmatic view of a man who could die at any moment, admitting that he tried not to dwell much on the future. Here, on the tribal frontier, where danger and slaughter intensified everything, England seemed a remote and distant concept—but he still hoped to make it back someday with a few medals pinned to his chest. Despite all he had gone through with the other men, he felt no sense of kinship with them and admitted to feeling lonely. Sir Bindon Blood proved to be his one social respite.

At 5:30 the following morning, when the first orange hint of daybreak cast the mountaintops into relief, Churchill and the brigade left camp to attack the village of Zagai. As the target took shape in the near distance, Churchill saw black clouds of smoke rising from a mountain behind the village. Similar clouds began to drift skyward from other peaks, as tribesmen communicated via smoke signals. The ominous sound of drumming drifted from the village, which sat between two rocky spurs overlooking the terraced huts. A creek ran past the village and fed patches of vegetation, lending the place an almost picturesque appearance. Some of the cavalry broke away from the main column and ascended one of the spurs to better survey the target. They quickly returned to report that the place was heavily defended from the upper slopes. Against the pale-yellow hills, tribal battle flags, brightly colored, unfurled in the warm breeze. Then the firing began.

Churchill cast his gaze to the distant peak of a nearby mountain. Through his looking glass he could see roughly forty Pashtuns—armed with Martini-Henry rifles—lying flat against the rock and firing with impunity. Somewhere behind him a man screamed. He turned to see a soldier fall to the ground; another two quickly followed. Those still standing took cover where possible. One British soldier eyed the enemy peak through the scope of his Lee-Metford rifle and estimated the distance to be fifteen hundred yards, prompting Churchill and others to comment on the enemy's shooting proficiency.

The cavalry moved into the village and quickly assumed control, while infantry climbed the hills to try to flush the enemy out. Sappers went about their work and readied the village to burn. At 11:00 that morning, Zagai ceased to exist. The primitive huts collapsed in burning heaps and smudged the blue sky with thick columns of smoke. When the tribesmen saw the Anglo-Indian force pulling back, they ran screaming from the hills and took cover in the burning village, shooting at soldiers falling back over flat, open terrain. The bullets scorched the air overheard or slammed into the ground—sodden from the previous night's rain—with a wet smack. The soldiers maintained a steady return fire, aiming at figures darting back and forth between the burning huts. On the slopes to the left of the village, Churchill saw more tribesmen scramble down to reinforce their brethren below. A charge by the cavalry, however, forced the Pashtuns back to their hiding places. After ten minutes of frantic firing, the soldiers were safely out of range. The tribesmen in the village did not give chase. It was, Churchill conceded, a minor engagement, but any impartial observer would have surely noticed "the strength and majesty" of the British soldier. In the melee, the brigade lost sixteen men.

Churchill found himself in combat on an almost daily basis. The day following the attack on Zagai was one of rest, but operations followed on September 22 against the village of Dag, which fell with relative ease. Marching to their target that morning, the men passed the village of Desemdullah, where Jeffreys and his party had so desperately fought for their lives on the night of the sixteenth. Churchill saw a sight that was "horrible and revolting": the British and Indian dead had been hauled from their graves and butchered. Churchill, mindful that the *Telegraph* was a morning publication and most likely read at the breakfast table, spared his readers the gory details. He was not a man easily shaken, but whatever he witnessed that morning left him deeply disturbed. It went beyond man's inhumanity to man and transcended a level of barbarity he found hard to fathom:

> These tribesmen are among the most miserable and brutal creatures on earth. Their intelligence only enables them to be more cruel, more dangerous, more destructible than the wild beasts. Their religion—fanatic though they are—is only respected when it incites to bloodshed and murder. Their habits are filthy; their morals cannot be alluded to. With every feeling of respect for the wide sentiment of human sympathy which characterizes a Christian civilization, I find it impossible to come to any other conclusion than that, in proportion that these valleys are purged from the pernicious vermin that infest them, so will the happiness of humanity be increased, and the progress of mankind accelerated.

There was more savagery to come.

In the final week of September Sir Bindon Blood—having secured for Churchill an additional two weeks' leave of absence from the 4th Hussars—posted the young journalist soldier to the 31st Punjab Infantry. The regiment, "badly mauled" in recent combat, only had four white officers left. "I have put him in," Sir Bindon wrote a friend, "as he was the only spare officer within reach, and he is working away equal to two ordinary subalterns." Although a cavalryman by training, Churchill had taken part in infantry drills at Sandhurst and felt confident of his abilities. The language barrier between him and the regiment's native soldiers was another matter. He passed orders to them primarily through hand gestures. His verbal commands were limited to three words: "'Maro' (kill), 'Chalo' (get on), and Tally ho! which speaks for itself."

On September 30 orders called for the 2nd Brigade to attack the village of Agrah on the western edge of the Mohmand Valley near the foot of the Hindu Raj range. Churchill saw several blood-red standards appear against the flesh-colored rock of the surrounding hills as the brigade closed in. Through his field glasses he saw a great many tribesmen brandishing rifles and lining the rocky ridges above the village. Under a sun already blazing hot before 9:00 that morning, the 31st Punjab was ordered to secure a series of spurs on the village's right flank. They advanced under Lieutenant Colonel J. L. O'Bryen, who urged the men on with apparent disregard for his own safety. Tribesmen smothered the line of advance with heavy fire from a cluster of nearby boulders. Colonel O'Bryen, seemingly oblivious to the mayhem, moved among his men, barking orders and directing the return fire. Churchill admired the man's tenacity.

The tribesmen, observing the colonel's preening and animated figure, made him a primary target—and still O'Bryen refused to take cover. One round after another kicked up geysers of dust at his feet or sliced the air on either side of him with a sharp whistling sound. No more than a hundred yards of hard ground separated the two opposing sides. As O'Bryen moved forward, pistol in hand, a bullet ripped through his gut and killed him. Although Churchill thought dying while leading your men into battle was how any soldier would wish to go, he mourned the loss of an exemplary character who clearly had much to offer his country and empire.

And still the Punjabis pushed forward, clashing with the enemy at close quarters, stabbing with bayonets and unloading their side-arms. Tribesmen blazed away from the slopes above, wreaking havoc but simultaneously drawing the attention of a British battery on the plain below. Artillery shells screamed over the heads of the Punjabis and slammed into the mountainside, scattering great chunks of rock and earth and reducing enemy combatants to shredded ruins. While the Punjabis waged a vicious struggle above, British soldiers below advanced on Agrah across open ground. They entered the village and unleashed havoc with sword and bayonet. Men on both sides fell with gaping wounds and missing limbs. Blood pooled and flowed in thick rivulets on the hard, cracked ground. The tribesmen appeared to be countless in number. Jeffreys, worried the British and Indian troops would soon be overwhelmed, ordered a withdrawal. As the soldiers pulled back, the village burning behind them, the artillery moved forward to provide covering fire. The shells burst low above the village in clouds of black and gray, unleashing a storm of hot shrapnel on the enemy below. It churned the ground, scarred the primitive mud dwellings, and maimed and mutilated those Pashtuns caught in its devastating radius.

Jeffreys's men, in the meantime, focused on evacuating their own casualties from the front. Every possible conveyance, from stretchers and blankets to mules and wagons, was employed for the task. A long, bloody convoy of stricken men—some dead, others in torment from their wounds—flowed from the fighting line. The withdrawal proved to be a grueling task for all involved. Those doing the carrying struggled to maintain their balance on the uneven ground and not spill their delicate cargo. Every jostle and bump, every attempt to ease the passage down the slope, brought forth pitiful cries from the wounded and desperate pleas to stop. It came as only a small mercy when the brigade reached the relatively level ground of the plain and began the journey back to camp. As a precaution, the cavalry hung back to deter any attack on the rear flank.

Churchill observed the bodies of the sixty-one men killed in action and tied with cord to mules—their heads hanging over one side and their legs the other. It was a gruesome spectacle, one that seemed to accord little respect to the fallen, but the alternative would have been desecration at the hands of the tribesmen. The dead Sikh troops were particularly disturbing to Churchill's eye. Their hair, long and black, stiff with dirt and blood, dragged along the ground and lent the already grotesque scene an added element of the macabre. Back at camp, surgeons pushed several large crates together and draped them in waterproof sheets to create two operating tables. Then, waiting at the camp's entrance, they rolled up their sleeves in anticipation of the wounded and the long hours of surgery ahead.

The 2nd Brigade had been at the Inayat Kila camp for three weeks. The small shelter trench that initially surrounded the compound had been turned into a deep, wide dugout, creating, in Churchill's words, "quite a formidable defense." Foxholes and trenches honeycombed the camp's interior, yet the place possessed a strange and undeniable beauty. From this vantage point, one could see the whole Mohmand Valley, its great plains of green and brown and its many scattered villages, some of which still burned in the distance. Churchill, having been under fire for five hours, was thankful to behold the view once more. The clean atmosphere and unobstructed light of the sun seemed to magnify everything. How strange, he thought beneath a cloudless sky of startling blue, that a place wracked by such violence could possess such beauty.

The vista gave him pause. He was living life day-to-day and concerned only with survival, which pushed most other considerations aside. Although he tried not to invest too much thought in the future, Churchill believed destiny would see him through. He realized that war fundamentally changed a man. It scarred him with visions and memories that would haunt him forever and rendered the monotony of a quiet life at home something to cherish. Churchill still thrived on the danger of it all.

Sitting in his foxhole in the middle of camp on the night of October 2, he wrote a letter to his mother and included his two most recent dispatches for the *Telegraph*. The tribesmen, he confessed, were proving to be worthy adversaries. They scaled the rocky slopes with cat-like agility, were lethal marksmen, and knew absolutely nothing of mercy. Neither did the enraged British, who executed the enemy wounded without hesitation. Although he did not elaborate, Churchill admitted to witnessing acts of barbarity—but promised his mother his hands and conscience were clean. He did not condemn those who perpetrated such deeds. War often required men to abandon their civility. And yet despite all this, he was enjoying himself and hoped to stay with Blood's force as long as possible. Life was strange, but what passed for normal under such circumstances?

More blood spilled in the days that followed, as the 2nd Brigade—soon to receive substantial reinforcements from Sir Bindon Blood—marched against one village after another. In the evening the men gathered in camp and listened to the Scottish pipers play or smoked their cigarettes and drank whisky, enjoying the quiet hours before the enemy snipers commenced their nocturnal ritual.

For Churchill, time on the frontier was running out. He had been absent from his own regiment for nearly two months. Jeffreys praised Churchill in dispatches for the young lieutenant's "courage and resolution." It was nice recognition, but did nothing to earn Churchill his desired Victoria Cross or Distinguished Service Order. There were some in the army high command who did not take kindly to Churchill's pursuit of glory and labeled him a "medal hunter." While this criticism contained an element of truth, it was ultimately unfair. Even had Churchill's ambitions not been political, he would still have craved the combat experience. Under no circumstances would he have been content living the peaceful life of a gentleman officer. Nevertheless, he seemed ambivalent in later years about the whole adventure. He estimated that three British officers had died for every twenty tribesmen killed. Who could say if any of it meant anything? The British aim had been to punish the Pashtuns for their aggression. The number of smoldering villages Blood's men left behind suggested they had succeeded in their mission. The campaign would officially end in late October with the tribes of the Mohmand Valley surrendering their arsenal of Martini-Henry rifles and promising to be on their best behavior. British prestige had been restored at a cost of 245 men killed or wounded—a substantial figure when one considers the frontline strength of the Malakand Field Force never exceeded 1,200 men. Churchill was not around to witness the peace negotiations. In early October he received orders to rejoin the 4th Hussars in Bangalore.

He tried at the last minute to join another campaign. An expeditionary force under the command of General Sir William Lockhart was being dispatched to "the Tirah region east of the Kyber Pass," where the Afridi tribes were in open rebellion. Churchill's superiors, however, believed he had taken part in more than his fair share of extracurricular adventures and denied his request. He returned to Bangalore with a heavy heart, telling his mother his time on the frontier qualified as the most enjoyable of his life. He had seen things that would forever stay with him, but never flinched in the face of danger and escaped death on multiple occasions. When he considered the close calls, the bullets that had missed him by inches, he marveled at his luck. But such were the experiences that made life a wonderful pursuit. If Cuba had offered but a subtle taste of war, the North-West Frontier was a feast—and it only stoked his appetite for more. It was not violence that enthralled him, but the excitement of life on the precipice. No other endeavor but war offered the same kind of risk and reward. It stripped away all pretense, blew away the façade, and exposed a man for who he really was.

Churchill was back in Bangalore by October 21, 1897, and once more ensconced in his pink stucco bungalow. When he finally received copies of his *Daily Telegraph* articles, he was dismayed to find his byline missing. The whole point had been to get his name out there and earn some political capital. He had agonized over every word, reworked sentences to ensure the narrative's flow and rhythm, and gone to great lengths not to make the articles all about him. It was stellar work for which he received zero credit.

He found more to gripe about when he saw that in one dispatch the word "exterminate" had been used in place of "extricate." He admonished his mother for not proofing the pages before they went to press. Two dispatches were printed out of sequence, piquing Churchill's ire—and "another stupid misprint" only further sullied his opinion of the paper. Of his writing abilities, Churchill—rightfully—had few doubts. He wrote home in late October and told his mother he would like an expert—perhaps a professor of classic English literature—to review his articles and render an opinion. His work, he opined, was perfection on a page. He planned to put his journalistic skills to the ultimate test. In November he decided to write a book on the campaign—from the native uprising to the crushing of the rebellion—with the not-so-gripping title *The Story of the Malakand Field Force*. He would dedicate it to Sir Bindon Blood. Tackling this new project would mean shelving his novel, of which he had completed eleven chapters. He did not like sacrificing one story for another but realized he needed to complete the Malakand book while the campaign remained fresh in the minds of the reading public. Never one to shirk a challenge, he hoped to have the manuscript finished and ready for publication by Christmas if at all possible, but definitely no later than February 1898.

He set to work immediately, spending six hours a day on research and composition. He put his mother to work as a de facto literary agent and charged her with approaching publishers to gauge their interest. Whereas most authors are wracked by self-doubt, convinced what they have done is subpar at best, Churchill had no such qualms. He radiated self-confidence in everything he tackled. In a letter to his mother on December 2, he told her the work-in-progress would rank as a great piece of literature. He would send her the manuscript shortly and expected it to be published without delay. Time was of the essence, for he had learned another lieutenant was also writing a book on the campaign. He pushed himself to his utmost limits and increased his writing time to eight hours a day, hoping the stress didn't impact the quality of the final product. Whatever the result, he had a right to be proud of his productivity and self-discipline. Three days before Christmas, the manuscript was nearly done. Writing the book revealed to Churchill a side of his character he never knew existed. For two straight months he dedicated at least five hours a day to his writing. Never had he known such intense focus. His frontier adventure had been well worth the risk. In prophetic words he wrote: "Bullets—to a philosopher my dear Mamma—are not worth considering. Besides I am so conceited I do not believe the Gods would create so potent a being as myself for so prosaic an ending. Any way it does not matter . . . I shall devote my life to the preservation of this great Empire and to trying to maintain the progress of the English people."

On December 31, roughly eight weeks after starting it, he sent his mother the completed 85,000-word manuscript. He was, quite understandably, tired of writing. Although a publisher had yet to be found,

Churchill believed £300 for the first edition—plus a royalty for each copy sold—was more than reasonable compensation.

Even before she received the package, Jennie had been hard at work on her son's behalf. Through Arthur Balfour, fellow Tory and future prime minister, she was put in touch with literary agent A. P. Watt, who didn't even need to see a sample chapter before agreeing to represent the work. Watt had read Churchill's dispatches and knew talent when he saw it. He had already mentioned the book to one respectable publishing house that was eager to see it. Watt felt confident a generous offer would be made—and indeed, a publisher quickly took the bait. Longmans purchased the book for £50—a far cry from Churchill's asking price, but at least it would get his name out there.

Churchill was adamant the title should hit shelves as soon as possible. He did not want to waste time mailing page proofs back and forth between England and India, so he asked an uncle—supposedly talented with the pen—to review the proofs and make the necessary corrections. A solid writer Uncle Moreton may have been, but a copyeditor he was not. Receiving the revised and final proofs in March 1898, Churchill spent one horror-filled afternoon flipping through the pages, spotting one miserable mistake after another. Had Moreton actually read the pages? In their current state, Churchill could not see how that was possible. He counted two hundred mistakes, though he conceded that half of them would only be apparent to the author. In some cases, Churchill discovered, Moreton had reworked some of the writing so that an "idiot in an almshouse" would have no trouble comprehending it.

He tried to delay the book's release, but to no avail. Its publication proved to be an event of great satisfaction and incredible frustration. Reviewers made note of the sloppy copyediting but praised the book's scope and subject matter. Reading the positive press served as a great tonic. Never before had Churchill been praised in such fashion. He had grown accustomed as a student to hearing his father and teachers voice their disappointment. Finally, he seemed to be living up to his true potential—but for those damned typos. He could hardly flip through the book without cringing with embarrassment. Like stains on white linen, the blunders were all he could see. Mistakes aside, the book benefited from the strong reviews and lined Churchill's pockets in a way the army never would. He received a 15 percent royalty for each copy sold and made nearly £400 in just a matter of weeks—something it would have taken four years to do on his subaltern's salary. The book did what his dispatches for the *Telegraph* had failed to do: increase his public profile. Such publicity, however, did not save him from what he once again found to be the monotony of life in Bangalore. Most men, having survived the horrors of conflict, would likely revel in quietude.

Not Churchill. He once more sought a new distraction and turned his attention to the Middle East, where Major General Horatio Herbert Kitchener was leading an Anglo-Egyptian army in a reconquest of the Sudan.

CHAPTER 7

The River War

S irdar (commanding officer) of the Egyptian Army, Major General Kitchener was a man of fierce reputation and scant humor. His invasion of the Sudan began in March 1896, when he set off from Egypt with an army of mostly Egyptian troops. Over time he would strengthen his ranks with British units, but even then his force would ultimately number no more than twenty-six thousand men. Theirs was a mission of conquest against a rebelling Islamic state. What the general lacked in manpower, he made up for in military hardware. His army stomped across the desert with "fifty pieces of artillery" and forty Maxim machine guns, "each capable of firing six hundred rounds a minute." On the Nile, following the Anglo-Egyptian army's line of advance, a flotilla of ten British gunboats bolstered the general's arsenal. Kitchener would need all he had. Awaiting him out in the desert plains was a force of some sixty thousand Muslim tribesmen: "ansars, or servants of Allah, referred to as Dervishes by the British."

Kitchener's march deep into Sudan proved slow going, as a railway line was simultaneously constructed across the arid landscape to keep his army supplied. As a commander who preferred meticulous planning to aggression, Kitchener was in no rush. This seemed fitting for such a campaign, the origins of which dated back more than a decade.

It began in 1881 when a Sudanese priest turned religious zealot named Muhammad Ahmad al-Mahdi proclaimed himself an "Ashraf" (descendant of the Prophet) of Islam. Sudan was then ruled by an Egyptian administration under British authority, which irked the native population. Ahmad rallied the disparate tribes of the Sudan and raised an Islamic army to wage war against their foreign oppressors. Beset by poverty and deprivation, most Sudanese had never given much thought to religion—but now came a rallying cry, a summons to overthrow their masters no matter how desperate and bloody the struggle.

The Mahdi whipped his Dervish minions into a frenzy of religious fanaticism, devotion to their cause making up for what they lacked in military skill and hardware. In November 1883 the Mahdi and forty thousand of his followers overwhelmed an Egyptian army of less than ten thousand and were soon advancing on the capital of Khartoum. The British government, alarmed by these developments, dispatched a small force under the command of Major General Charles Gordon to evacuate British and Egyptian subjects. In the process Gordon—and his thousand-strong army—died, on January 26, 1888, when he opted to defend the city "in the name of Christianity." The general's death staggered the British public, who promptly demanded "Gordon of Khartoum" be avenged. The job ultimately fell to Kitchener, who had assumed command of the Egyptian army in 1892.

Temperamental and arrogant, Kitchener was a law unto himself. He ignored orders from the War Office whenever he deemed fit and commanded his men with a stranglehold on authority. The only opinion that mattered in Kitchener's army was his own. He was an intimidating presence, standing more than six feet tall, who had "no tolerance whatsoever for failure." And so he took his time crossing the Sudanese desert, until, in April 1898, his men defeated a Dervish army of sixteen thousand near the confluence of the Nile and Atbara rivers. Ahead lay a two-hundred-mile march to Khartoum, where Kitchener could avenge Gordon and crush the uprising.

Churchill, upon hearing the news, was naturally eager to join the enterprise. This did not prove to be an easy task, for his reputation as a publicity hound rankled with a good many people, Kitchener among them. Although his book on the Malakand Field Force had been well received, there were still some in the military high command—the old school, as it were—who disapproved of Churchill's seemingly endless quest for publicity. Was Churchill a soldier or a journalist, and what right did he have to pass judgment in print on senior officers and military campaigns? Surely it was unfair to keep granting this glory seeker and self-promoter extended leave from his regiment so he could go off on adventures of his own choosing.

None of this dissuaded Churchill, who saw no reason that he could not be a soldier *and* a journalist. One function benefited the other. His military adventures provided great copy, while his articles helped him establish a name and voice his admiration for the cause of empire. To this end, he urged his mother in January 1898 to once more plead on his behalf. Jennie dutifully wrote a letter to Kitchener, but warned her son she did not expect a response. She had learned that only soldiers with at least four years' service would be allowed to join the campaign. At any rate, even if Churchill did get approval to go, who was to say he would arrive in time to see any fighting? Churchill, unperturbed, urged his mother to exert her influence in all quarters. From Bangalore at the beginning of February, he told Jennie he would take three months' leave starting June 15 and travel to Egypt. He did not anticipate the march on Khartoum would start until autumn. If he could not be temporarily attached to Kitchener's army, then he would try to get there as a correspondent. Only death, he said, would prevent him realizing his ambition.

He was eager to take his leave and see England again before shipping off to another war zone. He set sail from Bombay on the SS *Oriental* on June 18 and arrived at Victoria Station two weeks later. Although it was wonderful to be back in London, he did not plan on pursuing any social engagements. Time was a commodity in short supply if he hoped to be in Egypt for Kitchener's final offensive. Kitchener, responding to Lady Randolph's letter, said he had more officers than he knew what to do with and was up to his neck in applications from eager men far more experienced than young Churchill. The fact is that Kitchener did not like war correspondents—and he made no secret of his feelings. He considered them a hindrance and did his utmost to keep them away from the action. In his opinion they cared nothing for the truth and sensationalized the serious matter of war in order to sell papers. More than a dozen war correspondents were already attached to Kitchener's army, and he did what he could to make their lives miserable. He would keep them waiting outside his tent for hours in the hot Egyptian sun. When he finally emerged, he would walk past them and bellow, "Get out of my way, you drunken swabs!"

But Churchill was a special case. Kitchener was well aware of Churchill's quest for glory and thought it bad taste that a soldier should be shilling for the press. The response did little to discourage Churchill— on the contrary, it only stoked his determination. He launched a major charm offensive on all fronts—as did Jennie, who worked tirelessly to see her son's wish come to fruition. Lavish lunches and champagne dinners were hosted for those who could make things happen. Mother and son did their utmost to cajole and conquer the decision makers.

In the end, it proved to be Churchill's writing ability—and not Jennie's connections—that served him best. Lord Salisbury, the third-time prime minister, had read *The Story of the Malakand Field Force* and was duly impressed. He had his private secretary send Churchill an invitation to the Foreign Office to discuss the book. At four o'clock on the afternoon of July 12, 1898, Churchill entered the Foreign Office for the first time. Shown to a large, well-appointed room overlooking Horse Guards Parade, he found himself face to face with the most powerful man in the British Empire.

Salisbury greeted Churchill with a salute and ushered him to a sofa. For half an hour the prime minister praised Churchill's book for not only its content, but also its clear and concise style. Salisbury told the young author he had learned more from the book about the savage nature of fighting, the unforgiving landscape, and the overall complexities of the expedition than he did reading the voluminous War Office reports that swamped his desk. Churchill glowed on the inside but did his utmost to maintain a cool façade, for here was the highest praise. Their meeting finally over, Salisbury escorted Churchill to the door. He put a hand on Churchill's shoulder and—after uttering a few kind words about Lord Randolph—said if there was anything he could do to help in the future, Churchill should just let him know. Never had anything sounded so sweet to his ears.

He wrote Salisbury a letter shortly thereafter, explaining his desire to ride with Kitchener. He wanted to be a witness to history when British troops recaptured Khartoum. More important, he believed the adventure would make an excellent book—one that would greatly benefit his finances and further boost his literary reputation. Kitchener had proven himself to be a stubborn hindrance to Churchill's ambition. Jennie had failed to sway him, as had notable friends of the Churchill clan. Not even Sir Evelyn Wood, adjutant general at the War Office, could persuade Kitchener to change his mind.

True to his word, Salisbury approached Lord Cromer, the civil administrator of Egypt and Kitchener's superior, and asked him to try to make things happen. He warned Churchill in a letter, however, not to get his hopes up; everything rested with Kitchener. Quite frankly, if the adjutant general of the War Office had failed to change Kitchener's mind, Salisbury doubted Cromer would fare any better. The prime minister could do no more.

Still Kitchener refused to budge, effectively putting an end to Churchill's scheme. But grim luck proved to be on Churchill's side when a lieutenant with the 21st Lancers, a British cavalry regiment in Cairo, died shortly after Kitchener's response. Two days later Churchill received a telegram from the War Office saying he had been temporarily attached to the Lancers as a lieutenant. He was to leave immediately for Cairo and report to the regimental headquarters at the Abbasiyah barracks. The army would not be paying any of his traveling expenses—nor, in the event of his being killed or wounded in the course of the campaign, would it cover any costs associated with such misfortune. Churchill shrugged aside any financial concerns and began preparing for his departure. There was one slight catch. Lady Jeune, a prominent London socialite and friend of the Churchills, had been one of the many to write Kitchener on Winston's behalf and perhaps overstepped her bounds when she proclaimed, "Hope you will take Churchill. Guarantee he won't write." That was a guarantee no one could make.

Before setting off Churchill met with Oliver Borthwick, the son of the proprietor of the *Morning Post*, and secured a commission to write articles for the paper at £15 apiece. To avoid getting on Kitchener's bad side—if such a thing was possible—the dispatches would be published anonymously as letters written to "Dear Oliver" by a friend serving in the 21st Lancers who supposedly would have no knowledge they were making their way into print. His journalistic commission secure, Churchill was ready for his next adventure.

At a social gathering one evening before his departure, he wound up in conversation with the president of the Psychical Research Society, who made Churchill promise somewhat begrudgingly that if he died, he would send some sort of message about how things really were in the Great Beyond. On the morning of July 27—with his mother waving him off—Churchill caught the 11:00 train to Marseilles, where he boarded a ship bound for Egypt. He arrived in Cairo on the evening of August 2 and reported to the 21st Lancers' barracks, relieved to find no awaiting orders demanding his return to India. He was attached to "A" Squadron and told they would be moving out the following day. Two squadrons had already set off up the Nile to join Kitchener. It would take almost two weeks to reach Atabara, a journey made by rail and paddle steamers. At first light on August 3 the men moved out as the regimental band struck up "Auld Lang Syne."

The entraining of the regiment proved to be an exercise in organized chaos. Men burdened with cavalry swords, packs, bottles, rifles, and the like formed long lines and waited to board their carriages. Not only was there ample luggage and provisions to contend with, but also the horses—Arabian stallions—and all the supplies and equipment they needed: food and water, saddles, harnesses, and bridles. Churchill watched the steeds kick, stomp, snort, and resist all efforts to load them into the trucks. They were, he mused, as stubborn and ill-tempered as the indigenous people of the region. But slowly order seemed to assert itself, and after several hours men and beasts were all on board. The train took them to Aswân, where the process would be repeated when it came time to board the transport ships.

The river voyage was an almost leisurely adventure, with the boats moving at a laborious four miles an hour against a six-knot current. A large red paddle wheel protruding from the back of each boat pushed the steamers downriver, the blades of each wheel splashing muddy water all over the stern with each rotation. An awning on the roof provided shade during the days and a place to sit and gaze at the stars by night. It was under this awning that Churchill spent most of his time, watching the scenery slide by while scribbling notes for the *Morning Post* and writing letters home. At one point, where the river narrowed, the current almost brought the steamers to a complete stop. The men didn't mind, for the boats were comfortable and the weather pleasant. The days, although hot, were nothing compared to the sizzling temperatures of the North-West Frontier. The nights were cool and clear.

It seemed to Churchill that the campaign would be a luxury compared to all he had endured in the Swat Valley. During the Malakand expedition, soldiers traveled with no more than eighty pounds of baggage; the allowance in Egypt was two hundred pounds. Soldiers simply crammed whatever possessions they had into as many trunks and cases as possible and brought them along for the ride. This struck Churchill as overkill, but perhaps it was better to overpack for a war zone than be left wanting. Nevertheless, here on the water, conflict seemed another world away. The only horrific thing forced upon him was the food, which bore testament to the cook's total lack of interest in the culinary arts. Fortunately, there was plenty to keep one's mind off the disappointing diet. The scenery possessed a kaleidoscopic quality: the mud-colored water frothing white as the boat made its way downriver, the yellow desert with its flashes of greenery stretching beyond the horizon, and all this beneath an unblemished sky of radiant blue. Twilight colored everything in fiery "shades of red and orange." The mud-brown waters of the Nile, in the last light of day, turned gunmetal gray in color. The sophistication of London, with its dance halls, theaters, and glittering dinner parties, was a realm of make believe in these ancient surroundings. The slapping of water against the hull of the ship and the ceaseless neighing and stomping of horses in their barges, the swaying palm fronds along the river bank, the soldiers in their knee-length khaki shorts and sun helmets, made it hard to believe London could exist at all.

They stopped at Luxor on August 5 for a couple of hours and dropped anchor near the temple on the east bank of the Nile. Churchill toured the ruined complex and marveled at the weight of history pressing down on the place. Walking its halls and chambers, he could easily imagine "awestruck worshippers" on their knees, praying to their Egyptian gods. As he made his way back to the steamer, he encountered another officer from his squadron and asked the man if he had explored the temple. The officer waved his hand in dismissal. Why, he countered, would he want to spend his afternoon staring at old rocks and stone when he might be killed in the coming days? To Churchill, a lover of history, the possibility of pending death was all the more reason to tour the ruins.

The journey downriver resumed. The days passed slowly and seemed to blend into one another with no noticeable change. Sitting on the steamer's deck, listening to the monotonous slap of the water against the hull, Churchill continued working on his dispatches. "One idea grows steadily in the mind until it fills it altogether—the Nile," he wrote. "It is everything. It is all there is." He continued:

> It is the great waterway of Africa. It is the life and soul of Egypt. It is Egypt, since without it there is only desert. . . . On its waters we shall be carried southwards to the war and onto Khartoum. It is the cause of the war. It is the means by which we fight. It is the end at which we aim. Through every page which I write to you about the campaign, your imagination must make the Nile flow. It must glisten through the palm trees during the actions. You must think of the lines of animals, camels, horses, and slaughter cattle that march from camps every evening to be watered. Without the river we should never have started. Without it we could not exist. Without it we can never return.

Although Churchill enjoyed the experience, he worried Kitchener might find out about him at any moment and send him packing. This proved to be a fear he found impossible to shake. He imagined the

general writing angry letters of protest to the War Office, demanding
Churchill be recalled to London or banishing him to Cairo. Kitchener would not think twice about doing such a thing. The War Office had, after all, ignored his wishes. But as the journey progressed,
it became obvious Kitchener had more important things on his mind.
When told Churchill would be tagging along, the general shrugged
it off and turned his attention to other matters. Finally, on August
10, the steamers arrived at Aswân. The Nile's first cataract—a shallow,
rocky stretch of rapids—prevented the boats from traveling any further, but other steamers were waiting beyond the cataract in Shellal,
just six miles away.

The horses, having been cooped up on board for so long, were
happy to be disembarked. Once on land they stomped their feet and
"stretched their limbs," oblivious to the heat and swirling dust. Aswân,
hot and dirty, did not impress Churchill. He heard that some people
enjoyed visiting the place for pleasure, but could not fathom why any
sane individual would choose to do so. It was like languishing in a blast
furnace. Perhaps such individuals might enjoy a blazing summer jaunt
to Jacobabad, one of the hottest spots in India.

Native laborers hauled the regiment's luggage from the steamers
to a waiting train, which made the short trek to Shellal under heavy
escort and arrived as the sun began to set. Beyond a row of palm trees
at the river's edge, Churchill could see from the train several "fresh
steamers" ready to take the regiment to Wadi Halfa. Crates of ammunition, shovels and picks, medical supplies, and other necessities of war
crowded the riverbank. Convicts—with heavy shackles fastened around
their ankles—and native laborers approached the train ready to unload
the luggage and transfer it to the waiting steamers. Soldiers dressed
in their khaki and natives in blue robes worked side-by-side, lugging
cases, stocking supplies, and corralling the horses, pulling and kick-
ing, once more into the cramped confines of barges pulled alongside
the steamers. There were shouts and swearing, the bellowing of orders,
and the shriek of boat whistles as the shadows lengthened and the sky
darkened. The ruins of the temple of Philae served as a backdrop to the
bustling scene. It was, Churchill noted, as if "the past looked down on

the present and, offended by its exuberant vitality, seemed grimly to repeat the last taunt that age flings at youth: 'You will be as I am one of these days.'" The men boarded the steamers and once more set off on the water as the sun slipped from view. The novelty of river life still tempered the journey's monotony. Churchill was struck by the primitive nature of existence along the river.

As the steamers passed by, small children ran naked from huts down to the shore and begged those on board for alms. Their pitiful cries were made even more so by the knowledge that they would receive nothing. Village elders, wrapped in gowns of dirty white and blue cloth, stood back from the water and watched, expressionless, as the boats continued on their way. It amazed Churchill that people could live with so little. Even by the standards of what he had seen on the Indian frontier, life along the Nile appeared incredibly Spartan. Those who called the riverbank home got by with a meager patch of corn, a few date palms, and a water wheel.

Although this was a fascinating slice of life, Churchill knew his readers really wanted "to hear about war and bloodshed." They would not have to wait much longer. On August 15, after transferring yet again from river to railway at Wadi Halfa, the squadron finally reached the fortified camp at Atbara, the army's railway staging point, where they spent the night before marching south the following morning. Churchill had some unspecified business to attend to and did not leave with his squadron. He planned to catch up with the column that evening at their first camp, some fifteen miles away.

By the time he was done and ready to set off, daylight was already fading. He took a little steamer, the *Tahra*, across the river to the west bank and asked someone for directions to the campsite. Simply head south, he was told, until you see the campfires. Churchill had gone no more than a mile when the last sliver of daylight disappeared and left him in total darkness. Churchill maintained his southern heading by following the polar star, but kept his distance from the river to avoid entanglement in the large, thorny bushes that grew along the banks. For two hours he continued on his course, all the while thinking what a relief it would be when he could finally sit down to a meal and

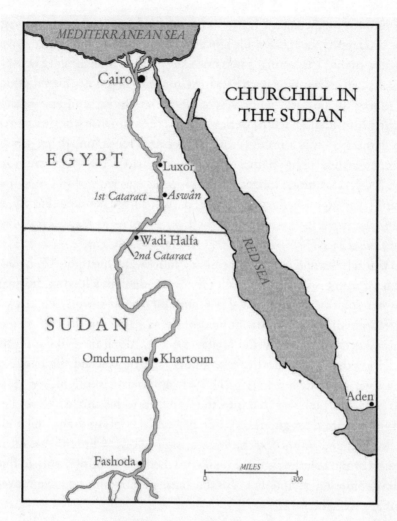

Map 4: Churchill in the Sudan

well-deserved drink. At any moment, he expected to see on the horizon the telltale glimmer of campfires—but the minutes, and then hours, passed with no such sighting. Much to Churchill's dismay, clouds began to move in and obscure the stars. He pressed on, hoping he was guiding his pony in the right direction—but the farther he traveled without spotting a break in the Stygian darkness, the more he realized he was lost. There was no point continuing; to do so would only worsen his predicament. He found a patch of soft sand behind a large rock, wrapped the reins of his horse around his wrist, and settled down for the night. The animal's nervous stomping and neighing effectively derailed all attempts at sleep, leaving Churchill to ponder his situation.

Lying in the dark, a hot desert wind stirring the sand and exacerbating his thirst, he felt powerless against the immensity of this barren wilderness. It was a unique, and unpleasant, sensation. What would happen at first light should he discover he had wandered away from the Nile? How much longer would his pony survive without food and water? The night seemed endless, its darkness impenetrable. Finally, at half past three in the morning, the clouds began to scatter, revealing the constellation Orion.

Churchill could hardly remember a more welcome sight. He hauled himself into his saddle and took off at a steady clip, allowing the great hunter to point the way. It was Churchill's good fortune he knew a little something about astronomy, for he remembered that Orion—at this time of year—lay in the predawn hours "along the Nile" with his head looking to the north. Two hours later he reached the banks of the river, its waters catching the first glimmer of sunlight. He leapt off his pony and staggered into the water up to his thighs. Never had anything tasted so good, as Churchill and his pony drank their fill. Refreshed and imbued with a new sense of hope, Churchill set off in search of the column. He eventually reached the campsite, only to find the smoldering remnants of several fires. The men must have moved out at first light.

Churchill continued south and came across a depressing village of mud huts and few inhabitants. He spotted one man whose fez "proclaimed him a man of some self-respect and, perhaps, even of some local importance." Navigating the language barrier to the best of his ability, Churchill asked for some breakfast and inquired about a guide to see him through the desert. From inside his hut the man produced a stash of dates served on a white cloth. Three women emerged from the squalid dwelling and began feeding Churchill with "fingers whose dark skin alone protected them from the reproach of dirt." Several children drew near to observe Churchill, dressed in his khaki shorts and tunic.

The dates quickly consumed, Churchill was offered a bowl of sweet, dirty milk. The liquid did nothing to satisfy his palate, but it helped fill his stomach. Now full, Churchill required help to rendezvous with his column.

With the tip of his sword Churchill drew a crude sketch in the sand of an English soldier. The villagers nodded excitedly and pointed to the south, indicating Churchill's squadron had passed through that morning. Churchill mounted his horse, snapped the reins, and galloped off, riding for the better part of the day. He occasionally stopped in a random village for another native meal of dates and dirty milk, which he only consumed out of desperation. Not until nightfall did he finally catch up with his column, happy to regale the men with his tale of adventure and rinse away the taste of native cuisine with a strong whisky.

Joining the column did nothing to ease the savagery of the desert. The men marched up to thirty miles, at a cost of six horses, every day. Churchill thought it poor planning on Kitchener's part. By the end of August the army—some twenty-five thousand soldiers from Britain, the Sudan, and Egypt, backed by a lethal arsenal of heavy field artillery and a fleet of gunboats on the river—was fast approaching Omdurman, across the Nile from Khartoum. The march from Atbara had been surprisingly uneventful. This war, Churchill mused, was far different from anything he had experienced in Cuba or on the North-West Frontier.

A great sense of expectation had characterized his past military campaigns. One knew an engagement with the enemy would soon take place. Each day would bring with it a foretaste of the impending clash of arms: an outpost might be attacked or a reconnaissance party might exchange fire with an enemy patrol. Such things blatantly suggested the shrinking distance between armies. The closer the two sides drew to one another, the more violent the encounters, until the inevitable denouement. But here in the desert, patrols had failed to locate any sign of the enemy within a thirty-mile radius. In fact, Kitchener's army had not fired a shot in anger since April. Some men began to wonder if there remained a war to fight.

In the early morning hours of September 1 the army broke camp and continued its trek toward Khartoum. The 21st Lancers, serving as scouts, rode eight miles ahead of the main force. Vultures circled above, large and black against the sky. Churchill counted at least one hundred and watched as some landed in nearby brush to eye the procession of men and horses. The ugly beasts were a harbinger of bloodshed. The men marching past knew full well the birds had gathered in anticipation of a meal—a fact that unsettled many in the ranks. Much like the vultures, Kitchener's army was confident the day would bear witness to battle—but such hope diminished as the miles passed with no sign of the enemy.

At about nine o'clock that morning the Lancers reached the foot of a hill. The commander, Colonel Rowland Martin, barked some orders and scrambled up the slope with a few officers and signalers in tow. A signal flag soon unfurled atop the hill and, flapping in the breeze, spelled out a message that sent a jolt of excitement through the waiting regiment below: "Khartoum in sight." It had been, Churchill reported, thirteen years since "an Englishman could have said that with truth."

The march resumed with a new sense of urgency to cover the ten miles of blistering desert between Kitchener's men and Omdurman. Soon a strange form began taking shape in the shimmering middle distance: a pointed dome, the color of sun-bleached sand. This was the tomb of the Mahdi, the man who had whipped the Sudanese tribes into rebellion. He had died in June 1885, six months after taking Khartoum. In his place, according to the Mahdi's own wishes, ascended Khalifa Abdullah, a "shrewd and energetic man," who was nevertheless "unbelievably cruel and despotic." He lived in Omdurman, with "a retinue of eunuchs" at his beck and call and a harem of wives to satisfy his needs. Churchill dismounted from his charge and climbed to higher ground. The Mahdi's tomb stood tall in the heart of the city, dwarfing cluttered rows of mud houses. The river flowed past Omdurman to the left, where it forked into the Blue and White Niles. Squinting against the sun and looking across the river, Churchill could also see Khartoum. It appeared, he noted, to be nothing more than "a straggling mud village." He saw no signs of life among the squalid dwellings and wondered if he would actually see any combat. Where was the Khalifa's army? Perhaps none existed. How else could Kitchener have advanced unhindered this far?

Churchill rejoined the regiment. There was little to hold the men's interest as they trailed across a barren, sandy plain of rolling hills and low ridges. Nothing about the landscape, or the drab outer walls of Omdurman, offered much to fix one's attention. Churchill settled his gaze on the horizon and soon noticed something four miles ahead to the army's right, atop a slight hill. It looked, initially, like a giant black-and-white snake—but Churchill soon recognized it for what it was: the Dervish army. It appeared to be roughly three thousand men behind a zareba—an improvised stockade made of dense, thorny bushes. As the distance between the two armies gradually closed, Churchill realized he had vastly underestimated the number of enemy warriors.

What he had at first believed to be the long line of zareba—the black part of the snake—separated from the main body and began running down the hill: countless thousands of warriors clad in black robes. In their wake followed "other immense masses" of men, who swarmed unceasingly over the crest until the slope appeared to be some writhing, living thing. Churchill and his fellow Lancers, both mesmerized and alarmed by the stunning display, brought their horses to a halt. Never had they seen such an awesome spectacle, nor did they think they would ever see one again. Churchill guessed the enemy horde stretched four miles from one end to the other.

Colonel Martin ordered Churchill to report the situation to Kitchener. Churchill rode forward and ascended a hill to get a better view through his field glasses. Thousands of razor-sharp spears glistened in the blinding sun, while some twenty thousand men appeared to be armed with outdated, but effective, single-shot Martini-Henry rifles. Despite its immense size, the Dervish army looked minuscule in the vast openness of the battlefield. To the east of his hilltop position Churchill could see the Anglo-Egyptian army approaching in a giant cloud of dust, an enthralling spectacle of imperial power.

"The British and Egyptian army was advancing in battle array," he later recalled. "Five solid brigades of three or four infantry battalions each, marching in open columns, echeloned back from the Nile.

Behind these great blocks of men followed long rows of artillery, and beyond these there trailed out interminable strings of camels carrying supplies." He mounted his horse and rode in Kitchener's direction. He had six miles of desert to cross but did not want to push his horse too hard in the blazing heat. It took him forty minutes to reach the first lines of infantry. Kitchener was riding several horses' length in front of his headquarters staff. Soldiers on either side of him carried the Union Jack and Egyptian flag. Churchill brought his horse alongside the general's, saluted, and—without mentioning his name—said he had an update on the enemy's disposition.

Kitchener nodded, signaling the young lieutenant to continue. The enemy, Churchill explained, superior in numbers, was roughly seven miles ahead and positioned midway between the Anglo-Egyptian forces and the city of Omdurman. When last spotted, they were advancing rapidly. Kitchener did not immediately respond, nor did he seem too concerned. He pondered the matter before asking how long he might have before the two armies collided. An hour at the very least, Churchill said without hesitation, maybe an hour and a half. Kitchener again nodded. Churchill saluted once more, pulled away from the general, and watched the Egyptian and British soldiers pass on their way to an unknown fate.

As Churchill considered the pending battle, Sir Reginald Wingate—Kitchener's head of intelligence—approached with an invitation to lunch. Stacked biscuit boxes covered in clean, white linen served as a makeshift table, upon which were arranged platters of bully beef and pickles and bottles of drink. It was, Churchill mused, a nice touch of English civility in the heart of savage country. Although the enemy far exceeded the Anglo-Egyptian army in size, no one appeared overly concerned. The jovial mood around the table seemed better suited for a London dinner party. Churchill, busy shoveling bully beef into his mouth, could hardly believe a major battle was imminent.

As it transpired, there would be no heavy fighting that day. Churchill, his stomach full and spirits high, returned to his squadron. The enemy halted its advance a mere mile and a half from the 21st Lancers shortly before two that afternoon. Standing on a summit overlooking

the plain, Churchill and other members of his squadron watched as
the Dervish soldiers fired their rifles in the air with "a great roar—a
barbaric *fue-de-joie*." When the smoke cleared, they sat down on the
ground. This came as something of a relief to the Lancers, who would
undoubtedly have been overwhelmed had the Dervish horde continued
forward. Several minor engagements ensued throughout the afternoon,
as scouting parties from both sides clashed amid the rocky ridges and
desert brush. British casualties—"one man wounded and one horse
killed"—were negligible.

On the river British gunboats began shelling enemy batteries along
the Omdurman shore. Thick clouds of black-and-white smoke from the
boats' funnels and artillery pieces drifted across the water. The gunboat
crews fired with deadly efficiency, reducing the Dervish emplacements
to splinters and ash. Enemy fire proved stubborn but ineffectual, and
soon the shore batteries fell silent. The great dome atop the Mahdi's
tomb now presented too irresistible a target.

A British shell roared overheard and detonated in a blinding flash
just above the tomb. More shells followed in a storm of thunder and
fire that blew the top of the dome to pieces. Massive plumes of red dust
rose up from the battered structure as it took the relentless beating.
Large cracks spread across the dome's surface, the tomb's cupolas dis-
integrated, and where once solid walls had stood, there was now open
space. Churchill admired the precision of the gunboat crews, but found
the exercise to be not only pointless but a waste of good ammunition.

Late in the day the Lancers descended to the water's edge and—
with the rest of the army—set up camp. "Somewhat removed from
the zereba and trenches, and nearer the Nile," noted one soldier, "were
the hospitals, the transport, the stores, nearly 3,000 camels, and about
500 mules." The 21st Lancers were picketed at the southern end of the
encampment. That evening Churchill and a fellow officer walked the
shore. "All along the river's bank beside the camp were moored gunboats, steamers and barges, with a fleet of a hundred or more native
sailing boats, at once a means of defense and a supply column." As
Churchill gazed across the water, someone yelled at him from a passing gunboat and asked if he wanted a drink. Before Churchill could

reply, the officer tossed a large bottle of champagne over the deck's railing. It cut a graceful arc through the darkening sky and landed with a splash just shy of dry land. Churchill charged knee-deep into the water and rescued the blessed prize, holding it aloft like some trophy as he emerged from the river and hurried back to the mess.

That night the gunboats, moored nearby, swept the riverbank and the desert plain with powerful searchlights. The dazzling illumination made it difficult for some soldiers to sleep. A restless Churchill decided to inspect the camp's perimeter, protected by thorn brush and sentries. All was quiet. The desert was a black void, save the occasional glare of searchlights. At sunrise it would become the final resting place for many.

CHAPTER 8

Last Charge at Omdurman

The sounding of bugles brought to a close a night of fitful sleep for twenty-two thousand men at half past four on the morning of September 2, 1898. The sky was still dark, though a full moon bathed the Anglo-Egyptian camp in pallid silver light. The banging of drums and the blare of cavalry trumpets soon joined the bugles in signaling the day of battle. The men of Kitchener's army dressed by the light of the moon and lanterns "with an eager desire permeating all ranks to have it out with the Dervishes then or never." They ate a hurried breakfast of sausage, biscuits, porridge, and bully beef, all the while discussing the imminent action. "Everything was in readiness in our camp by 5 a.m.," recalled one soldier. "Camels, horses, mules, and donkeys had been watered and fed, and the men had disposed of an early breakfast. . . . Infantry and artillery had made sure of their full supply of ammunition, and the reserve was handy to draw more from. [They] carried 100 rounds of the new hollow-nosed Lee-Metford cartridges. Behind [each British soldier] were mules loaded with a further twenty rounds for him. The [Egyptian] soldiers had 120 rounds of Martini-Henry cartridges." Within half an hour the 21st Lancers mounted their horses and rode out of camp. Churchill galloped ahead with orders from his squadron leader to take an advance team forward to reconnoiter the area. With his seven-man scouting party, Churchill charged across open desert toward a nearby hill. As they ascended the slope, Churchill wondered whether the enemy would still be there, or would they have "melted away into the deserts" during the night? When they reached the top of the ridge—dubbed Heliograph Hill—he had his answer. As he reported in his dispatch:

> It was quarter to six. The light was dim but growing stronger every minute. There in the plain lay the enemy, their numbers unaltered, their confidence and intentions apparently unshaken. Their front was nearly five miles long, and composed of great masses of men joined together by thinner lines. Behind and to the flanks were large reserves. They looked from where I stood dark blurs and streaks, relieved and diversified with odd-looking gleams of light from the spear points.

Churchill jotted down a quick report for Kitchener, describing the scene, and scrawled his name at the bottom. He wondered, if only briefly, what the general might think when he saw the signature. Tasking a corporal with the report's delivery, he turned his attention back to the massive, chanting army below. Even from a mile away the enemy's battle cry was disturbing—almost elemental, like the sound of the sea whipped into a fury. "Allah el Allah! Rasool Allah el Mahdi!" It crested the hill and swamped the summit, drowning Churchill in its ferocity and promise of slaughter. Glancing at his small party, he suddenly felt very insignificant. Although confident of ultimate victory, he sat in awe of the grand spectacle. At 5:50 the great Dervish mass surged forward beneath five hundred waving flags embroidered with passages from the Koran. Churchill fired off a second report to Kitchener, letting him know the enemy was on the move.

Behind the Lancers, back near the river, the Anglo-Egyptian army "was drawn up in line" with the Nile behind them and the gunboats protecting their flanks. Two thousand Dervishes swarmed to within five hundred yards of Churchill's vantage point. A dozen enemy riflemen scrambled up the slope and fired without respite, forcing Churchill and the others to take cover, the .45 caliber rounds chipping away at dirt and rock. Churchill leapt from his horse and fired blindly down the slope. The air reeked of gunpowder, as an unceasing fusillade hammered the Lancers' hilltop position. The Dervishes' aim improved as they climbed, gaining an accuracy that prompted the men to move to the other side of the hill, out of the enemy's line of fire.

The situation hardly improved. Looking down, Churchill saw more riflemen working their way up the southern slope. He and his party took shelter among some large rocks and watched the Dervishes continue their ascent under fluttering banners. The relentless firing seemed to come from all directions. A thunderous boom echoed from the desert plain below, distracting Churchill from his own dire predicament. Kitchener's artillery had unleashed a deadly salvo into the center of the Khalifa's advancing hordes. It had the effect of a sharp blade mowing through long glass. Men and tattered banners fell in a wide swath, only to be trampled by those charging undaunted from behind. From Churchill's elevated position some two miles away, the army fast approaching the Anglo-Egyptian line looked like an angry swarm of insects infesting the desert floor. He admired their bravery but nothing else.

Returning to his own problem, Churchill saw that the Dervish riflemen climbing the slopes were about to breach the crest. He and his party sat sheltered behind boulders some three hundred yards off to the side. It was a good place to be, for he knew what lay in store once the artillery men and the gunboat crews—some two thousand yards away—saw the enemy flags fluttering atop the hill. The Dervishes reached the summit and fired their rifles skyward in a celebratory gesture, chanting war cries at the sight of Kitchener's troops below. Churchill, wanting a better view but not daring to leave the safety of his shelter, eyed the enemy warriors through his field glasses. He watched as they charged down the hill toward the Anglo-Egyptian army. They made little progress. The roar of big guns signaled their gruesome fate. Churchill, awestruck, witnessed the grisly spectacle unfold. Within the span of a minute twenty shells fell among the enemy ranks, blowing men apart. Some shells detonated above their heads and sent hot shrapnel through skin and bone, while others slammed into the sand and launched bodies skyward in clouds of burning earth.

Even against such murderous fire, the Khalifa's men pushed forward, picking up the fallen and bloody flags and continuing the charge. They showed no fear, Churchill wrote, and seemed more than willing "to die for Allah's sacred cause." From where they remained sheltered, Churchill and his men could have easily fired into the rear flank of those being slaughtered by Kitchener's artillery—but they opted not to do so, as their advantage seemed grossly unfair. As Churchill sat in the saddle and watched the carnage unfold, three enemy horsemen came charging in his direction. They raised long spears as they closed the distance, their dark, monk-like cowls flapping behind them. Churchill drew his Mauser and fired several rounds, prompting the horsemen to scatter. As he holstered his smoking sidearm, a major arrived on horseback and ordered Churchill to rejoin the main force. Kitchener was preparing to unleash everything he had.

Churchill led his party down to the Nile and took cover with the rest of the cavalry behind the zereba. They watered and fed their horses, all the while hearing the tumult of the battle beyond the camp's perimeter. For the better part of an hour Churchill listened to the roar of artillery, the clatter of Maxim guns, and the deafening, whip-like crack of twenty thousand rifles. The Khalifa—who watched the battle atop a donkey "attended only by a small retinue"—had thrown his men against the main body of the Anglo-Egyptian army in a "suicidal frontal attack." Charging and screaming across the desert plain, the Dervishes slammed headlong into nearly three full infantry divisions. Kitchener's men were "ranged two deep in front with a partial second double line or supports placed twenty yards or so behind them. These assisted in the fight to pass ammunition to the firing line and carry back the dead and wounded." The shooting prowess of the British and Egyptian soldiers ripped the Khalifa's army to shreds. Belief in their cause and religious fanaticism were completely ineffectual against late nineteenth-century weaponry. The battle would later inspire the historian and poet Hilaire Belloc to write:

> *Whatever happens we have got*
> *The Maxim Gun and they have not.*

Wave after wave of Dervish men went to the slaughter, falling in torn and tattered heaps, the yellow ground beneath them turning red as their line of advance burst "into flame and smoke." Seven hundred yards from the Anglo-Egyptian line, the enemy's attack faltered. "They came very fast, and they came very straight," noted the *Daily Mail* correspondent, "and then presently they came no farther. With a crash the bullets leaped out of the British rifles . . . they poured out death as fast as they could load and press the trigger." Thousands of men lay dead or screaming in agony, waiting for death to bestow a final mercy. Among the British and Egyptian forces, no more than sixty men had been killed or wounded.

Enemy riflemen dropped to the ground and advanced on their stomachs while maintaining an erratic fire. Although some of their rounds struck home, it was clear the Khalifa's offensive had been thwarted. At 8:30 the cavalry were ordered to mount up and take up position on the left flank of Kitchener's front. For a quarter of an hour the men prepped their weapons, all the while observing the thousands of Dervishes approaching once more on the desert plain. Churchill bristled with excitement. The four hundred cavalrymen of the 21st Lancers started off in the enemy's direction, with Churchill leading a troop of twenty-five men. Between the Lancers and the object of their attack were 150 Dervishes crouching in a shallow depression. Churchill assumed they were spearmen, but they attacked with rifles when the cavalry closed to three hundred yards. Up and down the enemy line, Churchill saw flame flicker from countless muzzles. With only two options available to them—retreat or attack—the Lancers rode into history, executing one of the last great charges of British cavalry.

A trumpet sounded the order to gallop. The Lancers thundered forward, hooves beating the ground and lances at the ready. Because of his old shoulder injury, Churchill could not hold a lance. Instead, he pulled his Mauser pistol and cocked it. The noise of the horses, the trumpet, and the yelling of men drowned out the sound of the enemy's fire. All Churchill could see in front of him were the crouching Dervishes in their blue robes and clouds of white smoke drifting up from their rifles. One round struck a private named Byrne. The round passed through his right arm, forcing him to drop his lance. Although severely wounded, he managed to draw his sword and continued galloping forward.

The Lancers broke through the line of riflemen with minimal casualties. Churchill looked over his shoulder to see a few men falling from their horses—but what he saw when he glanced forward was a terrifying sight: "a long, dense, white mass of men," initially obscured from view by a "deep fold in the ground." Armed with spears and rifles, they numbered at least three thousand and crouched twelve deep, extending the entire length of the Lancers' line. Fully committed to their present course of action, Churchill and the others urged their horses onward, hoping to hit the wall of men and gleaming points with enough force to break through to the other side. The Dervishes, their spears ready and rifles coming to aim, showed no sign of dispersing. As the cavalry closed in, bright battle flags appeared above the enemy mass. Reported Churchill:

> The Dervishes stood their ground manfully. They tried to hamstring the horses. They fired their rifles, pressing their muskets into the very bodies of their opponents. They cut bridle-reins and stirrup leathers. They would not budge till they were knocked over. They stabbed and hacked with savage pertinacity. In fact, they tried every device of cool determined men practiced in war and familiar in cavalry. Many horses pecked on landing and stumbled in the press, and the man that fell was pounced [on] by a dozen merciless foes.

It took less than two minutes to break through the Dervish line, but it felt like an eternity. Sixty of the Khalifa's men lay dead or wounded under the relentless sun. Directly in front of him, Churchill saw a Dervish warrior drop to the ground and draw his curved sword, ready to slice the hamstring of Churchill's horse. Churchill pulled violently on the reins and slung himself low in the saddle. He fired two rounds into the man and turned to ride away. Another Dervish blocked his path and ran at him with sword raised high. Churchill thrust his gun forward, the barrel actually making contact with his target, and pulled the trigger. Then the sun glinted off something out of the left corner of his eye. It was a Dervish on horseback clad in tarnished chain-mail armor and helmet. Churchill put a bullet in the man and watched him drop. Around him, Churchill's fellow soldiers fought desperately against a fanatical enemy. One lieutenant thrust his sword through a foe with such force the blade "bent double and remained thus."

A Dervish approached the horse of Major Crole Wyndham, pressed the muzzle of his rifle into the animal's side, and fired. The horse fell dead, sending Wyndham to the ground and leaving him to fight and stagger his way to safety on foot "through a savage crowd." One Lancer, Lieutenant Nesham, seemed destined to die as the enemy swarmed around his horse, slashing and stabbing with their swords. Despite the ferocity of the attack—and his left hand dangling from the wrist by a flap of skin—Nesham remained in the saddle. An enemy blade sliced through his right leg; another drew blood on his right arm. Nesham's mount, suffering but still standing, "carried him through the Dervishes to fall fainting among the rallying Squadrons."

The sight of a sergeant named Freeman trying to rally his troop struck Churchill particularly hard. The man's face had been stripped of nearly all its recognizable features. His cheeks dangled on thin strips of flesh down either side of his neck, and his nose and lips appeared to be missing altogether. Despite such grievous injuries, he barked commands at his men, blood frothing in thick bubbles around the remains of his mouth. Private Byrne, wounded in the initial charge, found himself surrounded by thousands of screaming, fanatical warriors, stabbing with their spears. As Byrne struggled to fight his way free, he heard someone calling for help above the din. Looking through the mass of men, Byrne saw Lieutenant Richard Molyneux knocked from his horse and "streaming with blood." He was lying on the ground and trying to claw his way out of the maelstrom, while being attacked from all sides.

Byrne rode toward Molyneux and swung his sword to clear the Dervishes away. The weapon slipped from his hand, as a severe wound to his arm had weakened his grasp. At that moment a Dervish lunged forward and thrust his spear into Byrne's chest. Byrne remained in his saddle and managed to reach Molyneux. He pulled the wounded lieutenant to safety before fainting from loss of blood and was carried from the battlefield. Glancing over his shoulder, Churchill saw the Dervishes falling back into line. The enemy was only twenty yards away. He watched two of them drop to their knees and aim their rifles in his direction. He turned in the saddle and whipped his horse into a gallop, surprised upon hearing the rifles discharge that neither round found its mark.

He and the Lancers regrouped 150 yards away. Their swords smeared with blood, they prepared to charge again—but the extent of their losses soon became evident. Horses without riders ran aimlessly about the battlefield, while on others injured men slumped forward in their saddles. Many horses, having been slashed and stabbed, hemorrhaged blood and could scarcely support the weight on their backs. Some simply collapsed with spears still sticking in their sides. Churchill was lucky—neither he nor his horse had suffered a scratch. In a two-minute action, the Lancers had lost 71 men and 119 horses. Although having suffered heavy losses, they had no intention of retreating.

Churchill assembled the men of his patrol, who lined up on their panting, sweating steeds. Riding up and down the line, he ordered them to prepare for another charge—and quite possibly, one after that. A young subaltern, bloodied but determined, voiced his enthusiasm. The men, he said, would go as many times as needed. It was the kind of fighting spirit Churchill admired. He turned to his second sergeant and asked if the man had enjoyed himself. Enjoyed, the sergeant replied with mild humor, was not a word he would affix to the experience.

The enemy "prepared with constancy and courage for another shock"—but Churchill's superior officer, Colonel Martin, refused to order another charge lest the Lancers suffer more grievous casualties. Instead, they skirted the Dervish flank on horseback before dismounting and battering the enemy line with heavy rifle fire. Slowly the Dervishes began to pull back in a fighting retreat, returning fire as they moved toward Heliograph Hill, where the Khalifa's own personal standard—large and black—fluttered from the summit. Soon the Lancers were left to tend to their wounded and retrieve the dead. At first glance the desert looked much as it had before the confrontation. From a distance one would have been hard-pressed to tell a battle had even taken place. Closer inspection, however, revealed the detritus of war. It looked as if someone had scattered large mounds of trash all across the plain. The dirty white robes of the warriors, fluttering gently in the hot desert wind, reminded Churchill of discarded newspaper. Lying among the Dervish dead were the fallen British and Egyptian soldiers, their tattered khaki uniforms bringing to mind "bundles of dead grass." These were few in number when compared to the mass slaughter of the enemy.

The shredded remains of flags, spent shell casings, bloodied swords, rifles, broken spears, and other such items lay scattered among the dead. "In the foreground lay a group of dead horses and several dead or dying donkeys," Churchill recorded. "It was all litter." The whole ghastly episode struck Churchill as surreal. Here was the true nature of war. Almost immediately his mind seemed to rebel against the experience—muting his recollections to perhaps make them more bearable. Strangely, he could not recall any sound. The shouts of men and the thundering of hooves, the rifles firing and the blare of the bugle, the screaming of injured horses and trampled Dervishes, were all absent when he replayed the event in his mind's eye. Perhaps the brain filtered out such distractions to allow one to concentrate on only what was important: the steady aim, the firm grip on the reins, and the conquering of fear.

As Churchill helped with the fallen, he found out one of the dead was a man to whom he had been particularly close, Lieutenant Robert Grenfell. Charging through the Dervishes, Grenfell took a blade in the back. Churchill and another friend had often dined with Grenfell, an officer "of great personal charm and high courage." Earlier in the day Grenfell had braved a maelstrom of fire after being ordered to observe the disposition of enemy forces. News of Grenfell's death shocked Churchill, who, though fully aware of the horrors of war, still viewed combat through a romantic, if slightly bloodied, lens. On the one hand, it was a noble endeavor in the name of empire—on the other, he found it to be a "dirty, shoddy business, which only a fool would play at."

The Lancers retrieved their dead and laid them in a row. The survivors hung their heads in a moment of silence. Along the river, the hastily set-up field hospitals took in the screaming wounded. The thunder of guns rumbled across the desert, a clear reminder that the battle still raged elsewhere. As Churchill climbed once more into the saddle, he looked at his pocket watch. Back in comfortable, civilized England, it was only half past nine in the morning. He thought of people sitting down to breakfast and felt a slight pang of envy. Although thankful to be alive, Churchill dared not dwell on that thought too much. In the near distance long lines of Dervishes still moved across the desert plain against Kitchener. The Lancers, battle hardened, took off in that direction, anticipating more carnage. As the cavalry bore down on the enemy, Dervishes turned and ran toward them. Churchill, his Mauser loaded with a fresh ten-round magazine, prepared once more for a violent collision. But the Khalifa's men began tossing their weapons into the sand and throwing their hands up above their heads.

Having just paid his last respects to fallen comrades, Churchill felt little compulsion to show mercy. What compassion would these "savages" have shown to surrendering British soldiers? They lacked any basic element of humanity and knew only how to inflict suffering. He had only just seen this enemy slash, hack, and stab fallen men in a frenzy of bloodlust, rendering their victims unrecognizable as anything but pieces of bloody meat—yet here they were, seeking food, water, and medical assistance.

It was not long before countless Dervishes were presenting themselves to the Lancers in surrender. Not all enemy combatants, however, gave themselves up. Thousands fled across the plain into Omdurman, taking refuge among its cramped mud houses and narrow streets. The escorting of prisoners into captivity stalled the cavalry's advance. Churchill estimated some twenty thousand Dervish warriors consequently escaped the field of battle. Some of the Lancers leapt from their horses and harassed the fleeing hordes with rifle fire. The Dervishes, withdrawing into the city, fired back—but the range between the two sides was such that accuracy proved elusive.

All this while the main body of Kitchener's army continued pushing closer to the city walls. The Khalifa's men, although undoubtedly brave, were easy prey for the British Maxim guns and fell in startling numbers. Kitchener, sitting on horseback and observing his army's advance through field glasses, was pleased with his army's progress. By two o'clock he and his men were two miles from Omdurman, where the geography favored a house-to-house defense. British and Egyptian soldiers would be at a disadvantage in the streets. On the open floor of the desert, the Dervishes didn't stand a chance, but sheltered in Omdurman, their prospects were slightly improved. With their prisoners now sitting behind Anglo-Egyptian lines, the Lancers rode forward to join Kitchener. The army was taking a rest near a large hollow filled with Nile floodwaters. "The scene," Churchill reported, "is a strange one."

Scores of men, horses, and mules crowded at the water's edge to relieve their thirst; some staggered into the murky, crimson pool and submerged themselves. No one seemed to care—or notice—that three dead horses, rapidly approaching a state of decay, lay in the water. Hundreds of soldiers, content with a moment's rest, lay in utter collapse on the sandy slopes leading down to the pool. It seemed fitting to Churchill that it should be the Nile, the lifeblood of the desert, reinvigorating the men.

Soldiers washed the grime of battle from their skin and filled their canvas bottles. Churchill and the other Lancers let their horses drink until they could drink no more. The sun blazed overhead, drying man and beast in minutes. Bugles sounded at four o'clock. Men heaved themselves off the sand, some taking one last swig of water before falling into their columns and setting off for the city. Churchill checked his Mauser and climbed once more into the saddle. He wiped the sweat from the back of his neck and cast his gaze in the direction of Omdurman. The shattered tomb of the Mahdi appeared blurred in the heat shimmering off the desert sand. The men marched the short distance to the city's outskirts, where the Lancers and Camel Corps took up their positions. Churchill watched as the infantry, with Kitchener riding front and center, entered the Omdurman suburbs. Volleys of shots rang out here and there, but if Kitchener anticipated any fierce resistance, his expectations were dashed.

"The city presented some horrible sights," noted one contemporary account. "It was chiefly a collection of squalid mud huts. The streets were full of corpses of men and beasts." The British bombardment the day before had wrought terrible carnage. The shells had been indiscriminate in their slaughter. The mangled bodies of women and children littered streets and alleyways. Under the hot desert sun, the dead had already begun to bloat and decompose—the stench, cloying and sickly sweet like rotting vegetables, turned the men's stomachs. The cries and moans of the wounded drifted from the primitive huts. Dervishes who approached the column and did not surrender were gunned down or run through with bayonets. A hot wind blew litter across Kitchener's path and ruffled the clothing of the dead. Up ahead, three figures appeared seemingly out of nowhere. Kitchener ordered his men to a halt and watched the three individuals approach with caution. They stopped in front of Kitchener's horse and dropped to their knees in acquiescence, presenting the general with keys to the city, prison, and arsenal. Kitchener accepted their offering and surrender—the news of which seemed to magically bring the city to life. Whereas everything before had been desolation and silence, chanting and cheering crowds suddenly spilled into the streets. Men, women, and children staggered from their homes crying with relief and rejoicing that it was all over.

Kitchener had yet to enter the city proper, separated from the suburbs by a great wall. The shelling by British gunboats the day before had reduced many sections of the wall to piles of rubble. It quickly became apparent that not everyone was willing to surrender just yet. A number of Dervishes, armed with rifles, opened fire from the undamaged parapets and raked the street below. The infantry replied with Maxim guns, tearing great chunks from the wall, obliterating the parapets and knocking many Dervishes to their deaths. The exchange was short-lived, as the enemy no longer had the stomach to wage a lost battle. The city was Kitchener's for the taking, and he rode forward in triumph with his army—excited by its victory—marching close behind. British, Egyptian, and Sudanese soldiers, Churchill noted, entered the city "on a broad front" and fired their guns skyward in celebration. Some Dervishes still took random potshots at the victors, who responded in kind.

The army stomped through all of Omdurman, voicing its good cheer, before marching back to the suburbs and setting up camp for the night. Kitchener, eager to establish his headquarters, settled on the Mahdi's battered tomb and set the stage for one final tragedy. For some reason two British gun batteries outside the city opened fire when their crews saw the flag of Kitchener's headquarters staff raised above the tomb. In the Khalifa's abandoned house, adjacent to the tomb, *Times* correspondent Hubert Howard stood admiring the view from a top-floor window when a shell exploded above the home and struck him dead. It was ten o'clock at night when Churchill and the other cavalrymen returned to camp and learned of Howard's death. The waste of it incensed Churchill. He had long admired Howard's courage and would have pitied the man's misfortune had he not thought it would be an insult to Howard's memory.

Exhausted, Churchill dined that night on sausage and jam. When he lay down for the evening, he found his mind seized by the day's events and resistant to sleep. He got up and wandered over to the headquarters camp, where he witnessed a bizarre sight. Standing in the pallid glow of several lanterns was an emaciated figure, thin to the point of looking almost skeletal, his skin so white it appeared translucent. The man—although European—was dressed in a loose-fitting blue-and-white Dervish gown and was talking to a sergeant crouched at his feet. "I have forgotten how to walk," the man said in a weak, raspy voice that was more whisper than anything else. As Churchill drew closer, he saw the sergeant was hammering away at a thick chain that ran between the man's ankles. Several men standing nearby watched in silence.

Churchill inquired the identity of the human wraith. "Karl Neufeld" came the reply. Churchill knew the name. A medical student at the University of Leipzig, Neufeld had fled his native Germany in the early 1880s after shooting another student in a duel. He established a medical practice in Egypt before launching a merchant enterprise aimed at doing business with Sudan. In April 1888 he led a caravan through the

Sudanese desert, reportedly to trade with local tribes. The Khalifa, believing Neufeld to be on a mission to gather military intelligence, took
Neufeld prisoner and sentenced him to death. On the day of his execution, he was led in chains to the gallows. A subsequent article in the
Times noted, "He behaved there so courageously, asking to be executed
like a Mohammedan, instead of suffering death by hanging, that the
Khalifa was struck and respited him under the gallows. He was taken to
the general prison, with heavy chains on his hands and feet, and treated
in a most abominable manner." Kitchener's occupation of Omdurman
brought an end to Neufeld's ten years of captivity. Churchill watched
the sergeant continuing to bang away at Neufeld's shackles. Two sets of
chains ran between the poor man's ankles—one of them he had worn
continuously since his capture. The other was much larger and heavier.
"I could just lift the shackle with one hand," Churchill reported. This
had been strapped to Neufeld for two years.

Neufeld informed his rescuers the Khalifa had fled with the remnants of his army when Kitchener entered the city. Churchill jotted
down his observations in a notebook and returned to his camp. By now
not even his active mind could hold off sleep. He had purposely refused
throughout the day to dwell on his survival during the battle, lest he
tempt fate. Stretching out on the ground, surveying a brilliant canvas
of stars, he allowed himself to "make the fitting acknowledgements to
Providence."

On Saturday, September 3, 1898, Kitchener's army buried its dead.
To the mournful wail of bagpipes, British soldiers carried their
fallen comrades to a small hill on the banks of the Nile. From this vantage point they could see the dirty squalor of Omdurman and—key to
the whole drama—Khartoum. The Nile coursed between the two cities
and passed beneath the burial site with its row of white wooden crosses.

The grave markers, held upright by piles of red stones, stood in
startling contrast against the colors of the desert. Churchill lowered his
head and felt a lump rise in his throat. The freshly dug graves swept
away his infatuation with war, and he allowed himself to cry for the
fallen. Hubert Howard was also buried that day. His funeral made

international headlines. Noting incorrectly the manner of Howard's death, the *New York Times* reported: "Representatives of the Reuter Telegraph Company, the *Standard, Daily News, Daily Graphic*, and *Daily Mail* carried to the grave the remains of the Hon. Hubert Howard, second son of the Earl of Carlisle and correspondent of *The Times*, who was killed in Omdurman by the natives on the day the city was captured."

Funerals aside, the day was one of minimal activity. The Lancers patrolled the outskirts of Omdurman, which proved to be an uneventful exercise. At 6:35 p.m., back in camp, Winston sent his mother a telegram. It arrived at the post office in Spring Street, Paddington, just before one o'clock the next day. It simply read, "All right—Winston." The next day, September 4, representatives from every regiment in Kitchener's army descended on Khartoum. Gunboats ferried them across the river for a flag-raising ceremony. The Union Jack, naturally, was four times larger than the Egyptian Khedive raised alongside it. A brass band played the national anthems of both countries, after which those gathered—Churchill among them—cheered three times for Her Majesty. "For my part," reported Churchill, some forty-two years before that desperate summer of 1940, "I raised my voice and helmet in honor of that persevering British people who, often affronted, often checked, often delayed, usually get their own way in the end."

General Gordon was avenged; the war in the Sudan was over. That afternoon Churchill wrote his mother a letter. "Khartoum and be damned to it" was the return address. He told her of the cavalry charge, but said details were hard to recall. The whole thing, upon reflection, seemed almost unreal—as if it were a dream. But the deaths of Grenfell and Howard wielded the sharp edge of reality and cut him deeply. Their fates haunted his sleep and cast a depressing pall over his Sudanese adventure.

On September 5 Churchill toured the battlefield. Despite his considerable gifts as a writer, he realized it would be impossible to convey the horror and misery scattered across the sandy plain. Even if he could muster the words to do the visual impact justice, there was no way to adequately communicate the heinous stench that hung over everything.

It was so strong, so thick, it seemed to be an almost physical presence. Perhaps his readers would benefit from not knowing the details. Churchill estimated that eleven thousand bodies lay bloated and rotting in the sun. Their advanced state of decomposition rendered the bayonet and bullet wounds even more gruesome.

Of particular interest to Churchill was the scene of the Lancers' epic charge. He saw that the depression in which the enemy had concealed itself was five feet deep and roughly twenty feet wide. Bodies of men and horses littered the ditch. Other corpses were scattered about the surrounding area. He climbed to the top of Heliograph Hill. Here lay the Dervish victims of British artillery—or, as one witness described it, "the murderous tornado of exploding bombs and pitiless lead." The bodies had bloated to grotesque proportions and looked like balloons ready to burst. Those in a more advanced state of decay had inflated beyond anything that looked remotely human. Never before had Churchill witnessed such a sickening sight. Everywhere he turned, he saw signs of slaughter. The dead, in some areas, lay two or three deep and completely obscured the ground.

In life the Dervishes had been fearless warriors—a trait Churchill admired. In death they were human wreckage. The glory of their cause and the strength of their convictions meant nothing in the battle's aftermath. The British and Egyptian dead were at least provided a measure of honor in their military burials, laid to rest beneath the flags of their nations. The Khalifa's men were left to rot in the wild. There would be no monument to their ultimate sacrifice. It dawned on Churchill that perhaps the fallen enemy deserved as much respect as those who fell for the empire. It was an exceedingly unpleasant thought. Cuba had been a game to Churchill—a novelty and adventure. The brutality of the North-West Frontier had struck a stronger chord, but the carnage evident on the desert plain outside Omdurman made him truly see war for what it was. It rendered victory, for the moment, a hollow concept: For what glory was there to be found in any of this? Such a nightmarish panorama underscored the futility of war. And what of the wounded?

British soldiers returning home with physical or mental wounds would receive state benefits and medicine to help them heal. There would be no such help for the surviving Dervish casualties, many of whom lay helpless among the dead. With pistols drawn, Churchill and a companion—Lord Tullibardine—began picking their way among the fallen, looking for any who might still be clinging to life. They found "many scattered about the plain." Lord Tullibardine knelt beside those they found and offered a few drops of water from his canteen until it was finally empty. Three days had passed since the fighting—three horrific days for the Dervish wounded left lying in the sun. Churchill had never felt such pity. He wondered what would benefit these poor creatures more: a bucket of cool, clear water to soothe their parched and swollen throats, or an angel of mercy armed with a revolver and a bottomless sack of ammunition to put each one out of his hellish misery.

As Churchill and Lord Tullibardine picked their way among the human detritus, they came to a bush offering a small measure of shade. Four men lay beneath it. Judging from the drag marks in the sand, they had crawled a considerable distance before finding this pitiful refuge. One of them had spread the torn remnants of his robe across the bush's thorny branches in a sad attempt to create more cover. Upon closer inspection, Churchill saw that three of the men were dead. The fourth man lay bleeding and sunburned with a British round buried in his right knee. Lord Tullibardine knelt beside the man and dug the bullet out of the bone with his knife—but there was only so much they could do for the stricken. "Would you be further sickened with the horrors of the field?" Churchill asked his readers.

They came across one man, who, in limited English and pained speech, said he had been crawling three days to try to reach the river. Separating him from the water's edge remained another two miles of blistering desert—a distance rendered almost insurmountable by the man's missing foot and deteriorating state. Churchill and Tullibardine left the man to his exertions and forever wondered if he completed the journey. Another shattered warrior with mangled legs of broken bone had dragged himself through the sand in a sitting position. Churchill guessed the man was averaging no more than several hundred yards a day. As pitiful as such displays were, none was more so than the dead

Dervish warrior they found along the river's bank. The tracks in the sand suggested he had pulled himself miles to reach this point, only to die where the water wet the sand. "Let us hope," Churchill wrote, "he had drunk his drink first." These displays of vitality and stubbornness despite grievous injuries amazed Churchill, but it was this strength of body that had prolonged their agony.

Having witnessed suffering of this magnitude in the wake of battle, perhaps it's not surprising that Churchill, as Britain's later wartime leader, believed in magnanimity in victory. He would become a firm believer in the Roman saying, "Spare the conquered and confront the proud."

The sun was setting, draining colors from the grisly landscape. Churchill and Tullibardine returned to camp in the gathering gloom. The images of the day were forever seared into Churchill's memory. How strange, he thought, that men so full of aggression and courage just days ago lay, soon to be forgotten, rotting in the middle of nowhere. In a dispatch for the *Morning Post*, he wrote a final epitaph for the vanquished: "There they lie, those valiant warriors of a false faith and of a fallen denomination, their only history preserved by their conquerors, their only monument their bones—and these the drifting sand of the desert will bury in a few short years."

There was little else to report. The war finished, the long journey home would soon commence. His reporting had come a long way since the campaign in Cuba. While still jingoistic in places and promoting a romantic view of Britannia, his writing had taken on a stronger emotional edge.

Although he still loved the action of battle, he was more willing to acknowledge the dirty side of war—the horror and slaughter. In the past, having lost friends in combat, he had sought comfort in the belief that a soldier's death for queen and country was the noblest of fates—but now he wasn't so sure. The luster of war had dulled somewhat. Like the blacksmith shaping a sword's blade on the anvil, reality hammered at Churchill's preconceived notions of combat. Seen through the prism of history or imagined with lead soldiers in a playroom, war was the grandest of enterprises. But in the mountains of the North-West Frontier and the desert wasteland of Omdurman, Churchill could see cracks in the glorious façade and the ugliness it concealed.

On September 6 the 21st Lancers began their march back to Cairo, the first leg of which was a long slog through the desert back to Atbara. Churchill was ordered to stay behind and help load supplies for transport back down the Nile. Before the Lancers galloped off across the plain, Kitchener surprised them with a farewell visit. He rode into camp, resplendent on horseback and bristling with victory. Colonel Martin and his Lancers snapped to attention and gathered around the general. "Colonel Martin," Kitchener bellowed, "officers and men of the 21st Lancers, I am very proud to have had you under my command. The fine charge you made the other day will long go down in history in the annals of your regiment."

The Lancers galloped off across the desert, and Churchill busied himself with his dispatches, pondering the Lancers' daring action. Kitchener would certainly have achieved his aim whether the regiment charged or not. This does not discount their bravery—but even Churchill, in a dispatch dated September 11, argued the charge "did not greatly influence the fortunes of the battle." More than anything, he wrote, it was symbolic of the British Empire's fortitude: "From the study of the men—I mean the troopers—who charged on 2 September, 'the weary Titan' may rise refreshed and, contemplating the past with calmness, may feel confidence in the present and high hope in the future."

If the Lancers evoked in Churchill a sense of British pride, the same could not be said of Kitchener. On September 12 Churchill walked the reeking streets of Omdurman. He explored the Khalifa's house, damaged by shellfire and picked clean by looters. Shrapnel and gunpowder littered nearly every surface. From the top floor he looked out a shattered window at the city below, its streets still littered with the bodies of those killed in the British bombardment. The vista of mud houses and narrow alleys offered nothing to the eye but squalor and ugliness.

He next made his way to the Mahdi's devastated tomb, "destroyed and profaned" by British artillery. He did not approve of its destruction, for it smacked of pettiness.

One rumor he found particularly disturbing was that Kitchener, upon having the Mahdi's body removed from its crypt, demanded the corpse be decapitated. When Gordon was killed in Khartoum, the Dervishes mutilated his body in a similar fashion and delivered to the Mahdi, as a trophy, the general's head on a pike. Nevertheless, Churchill did not support the desecration of a holy relic—even one associated with what he considered a "false" religion. Besides, as far as Churchill was concerned, all pious beliefs were prone to suspicion. The followers of one religion were generally quick to denounce the followers of another. Whatever one believed, Churchill thought it poor form to wage war on the symbol of someone's piousness. Kitchener thought otherwise. He had ordered the exhumation of the Mahdi's body and its decapitation and then used the skull for an inkwell. None of this made it into Churchill's dispatches.

Churchill's time in Omdurman was at an end. Five days later he was in Atbara en route to Cairo. Kitchener, having never wanted the young upstart to join his expedition in the first place, had ordered Churchill to return to Atbara via long march. Churchill ignored the general—believing the order was issued out of sheer pettiness—and hopped a steamer with the Grenadier Guards for the return journey.

On September 20 Churchill penned his final dispatch for the *Morning Post*. He had taken readers on a voyage down the Nile and introduced them to a world far removed from the reality they knew. They had spent an unsettling night with him lost in the desert and accompanied Kitchener's army on a march through inhospitable country few civilized men had ever seen. He shared with them the thrill and horror of combat and the morally ambiguous realities of victory. With his journey home under way, it was time to say farewell.

But Churchill, naturally, had not undertaken this adventure to play tour guide; he craved action and sought to make a public name for himself on which to build a political career. That being the case, anonymous dispatches could hardly be expected to advance his efforts.

"Since in these letters I have only tried to write what is fair and true, and because no man should write that of which he is either ashamed or afraid," he wrote, "I shall venture in conclusion to subscribe myself." And so he concluded his farewell piece the only way he saw fit:

Yours truly,

WINSTON SPENCER CHURCHILL

CHAPTER 9

Literary Pursuits

hurchill left Egypt with a battle scar of sorts despite escaping Omdurman without injury. In Cairo he paid a visit in the hospital to friend and fellow Lancer Dick Molyneux, whose right hand had been nearly severed by a Dervish sword, the curved blade having sliced through tendon and muscle just above the wrist. Churchill arrived at Molyneux's bedside just as a tough-looking Irish doctor changed the wound's bloodied dressing. Molyneux, the doctor said, required a skin graft and volunteered Churchill to surrender a piece of flesh. Not entirely thrilled with the idea—but not wanting to abandon a friend in need—Churchill rolled up his sleeve. With a flourish suggesting he greatly enjoyed his work, the doctor produced a razor blade. In a thick Irish brogue, he told Churchill he would know what it felt like to be flayed alive. This proved to be no exaggeration. The doctor grabbed Churchill's wrist in a vice-like grip, applied razor to flesh, and sawed back and forth as Churchill's nerve endings screamed. After what seemed an eternity, the doctor had a nice patch of skin and Churchill, in the resulting scar, had a worthy memento of his Sudanese exploits. He was back in London by late October and established at his mother's house in Great Cumberland Place, with plenty on his mind.

The *Morning Post* had paid him a respectable £220 for his dispatches. Money, however, remained a pressing concern. He received a £500 annual allowance from his mother, but he wished to achieve financial independence. When he looked to the future, he saw nothing but money troubles for himself and his mother—something that caused him considerable dismay. They were both creatures of luxury, a typical Churchillian trait ill-suited for the family's constantly shaky finances. His allowance was not enough to cover his lifestyle with the Hussars, which included servants, polo ponies, and uniforms. Nor did his army pay of 14s. a day do much to ease the strain. His burgeoning writing career was yielding greater dividends than his military service. He was already writing a book about the Sudan campaign, which he hoped would keep the coffers full for the next couple of years. And so, after much thought, he decided to leave the army in favor of writing books and eventually pursuing politics—but not before competing in the Inter-Regimental Polo Tournament in India. He stayed around London long enough to celebrate his twenty-fourth birthday and send out letters to various knowledgeable people, requesting details for his Sudan book.

By December 4 he was in Brindisi, en route to Bangalore for the tournament. The journey by sea gave him little pleasure. The rickety boat rocked violently for most of the voyage. It proved too much for Churchill, who went two days straight without food. Even the ship's captain staggered about the deck with a green complexion. Not for the first time, Churchill promised himself he would never travel by sea again.

He arrived in Bangalore on December 22, happy to be back with his regiment, if only for the polo. In his new writing case he carried the partial manuscript of his latest book, which he called *The River War*. It remained his primary focus despite the upcoming polo tournament. He put all he had into the writing and set a grueling schedule for himself, working on it daily from first light to bedtime. No sentence was too inconsequential. Every choice of word proved a matter of deliberation, forcing him to rework some sentences three times before he moved on.

The work was not only mentally taxing, it took a physical toll. At times Churchill's hand would cramp to the point he could no longer hold his pen, but he deemed it worth the suffering. It was a stellar work, yet it would surely cause consternation in high circles. Progressing ever deeper into the manuscript, Churchill's dislike for Kitchener gradually revealed itself as the pages emerged. He thought the man indecent for desecrating the Mahdi's tomb, a grim episode he finally detailed in the book.

While Churchill toiled with pen and paper, a minor controversy erupted back in England. On December 17 a letter to the editor appeared in *Army and Navy Gazette*. The missive's anonymous author, "A General Officer," expressed umbrage with a certain young lieutenant. What special privilege allowed Lieutenant Winston Churchill to trot all over the globe reporting, at leisure, on wars of his choosing? It seemed every time one opened the paper, there he was—an officer with less than four years' active service to his name—critiquing the competence of senior commanders and opining on military action. How could the lieutenant be both a soldier and a correspondent? In the service clubs and military mess halls, Churchill's adventures left a bad taste in the mouth of many, according to the letter writer. Surely men of greater service and experience deserved at least half the opportunities afforded to Churchill. It was distressing to men of all ranks and damaging to morale. Whatever Churchill's family connections, the general officer stated, the young lieutenant should be treated no differently than others of equal rank.

Another letter appeared in the same publication a week later—this time from an anonymous "Field Officer," who echoed the sentiments of the previous letter writer. Churchill did not hesitate to respond when copies of the offending letters reached him in India. It was not so much the criticism that galled him, but that his detractors—particularly the general—refused to sign their names to the complaints. Nowhere in his "daily life," Churchill wrote, had he seen anything to suggest his fellow officers bore him ill will or considered his exploits in poor taste. Even if he had wronged his colleagues, he argued, he could take comfort in knowing he had never attacked the character of a stranger through the shield of anonymity. For anyone, he wrote, even a general, to assail another man in an unsigned letter was conduct "equally unworthy of a brave soldier and an honorable man."

Having addressed his mystery critics, he continued investing all he had in *The River War*. One sentence in particular stood out. Although he told his mother it was about the Mahdi, whose father had abandoned him as a boy, it carried a strong autobiographical component: "Solitary trees, if they grow at all, grow strong: and a boy deprived of a father's care often develops, if he escapes the perils of youth, an independence and a vigor of thought which may restore in after life the heavy loss of early days." Certainly this was true of Churchill. Deprived of paternal love and approval when Lord Randolph was alive, and denied the opportunity to forge a meaningful bond with the man, Churchill developed on his own terms. He had sought from an early age to establish his own identity and believed destiny would bestow greatness upon him. That his father never lived to see it would be a regret Churchill carried with him to the end of his life.

He put his writing aside in early February and traveled to Jodhpur to practice for the much-anticipated tournament. Shortly after his arrival he suffered a miserable misfortune when he fell down a flight of stairs, spraining both his ankles and dislocating his right shoulder. Not one to let physical incapacity get in the way, he still played, but with his right arm strapped to his side and in considerable pain. His team advanced to the final match and won, with Churchill scoring two goals. The bells sounding the end of the match came as a sweet and blessed relief. The 4th Hussars rode from the field as the uncontested champions of India. The celebrations, which involved vast quantities of wine, lasted well into the night. Then it was back to Bangalore to prepare for his permanent departure from the country and the army. He had completed his discharge papers and turned them in by the end of March. He may have stayed in the army had it not been such a costly enterprise. Civilian life, without its mandatory uniforms, bridlery, and polo ponies, would not be such a financial strain. In addition, he could make more as an author and journalist—professions to which he could devote more time—than he ever had in the military.

As for his book, he had roughly 135,000 words down on paper—about 450 pages—and hoped to be done with the manuscript in a month. On March 26, 1899, while traveling back to London, he stopped in Cairo for a two-week research trip and stayed at the Savoy Hotel. His choice of accommodation, he wrote his mother, was expensive—but one must always pay for comfort. More important, the hotel's central location made it ideal for his research excursions. Not everything, however, met Churchillian standards. He found the hotel's pens "horrid."

One man who provided Churchill with substantial background information was Lord Cromer, the British consul general of Egypt, who detailed the history of the Sudan campaign, starting with Gordon's slaying in Khartoum. In what he had written so far, Churchill had catered to the widespread notion of Gordon as a gallant soldier who died a hero's death. There was, after all, a statue of the man in Trafalgar Square. Cromer did not consider Gordon worthy of such an honor. He urged Churchill not to cater to popular opinion, saying the general was a victim of his own ego, erratic behavior, short fuse, and bull-headedness. His fondness for drink and drastic mood swings probably didn't help matters. Churchill informed his mother he would have to rework the chapter detailing Gordon's demise, though he refused to edit certain passages he believed sparkled on the page.

He arrived back in London by late April, intent on finishing his book by the end of May. He had it done by August and signed a contract with Longmans, publisher of his Malakand book, to release it in two volumes on the first of October. Unlike *The Story of the Malakand Field Force*, essentially a book-length piece of war reportage, *The River War* is a work of narrative nonfiction, epic in its sweep, a history of the Sudanese drama from the rise of the Mahdi to Kitchener's reconquest. He retired to Blenheim Palace to make final edits before publication. As always, he threw himself into the work and spent his days revising proofs, to the point of absolute exhaustion. The investment of blood and sweat was evident on the page. He had no doubt the book was his greatest work and marveled at his own productivity. Once free of the army, he had reconsidered going easy on Kitchener, but ultimately let the man have it. The desecration of the Mahdi's tomb continued to leave a bitter taste in Churchill's mouth, as did Kitchener's decision to take "the Mahdi's head in a kerosene-can as a trophy."

While finishing his manuscript that summer, Churchill entered his first political fray and ran for one of two parliamentary seats in Oldham, a "strongly cotton-dominated borough in Lancashire." He was wildly optimistic, for he was running against two Liberal candidates at the urging of the local Conservative association. Optimism, however, is not always enough. He suffered an inflamed tonsil early in the campaign, severely impacting his ability to deliver speeches, but he remained confident. A dislocated shoulder had not hampered his ability to win a polo tournament, he wrote his mother, so why should a sore throat cost him an election? He campaigned on a number of issues, including better care for the poor, opposing Irish Home Rule, and raising the standard of living for families across England. As a man who loved his drink, he opposed the idea of enforced abstinence "through the withholding of public house licenses." In global affairs, he promised to be a stalwart defender of the empire and safeguard the realm against foreign aggressors.

In a four-man contest, Churchill came in third with 11,477 votes when the ballots were tallied on June 6. His two Liberal opponents emerged triumphant, with "12,976 and 12,770 votes respectively," while his Conservative running mate came in last with 11,449. A reporter for the *Manchester Guardian* noted that Churchill "looked upon the process of counting with amusement. A smile lit up his features, and the result of the election did not disturb him."

Three months later, on September 18, the prospect of another wartime adventure arrived in the daily post. The editor of the *Daily Mail* wished to send Churchill to South Africa to cover the growing crisis between the Dutch settlers, or Boers, who had called the Cape home for nearly 150 years, and British imperialists with designs on the gold-rich country. Having previously established the Republics of the Transvaal and the Orange Free State, the Boers had no desire to live under the Union Jack. Various grievances between the two sides—among them the threat of British expansionism—had resulted in the First Boer War, fought between December 1880 and March 1881. The conflict proved an embarrassing defeat for the British, whose interest in the country only intensified with the subsequent discovery of gold in the Witwatersrand region of the Transvaal.

By the time Churchill received the *Daily Mail* offer, South Africa was the "single biggest gold producer in the world." Some British political entities feared that the rapidly burgeoning wealth of the Transvaal, if left unchecked, would "eventually topple Britain from its position of power in South Africa." Churchill followed the situation closely. Tensions between the Boers and the British—stoked by London's imperial ambitions, disputed control of the gold-mining industry, and the rights of British nationals in the Transvaal—had again reached a boiling point.

Churchill, convinced war was imminent, wired the *Mail*'s offer to Oliver Borthwick at the *Morning Post*, who, not wanting to lose a rising star, countered with extremely generous terms: £1,000 for four months' work, then £200 a month after that, with all expenses covered. Churchill accepted and prepared for his departure. His field glasses and telescope had taken a beating at Omdurman, so he put them in for repairs at W. Callaghan & Co. Opticians on New Bond Street. That same day, October 6, he wandered over to Randolph Payne & Sons—importers of wine, spirits, and liquors on St. James's Street—and placed an order for 6 bottles of champagne, 18 bottles of wine, 6 bottles of light port, 6 bottles of French vermouth, 18 bottles of ten-year-old Scotch whisky, and a dozen bottles of Rose's Cordial Lime Juice. Churchill had learned from past experience. When traveling to a potential war zone, one had to bring along creature comforts.

Five days later, on October 11, 1899, following London's refusal to withdraw troops from the Boer Republics, the Transvaal and Orange

Free State declared war on Great Britain. The Boers promptly invaded the British colony of Natal and proved to be a surprisingly formidable enemy. The Second Boer War, as history would christen the conflict, ushered in a new, bloody age of warfare and would thrust Churchill onto the world stage.

CHAPTER 10

Churchill Restrained

Thousands of well-wishers, fueled by a strong anti-Boer sentiment, crowded the dock at Southampton on the evening of October 14 to bid the Royal Mail steamer *Dunottar Castle* an enthusiastic farewell. Eager British soldiers, buoyed by the send-off, waved from the upper deck. Somewhere on board was General Sir Redvers Buller, their commander in chief. At the ship's railing, Churchill eyed the party-like scene along the water's edge. He found nothing to celebrate in the pending journey. Out there on the open sea, deprived of news from the war zone, he would be isolated from world events. The voyage was scheduled to last two weeks—an eternity in Churchill's opinion. He feared the war might be over by the time he disembarked.

Rough seas the first three days out only added to his general misery, as did the lack of decent company. As seemed to be the case more often than not when he traveled by sea, he found the people on board, a mix of journalists and soldiers, friendly enough, but incredibly boring. Nine days into the voyage the *Dunottar Castle* encountered a transport ship carrying Australian cavalry to the theater of war. The two vessels pulled alongside one another, enabling passengers to shout questions back and forth. One Australian asked if General Buller was on board. Churchill and the other steamer passengers yelled back in the affirmative. The

Australians roared their approval and waved their slouch hats above their heads, their boisterous greeting echoed by a high-pitched salutation from the transport's steam whistle. The two ships gradually drifted apart and continued on their respective courses. The encounter was, for Churchill, a brief respite from boredom. Growing anticipation of what lay in store and the pending release of his book also began to soothe his general malaise. He regretted not being in London for *The River War*'s publication—now scheduled for November—and urged his mother to send him any and all reviews. He was desperate to know details of the book's reception.

Eight days later, on October 31, he landed in Cape Town. As the harbor's guns fired a thunderous volley in welcome, photographers crowded the dock to catch General Buller descending the gangway. The atmosphere in Cape Town, much like Southampton, was one of celebration. Crowds choked the city streets to glimpse Buller in his carriage and cheered as he rode past. Union Jacks fluttered from the front of every building. After disembarking, Churchill hurried to the railway station and caught the evening train out of the city. His final destination was the Natal town of Ladysmith, currently the center of British operations against the Boers. The train worked its way up the mountains that night and by morning was clattering across the Great Karoo, a massive region of semidesert. Churchill stared out the window, impressed by its immensity but unmoved by the aesthetics. As far as he could see stretched a barren vista of parched land, withered scrub, and large, crumbling rocks. He discerned no beauty in the alien landscape, only desolation. The train and its occupants seemed out of place here in the middle of nowhere. It certainly made one miss the green fields of England.

When the train pulled into Beaufort West the following morning, grim news awaited. The twelve-thousand-strong British garrison at Ladysmith—under the command of Lieutenant General Sir George White and threatened with encirclement by a Boer army twice its size—had launched an offensive that had quickly soured. The end result was a British rout, with fourteen hundred men killed, captured, or wounded. All around Beaufort West, Churchill heard Dutch residents talking merrily about the Boer victory and doing little to hide their disdain for Britain and its fighting men.

In the town of De Aar Churchill saw the first signs of war. Military trains steamed in and out of the station with unceasing regularity beneath a permanent ribbon of smoke, while armed guards patrolled the streets. Many residents, panicked by the approach of the Boers from the north, clogged roads out of town with overloaded wagons, desperate to get away. Churchill found it all unsatisfactory but hoped Buller's arrival would soon turn British fortunes around. From De Aar he caught the last train bound for the southern coastal town of East London. A somber mood permeated the carriage. The British were falling back on all fronts. "Even the rattle of the train," noted Churchill, "seemed to urge 'Retreat, retreat, retreat.'" He believed a terrible conflict lay ahead, one that would eventually litter the South African veldt—wide open grasslands—with ten thousand corpses or more. He expressed these thoughts in a letter to his mother. The Boers, motivated by the defense of their land and homes, made a confident and dangerous enemy. Churchill knew better than to underestimate them.

He reached East London and boarded a steamer to Durban, where he hoped to catch a train to Ladysmith. A storm in the Indian Ocean made for a horrendous voyage and confined Churchill to his cabin, where he remained in his bunk, paralyzed by seasickness. It was nothing short of a blessing when the steamer docked in Durban at midnight on November 4. Churchill spent a long six hours waiting for daybreak and news of recent developments. As he roamed the docks, he saw the hospital ship *Sumatra* and went on board in the early morning hours to see if he could find any friends. Much to his surprise, he stumbled across Lieutenant Reginald Barnes—his companion in Cuba—who had been shot through the groin in a recent battle. Obviously in pain, Barnes told his friend not to believe any talk he might hear suggesting the Boers had no stomach for a long war. They will fight to the last man, Barnes warned. Churchill assured his friend that Britain would see things through to final victory. Barnes offered a weak smile. It was a race, he said, to see which side bled to death first.

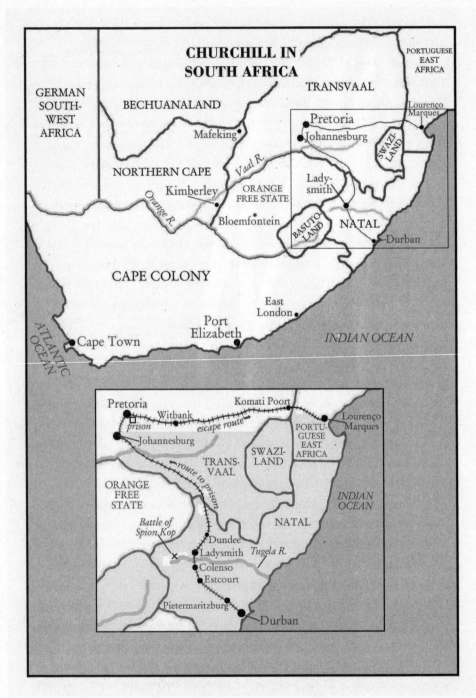

Map 5: Churchill in South Africa

At daybreak Churchill went searching in Durban for news from the front. What he heard shocked him. The Boers had laid siege to Ladysmith, severing the railway line in and out of town and trapping the remains of the garrison. A relief force, under General Buller, was on its way to put the situation right. Not wanting to waste another moment, Churchill was on a mail train by 7:00 that morning, heading for the town of Pietermaritzburg, roughly a hundred miles southeast of Ladysmith. The railway route, with its sharp bends and steep hills, took four hours to travel. Churchill did not think Pietermaritzburg a destination worthy of such an arduous route; he found it boring. Not even the wartime preparations of surrounding it with barbed wire, fortifying its hills, and installing gun emplacements could liven it up. He did not stick around for long. Because the Boers had effectively cut off Ladysmith, the closest Churchill could get by rail was Estcourt, some thirty-five miles from the besieged town. Estcourt was not so much a town as it was two neatly organized streets of roughly three hundred houses built of either stone or sheets of corrugated metal.

Churchill and other war correspondents set up a small tent city near the Estcourt railway station to await the arrival of Buller's army before the push on Ladysmith began. Churchill abhorred waiting. An armored train made daily patrols in Ladysmith's direction to the north. On the afternoon of November 8 he hitched a ride and went in search of his own adventure. The word "armored" suggests a beast-like machine bristling with guns and layered in steel, but the train did not present such a formidable sight. It had no guns of any sort, nor did the carriages have roofs. Churchill thought it "a very puny specimen." The train steamed out of the station at one o'clock in the afternoon with Churchill and a company of Dublin Fusiliers aboard. It pulled into Chieveley, five miles to the north, nearly two hours later; the prolonged journey was the result of making frequent stops to check with other patrols working the open land on either side of the tracks. From the station at Chieveley the train carried on, but at a reduced speed, the engineer and all on board wary of an ambush. Before the train crossed a bridge, the men would disembark to ensure it had not been rigged with explosives. Eventually they reached Colenso, less than twenty miles from Ladysmith. It was, Churchill reported, "a silent, desolate village."

In the middle of one street lay a dead horse, its legs sticking straight up in the air and its swollen belly seemingly on the verge of rupturing. Clothing and household items lay strewn everywhere, as if residents had tried to flee while holding in their arms all they could carry. Small flames still flickered among the wreckage of several buildings that had been burned to the ground; shop windows had been smashed and everything of value carried away. The Boers had looted the town from one end to the other. Turning down one street, Churchill spotted several dispirited locals who, believing more torment was heading their way, waved a stick with a white sheet tied to its end. Churchill, eager to leave, returned to the train.

They traveled further north from Colenso to where the Boers had severed the Ladysmith line. Getting off to inspect the damage, Churchill and the others eyed the nearby hills and wondered whether any Boers were lying in wait. The train would certainly be in range of any large artillery piece, a fact that made everyone ill at ease. The men made their inspection, noting that two lengths of track had been ripped away, before once more boarding the train and reversing back to Estcourt. The sun began its descent as the train sped through open country, belching black smoke into a red-and-orange sky. The soldiers seemed to relax more with each passing mile. Some lounged on the carriage floor, while others leaned against the sides of the car and smoked their cigarettes. The train rolled into the Estcourt station after dark.

His day done, Churchill returned to his tent for the night. He awoke the following morning, November 9, to a distant rumbling. From Ladysmith, the wind carried the clattering of field guns, interrupted every couple of minutes by the din of a large artillery piece. Churchill and two other correspondents, deciding to investigate, rode their horses to a hill on the outskirts of Colenso. It took more than an hour to reach the top, but when they did it offered an unobstructed view in all directions. Colenso lay quiet beneath them. In the distance, to the right of the town, smoke from bombardment and grass fires clung to a ridge of low hills. Below the black, drifting ribbon of smoke

Ladysmith suffered. Churchill observed the flash of artillery through his field glasses and heard the sound of the cannonade rumbling across the top of the hill seconds later. Even from this elevated vantage point, he could not see exactly what was going on. A local farmer soon joined them. "They've had heavy fighting this morning. Not since Monday week has there been such firing," he said. "But they are nearly finished now for the day."

After accepting the farmer's invitation to lunch at his homestead, Churchill and his comrades mounted their horses for the ride home. With nighttime threatening, no one had any interest in being out after dark. Safely back in Estcourt, Churchill wrote his *Morning Post* dispatch by lamplight. Nothing but bad news had filtered from the front since his arrival in South Africa. Nearly every clash between the British and Boers proved an embarrassment for Her Majesty's army. From points all across the frontier came word of British encirclement and retreat. The Boers, Churchill heard, held more than twelve hundred British prisoners. The fact is that Britain's army was ill-prepared for the struggle with the Boers. It was not so much a force for waging war, "but an institution" with aging traditions and a glorious history of victorious campaigns waged using tactics no longer suited for modern combat. Field training for soldiers had not changed much "since the muzzle-loading era." Conformity was stressed over individual thinking. Frontal assaults were still favored over flanking movements. Little to no emphasis was placed on the construction of fortifications and the building of trenches, for taking cover was considered an almost cowardly act and beneath the dignity of a British soldier. Looking good in ceremonial matters seemed to take priority over learning how to shoot straight.

Churchill voiced similar concerns that evening in a letter to Sir Evelyn Wood, adjutant general to the forces. "It is astonishing how we have underrated these people," he wrote. The Boers proved adept at coordinating infantry attacks with heavy artillery, while the number of British soldiers captured exceeded—by double—the number of casualties the Boers had suffered so far. This did not, lamented Churchill, reflect well on British military might. He opined that any commanding officer who surrendered should be punished, and—in words that would come back to haunt him—suggested the British rule out the possibility of prisoner exchanges.

On Tuesday, November 14, infantry patrols spotted enemy raiding parties advancing on Estcourt from the north and northwest. The following day the armored train operating out of Estcourt under the command of Captain Aylmer Haldane, an old army acquaintance from Churchill's time in India, steamed away to survey the line toward Ladysmith. With Haldane's blessing, Churchill wrangled a seat on board. This time the train went out equipped with a nine-pound, muzzle-loading naval gun and a detachment of sailors from the HMS *Tartar* to operate it. Passengers totaled 120 men, including soldiers from the Royal Dublin Fusiliers and the Durban Light Infantry. The train steamed away from Estcourt at 5:10 that morning and arrived at Frere Station shortly before 6:30. They stopped for fifteen minutes— just enough time for Haldane to meet with officers from the Natal Mounted Police, who informed him they had patrols reconnoitering Chieveley. Haldane ordered the train to go on, and it reached Chieveley at 7:10. At the station the train's telegraph operator received a message from Estcourt. Haldane and his men were to withdraw at once to Frere Station and remain there in an observational capacity until further notice. Only the night before, the Boers had been reported in Chieveley—so the locals were not to be trusted.

Haldane did as ordered. The train reversed out of the Chieveley station and began chugging back toward Frere. Less than two miles from their destination, they approached a hill overlooking the tracks. As it came more into view, Churchill—standing in a roofless carriage at the back and looking through his field glasses—could see Boer soldiers on the slopes. The enemy appeared to only have rifles, which would be useless against the train's armor. Quickly, the sailors readied the train's naval gun for firing. The soldiers on board checked their rifles and stuck the muzzles through loopholes running the length of the train's reinforced sides.

The Boers monitored the train's approach. As Churchill continued to watch, three large field guns appeared on the hilltop. The clatter of gunfire joined the rattling of the train and the barking of orders among the soldiers. Bullets clanged against the armor and hammered the carriages from end to end. From the top of the hill came the roar of artillery. An explosion buffeted the back of the train, sending white smoke and flame skyward. From a distance of no more than six hundred yards, the Boers had let loose with two artillery pieces and a Maxim gun. Boer riflemen quickly joined the action and fired with abandon. Churchill, having seen enough to fully appreciate the situation, dropped to the floor of his carriage and hoped for the best. Rounds continued hammering the side of the train, as the driver increased speed to escape the maelstrom. Explosions and the crash of guns drowned out all other noise. Churchill felt the train lurch forward and round a bend before hurtling down a steep hill, at the bottom of which the Boers had laid a large stone across the tracks.

The collision was violent. The first carriage slammed into the obstruction and went airborne, landing upside down on the embankment alongside the tracks. The second carriage, an armored car occupied by members of the Durban Light Infantry, flipped on its side and slid twenty yards along the line in a blaze of sparks, leaving in its wake a grisly trail of broken and bloody men. The third car spun on its axis and came to a grinding halt, half on the tracks and half off. Churchill's carriage remained upright but came to a sudden halt that threw its occupants to the floor with a bone-jarring thud. Aside from his rattled nerves and a few bruises, Churchill escaped major injury. The Boers continued blasting away at the wreckage. The sailors managed to fire three rounds from the train's paltry naval gun before an enemy shell to the barrel rendered it junk.

Although protected in his carriage from rifle fire, Churchill feared one well-placed artillery round would blow him and everyone else to smithereens. Believing his chances would be better outside, and curious to see the extent of the carnage, Churchill pulled himself up and climbed over the carriage's iron siding. He lowered himself to the ground among a hail of gunfire and ran toward the engine to inspect the damage. An artillery shell exploded overhead, sending hot shrapnel in all directions but missing Churchill. The train's driver, Charles Wagner, emerged from the wreckage, his head lacerated by a shell fragment and his face covered in blood. "I'm a civilian," he roared in protest. "What do they think they're paying me for—to be killed by bomb-shells? Not me!" Churchill urged the man to pull himself together and talked him into getting back behind the controls.

Churchill thrived in these desperate conditions. The engine and two cars still remained upright on the tracks. Clearing the derailed carriages from the line was vital if they hoped to escape. Churchill conferred with Haldane and hatched a strategy. Haldane and a number of rifle-men would lay down covering fire against the Boers' hilltop position. Churchill would oversee the effort to clear the line, which involved using the engine—operated by the wounded Wagner—to push the mangled mess free of the tracks. "The working of the engine itself was a difficult matter," notes a Home Office report on the incident, "because at each collision with the wreckage at which it was butting, it might have easily been derailed. The danger was exceptional. The heavy fire of shells & bullets inflicted many casualties, & more than ¼ of all the men in the train were killed or wounded."

As Wagner repeatedly backed the engine into the wreckage, a shell hit the front of the engine and set it on fire. Throughout the fifty-minute ordeal, Churchill stomped back and forth, barking orders, di-recting Wagner's efforts, and rallying the men. While many sought cover from the relentless enemy fire, Churchill appeared oblivious to it all; he seemed to have a total disregard for his own safety.

"Nothing was so thrilling as this," he reported for the *Morning Post*, "to wait and struggle among these clanging, rending iron boxes, with the repeated explosions of the shells and the artillery, the noise of the projectiles striking the cars, the hiss as they passed in the air, the grunt-ing and puffing of the engine—poor, tortured thing, hammered by at least a dozen shells, any of which, by penetrating the boiler, might have made an end of it all—the expectation of destruction as a matter of course, the realization of powerlessness, and the alternatives of hope and despair."

This was not hyperbole. As one private in the Durban Light In-fantry noted in a letter home: "Churchill is a splendid fellow. He walked about in it all as coolly as if nothing was going on, & called

2nd Lieutenant Winston Spencer Churchill of the 4th Queen's Own Hussars in 1895, the year he ventured to Cuba. *Photo Credit: The Churchill Archives Centre* (left); *The Imperial War Museum* (below).

One of several sketches Churchill made while in Cuba for the *Daily Graphic*.
This one shows a Spanish fort protecting a railway bridge near the town of Santa
Clara. *Photo Credit: The Churchill Archives Centre.*

A sketch by Churchill showing Spanish troops emerging from the jungle and
entering the town of Sancti Spiritus. *Photo Credit: The Churchill Archives Centre.*

The British under siege at Malakand in August 1897, as depicted in the French publication *Le Petit Journal. Photo Credit: Art Resource.*

Major General Sir Bindon Blood, who led the 1897 Malakand expedition against the Pashtun tribes on India's North-West Frontier, also saw action in the Anglo-Zulu War and the Second Anglo-Afghan War. *Photo Credit: Art Resource.*

Women and children sit outside a mud hut in the city of Omdurman, September 1898. *Photo Credit: Art Resource.*

The Mahdi's tomb at Omdurman stands in ruins after being blasted by British gunboats on the eve of battle. Muhammad Ahmad al-Mahdi proclaimed himself a "Descendent of the Prophet" and led an Islamic army against Egyptian and British rule in Sudan. He died in 1885 shortly after his forces killed Major-General Charles George Gordon at Khartoum, an event that sparked the British re-conquest of the Sudan. *Photo Credit: Art Resource.*

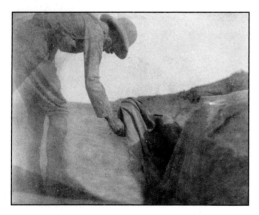

Captain Doran of the Royal Irish Regiment gives a wounded Dervish warrior a drink on the battlefield at Omdurman, September 1898. A major in the Royal Army Medical Corps took the picture. *Photo Credit: National Army Museum, London/Art Resource.*

A chromolithograph published in 1898 depicting the Battle of Omdurman, Sept. 2, 1898. *Photo Credit: National Army Museum, London/Art Resource.*

A painting by British artist Edward Matthew Hale (1852–1924) depicting the charge of the 21st Lancers at the Battle of Omdurman on September 2, 1898. Churchill took part in the charge in which 350 Lancers thundered headlong into some 2,000 tribesmen. *Photo Credit: National Army Museum, London/Art Resource.*

An 1898 photograph of Winston Churchill in desert uniform with pith helmet, spurs, and cavalry sword, taken around the time of the Sudanese campaign. *Photo Credit: Bridgeman Art Library.*

Long before his Finest Hour, Winston Churchill—war correspondent in South Africa for London's *Morning Post*—sits astride his horse, ready for action. *Photo Credit: Culver Pictures/Art Resource.*

Remains of the armored train attacked near the Blue Kranz River, Natal, on Nov. 15, 1899. The grave of four members of the Border Regiment killed in the ambush can be seen in the left middle-distance. Winston Churchill was among 58 men on the train taken prisoner. *Photo Credit: Imperial War Museum, London.*

Boer soldiers celebrate Christmas outside Ladysmith, 1899, during the Second Anglo-Boer War. *Photo Credit: Art Resource.*

Mr. Winston Churchill's Escape From Pretoria: Waiting for the Night to Come (image first published in *The Graphic*—a now defunct British weekly —on February 3, 1900). *Photo Credit: Bridgeman Art Library.*

A lithograph by British painter Frank Craig (1874–1918) depicting the stubborn resistance of Major Thorneycroft's men atop Spion Kop. *Photo Credit: Bridgeman Art Library.*

The bodies of British soldiers killed during the disastrous Battle of Spion Kop, January 23–24, 1900. *Photo Credit: Imperial War Museum, London.*

The intrepid correspondent outside his tent in Bloemfontein, South Africa, 1900. *Photo Credit: Bridgeman Art Library.*

for volunteers to give him a hand to get the truck out of the road. His presence and way of going on were as much good as fifty men would have been."

Haldane, in a subsequent report, also vouched for Churchill's bravery: "I would point out that while engaged on the work of saving the engine, for which he was mainly responsible, [Churchill] was frequently exposed to the full fire of the enemy. I cannot speak too highly of his gallant conduct."

As Churchill and others struggled with the wreckage, Haldane and his riflemen fought a desperate action to keep away the Boers advancing up the tracks until, with a loud grinding noise, the engine pushed the derailed truck from the line. The plan now called for linking the rear cab and gun carriage to the engine and hauling away as many men as possible—but an enemy round destroyed the couplings. Churchill and others attempted to push the trucks forward but abandoned the effort under severe fire. Haldane ordered his men to load as many wounded as they could onto the engine. Men still capable of standing were placed in the cab; others were laid gently in the tender, atop the coal, while some clung for dear life to the engine's cowcatcher. Through it all, enemy fire proved relentless. The plan called for getting the wounded to some houses near Frere Station, roughly eight hundred yards away, and to try to "hold out there while the engine went for assistance."

The Boers concentrated all their fire on the beleaguered engine. One round slammed into a metal plate inches from Churchill's face; another shattered the arm of a nearby soldier, leaving his hand dangling by a few strips of flesh. Infantrymen not injured followed on foot, using the engine as cover. The Boers doubled their efforts and battered the engine and tracks with everything they had. It proved too much for some. Much to Haldane's dismay, he saw two men waving white handkerchiefs. Enraged at this disobedience to his direct orders, Haldane ran in their direction and yelled at them to keep fighting. It was too late. Several Boers on the hill, noticing the surrender, mounted their horses and galloped down the slope to round up their catch. They reached the men before Haldane and encircled them on horseback with their rifles at the ready. The men, temporarily torn between Haldane's furious orders and the muzzles of the enemy guns, threw their hands above their heads and marched off into captivity.

Churchill leapt from the engine as it drew closer to the houses near Frere station. "I can't leave those poor beggars to their fate," he told Wagner before departing. He at once found himself alone in a shallow ditch, which ran alongside the tracks, and saw two figures in flapping coats and wide-brimmed hats on horseback about a hundred yards down the line. He turned and ran as the Boers squeezed off two rounds. His lungs burning, he pressed himself against the side of the embankment. One Boer quickly dismounted and dropped to his knees for better aim. Churchill scrambled up the embankment, flinching as two more shots kicked up dirt on either side of him. He rolled into a shallow ditch and caught the attention of another nearby horseman, who, yelling in a language Churchill didn't understand, galloped to within forty yards.

With blood on his mind, Churchill reached for his Mauser pistol, only to discover he had left it in the engine. He cursed and briefly contemplated running. He saw a hut for railway workers about 50 yards away, and 150 yards beyond that flowed the Blue Krantz River, which might afford some cover if he could reach its rocky banks. The distance, however, between him and the horseman—rifle drawn, aim steady—did not bode well. Giving up was a foreign concept to Churchill, but at that moment he recalled the words of Napoleon: "When one is alone and unarmed, a surrender may be pardoned." Churchill raised his arms. The Boer lowered his rifle and urged him to approach. Before marching off with his prisoner, the horseman fired several futile shots at the escaping engine.

It began to rain as Churchill walked silently alongside the Boer's horse. With nothing to do but think, two discomforting thoughts sprang to mind. The first was the letter penned five days earlier to Sir Evelyn Wood, discouraging the exchange of prisoners; the other concerned the two ten-round clips of Mauser ammunition in the pockets of his khaki coat. How could Churchill claim to be a correspondent and a noncombatant if they found the clips in his possession? He managed to discard one clip in the tall grass without being noticed. He palmed the other and was about to drop it, when the guard—speaking perfect English—addressed him in a sharp tone. The horseman marched Churchill back to the scene of the battle, where "fifty-six unwounded or slightly wounded men"—and a number of soldiers too injured to stand—were now prisoners. The rain fell in sheets and turned the ground to muck. Some prisoners seemed not to care and sat forlornly on the sodden earth, eating what meager rations they possessed. The Boers inspected their catch and soon ordered the men to their feet. On the order to march, the tattered-looking procession moved out. Those too wounded to walk were left at the scene to be gathered up later. Churchill turned as they climbed a small hill and saw the engine, smoke bellowing from its funnel in the foul weather, steaming away to Estcourt. Help would soon be at hand for those lucky few who had made it to the houses near Frere Station; for Churchill, Haldane, and the others, it was too late. Churchill hurried to keep up, but a Boer on horseback told him in a friendly tone there was no need to rush. Another offered him a hat to ward off the rain. Although dispirited, Churchill took comfort in this show of humanity.

The prisoners were brought to a halt at the top of the hill, near the artillery that had wrought so much devastation. Here Churchill learned the extent of the British casualties: five men were dead and would be buried by the Boers; sixteen seriously injured men had escaped on the engine; thirteen had been taken prisoner and would receive the necessary medical treatment in field ambulances or the hospital at Ladysmith. Among the prisoners currently gathered under the Boer guns, seven—including Churchill, who took a piece of shrapnel in the hand—were only slightly injured. So casualties numbered "between thirty-five and forty." Although he considered the numbers high enough, Churchill marveled that more had not been killed or injured.

An order to continue marching derailed his thoughts. As they crested one hill after another, Churchill realized the force responsible for attacking the train was actually a detachment from a much larger army. On the plain below he saw roughly three thousand Boers marching in the direction of Estcourt. The prisoners were soon corralled outside the tented headquarters of General Petrus Jacobus Joubert, the Boer commander in chief, and instantly surrounded by a crowd of curious onlookers. Not sure whom he should address, Churchill loudly proclaimed his role as a journalist and demanded to be released. A man stepped forward, took Churchill's credentials, and disappeared into the tent. The name on the papers caused a stir among the Boers, prompting one to ask if he was the son of Lord Randolph Churchill. Churchill answered in the affirmative, which caused more excited chatter. The Boer chuckled. It was not every day, he said, they caught the son of a lord.

Once again the prisoners resumed their march, dashing Churchill's hopes of meeting Joubert in person to plead his case. They soldiered on for six hours through the torrential downpour, the ground underfoot a thick sludge, before reaching the train station at Colenso. The Boers herded their captives into a "corrugated iron shed near the station, the floors of which were four inches deep with torn railway forms and account books." Churchill felt dejected. He had spent his life avoiding boredom and inaction, yet here he was, deprived of his war. For one so heavily addicted to adventure, captivity was akin to torture. He dropped to the filthy floor in a state of utter exhaustion and thought, almost enviously, of a soldier he had seen be struck down during the fight. Death at least spared one the ignominy of capture. Hours passed before the Boers let the men out to warm themselves by two large fires and gnaw on strips of ox meat. When they had finished they were put back in the shed for a cold, uncomfortable night. The conditions made sleep all but impossible. Churchill lay in the darkness, listened to the rain's relentless hammering on the tin roof, and cursed his predicament.

The morning sun, bleak and pallid, worked its way through the shed's dirty windows and skylight. Churchill sat up, his body aching. The hard floor, damp clothes, and cold night wind that whistled through the shed had all taken a toll. Guards opened the door and ushered the prisoners out. They ate leftover ox for breakfast and drank rainwater from a puddle before starting another long day's march. Men who the day before had fought so proudly for queen and country set off in a dirty and disheveled line. They marched through gullies swollen with water, marched up and down hills, and forded the Klip River, the men sinking up to their chests in the frigid waters. It felt to Churchill, starved and utterly exhausted, as though they were traipsing over all creation. They reached that night's laager—an encampment encircled by wagons—only five miles from Ladysmith after putting in a ten-hour day. Approaching the camp, they could see the British observation balloon floating above the besieged town. The men murmured their approval, proud, despite their sorry state, that Ladysmith still stood strong. Churchill could not take his eyes from the balloon, for it symbolized his possible salvation. He knew full well the dire conditions in Ladysmith—the disease and starvation, death and decomposition, the ceaseless bombardment—and yet he would prefer to be there than suffer the frustrations of imprisonment.

The prisoners dined on tea and bully beef that evening and retired to tents—luxurious accommodations compared to the previous night's shed—for some much-needed sleep. Two men with long, scruffy beards and threadbare clothing sat cradling their rifles outside Churchill's tent, which he shared with two other officers. Although much in need of rest, he obsessed about the British forces just miles away and considered making a break for it if circumstances allowed. Every now and then he quietly parted the flaps and braved a brief glimpse outside. A full moon bathed the camp in silver light, much to his chagrin. Any attempt at escape would have to be made in total darkness, but the odds would still be formidable. The tent remained under constant guard at all times by as many as four men. Often they sat quietly, other times they laughed and chattered, but at no time did they relax their hold on their guns. Even inside the tent, Churchill could hear them playing with the breech bolts as if sending some sinister message.

News of Churchill's capture did not take long to hit the press. The day after the event, Thursday, November 16, the story appeared in newspapers across Britain. Reported the *Guardian*, under the headline "Boers Wreck a Train. Churchill Is Missing," after detailing the initial attack:

[Mr. Churchill] set to work heroically with the engine hands and cleared the debris, and put many of our wounded men upon the locomotive and tender, which, though shelled, got back at ten in the morning. Mr. Churchill remained at Frere to assist the other soldiers. . . .

The Boers poured shot and shellfire into the crippled train. . . . A shell struck and hurled [the seven-pounder] away, overturning the truck. The only newspaper correspondent present was Mr. Winston Churchill, who distinguished himself by his courageous conduct, as did also Wagner, the driver, and Stuart, the stoker of the engine.

The troops, who had maintained a hopeless fight with great courage, were overpowered. A few managed to escape, but the majority were either killed or wounded or taken prisoners. Mr. Churchill was last seen advancing with a rifle among the Dublin Fusiliers. He is believed to have surrendered himself to cover the retreat.

The *Pall Mall Gazette* published a letter from Inspector Campbell of the Natal Government Railways to the railway general manager, thanking Churchill for his heroics:

The railway men who accompanied the armored train this morning ask me to convey to you their admiration of the coolness and pluck displayed by Mr. Winston Churchill, the war correspondent, who accompanied the train, and to whose efforts, supported by those of the driver Wagner, is due the fact the armored engine and tender were brought successfully out after being hampered by the derailed trucks in front, and that it became possible to bring the wounded in here. The whole of our men are loud in their praises of Mr. Churchill, who, I regret to say, has been taken prisoner.

The *Saturday Herald* ran a cartoon depicting Churchill trying to rally the men, its caption proclaiming, "Young Churchill, a newspaper correspondent, at the battle of the armored train, was obliged to seize a rifle and give the demoralized English soldiers a brave example. 'Can't ye stand like men' was his scornful cry."

Jennie received the news while in charge of a fund-raising campaign to equip and send a hospital ship to South Africa. Her efforts would later culminate in a charity event at Claridge's in Mayfair, transforming the whole first floor "into a garden of chrysanthemums, roses, and multicolored lights." The evening's entertainment included the "casts and orchestras" of two West End musicals. All of London high society was there, including the Prince of Wales and other members of the royal family "accompanied by an escort of the Life Guards in their brilliant white-and-scarlet uniforms, drummers and drum majors, and Scots Guards in tartans." But one person was noticeably absent that evening. Reported the London correspondent for the *New York Times*: "Lady Randolph Churchill looked in for a few minutes, but was deeply distressed, owing to her anxiety as to the fate of her son, Winston Churchill, believed to be a prisoner at the hands of the Boers, and left before the guests arrived. The absence of the leading spirit in the movement, due to the uncertainty as to the death or capture of her son, gave a tragic tone to the gathering."

In the predawn hours of November 17, 1899, Churchill and the other prisoners were roused from their tents and served a meager breakfast of tea and bully beef before setting off on a five-hour slog to the railway station at Elandslaagte. Churchill, his legs weak and his stomach cramped from hunger, felt his injured hand succumbing to infection. The wound itself was small, but two days of dirt, filth, and no medical attention had left it inflamed, raw, and pus-ridden. The men reached the station at eleven that morning to find a train waiting to take them to Pretoria. Once on board Churchill—ravenous with hunger—asked a guard for food and water. The guard urged patience. A railway official appeared several minutes later with a cart piled with meat, fish, bread, tins of jam, and pots of tea. Seeing their first real food in three days, the captives leapt on the feast like a pack of wild beasts and gorged themselves. As the men shoveled food and poured tea down their throats, Boers on the station platform watched the uncivilized display through the carriage windows. A doctor in the crowd, seeing Churchill's damaged hand, boarded the carriage to clean and treat the wound. For the first time since his capture, Churchill felt relatively human.

The train reached Pretoria late the following morning. At one point during the overnight journey, Churchill again considered escape. As the train passed through a tunnel near the town of Volksrust, he cast his gaze on the carriage's two open windows and thought perhaps he could climb through one. A guard sitting next to Churchill saw the prisoner's furtive glance and shut and locked the windows. Sitting back down, he flashed Churchill a grin and casually made a point of showing Churchill the fully loaded breech of his rifle. Churchill returned the smile and decided patience would be the wisest course of action.

A crowd of onlookers greeted the train when it pulled up to the dirt platform at Pretoria station. Churchill stared out the window and saw "ugly women with bright parasols, loafers and ragamuffins, fat burghers too heavy to ride at the front, and a long line of untidy, white-helmeted policemen . . . who looked like broken-down constabulary." The prisoners stood arranged on the platform by rank, as flashbulbs exploded and pictures were snapped. Churchill had always tried to keep personal feelings out of war, but—at this moment—he loathed the enemy.

The men marched off to their respective POW camps, the rank and file to a compound established at Pretoria's racecourse and the officers, including Churchill, to the State Model School a short distance away. It sat at the intersection of two dirt roads, a single-story structure built of red brick and surrounded by an iron-railing fence. A number of British officers sat in the shade of the building's slanted veranda and greeted the new arrivals with cheery salutations and questions about the war. The building was comprised of a dozen classrooms, each being put to a use far removed from its original intent. Eight of the rooms, furnished with beds, served as cramped sleeping quarters; there were a dining hall with long tables and benches and a meeting hall in which the inmates often played fives, a game not unlike racquetball, in which players use their hands for racquets. A large courtyard in the back housed a gym, a wooden shed where inmates could bathe, the outhouse, and twelve tents, which served as sleeping quarters for the guards. Walls ten feet high surrounded the whole compound. In truth, it would have been easy for any young man in decent shape to scramble over the top of them. The real obstacle proved to be the guards, all armed with rifles and revolvers, placed along the wall at fifty-yard intervals. They would shoot a man before he got one leg over.

Newly arrived prisoners received a suit, bedding, and toiletries. If they had money, they could purchase additional goods from the local shopkeeper. Churchill immediately bought a dark-colored tweed suit, which looked nothing like the clothes provided by the prison. It did not take long for him to succumb to the boredom of incarceration.

In captivity Churchill was miserable. He paced endlessly, like a caged lion, and considered the world beyond the bars. Out there was life, the war, both of which were passing him by. The Transvaal government allowed him to write his *Morning Post* dispatches while in captivity and send them off for publication. The Boers hoped that through Churchill's reporting the British public would learn about his civil treatment at the hands of the enemy. But Churchill could only write for so many hours a day, leaving plenty of time for him to ruminate on his dire circumstances. In the morning, the soldier servants brought the British officers their coffee in bed. The men would drink and smoke and ponder the mind-numbing day that lay ahead. After the nine o'clock breakfast, prisoners tried to distract themselves by reading or playing games of cards and chess. Smoking was a constant pastime. Lunch was served at one, after which the prisoners ambled about the schoolyard or gazed morosely through the iron fence. The heat—for November is summer in the southern hemisphere—added to the tedium and discomfort. The days dragged seamlessly into one another with no variation of routine.

Churchill walked the school's courtyard at dusk every evening and watched the last vestige of sunlight fade beyond the hills. The inescapable prospect of tomorrow soured the blessing of another day's passing. Strolling the yard's perimeter, he would keep one eye on the guards and another on the fence, looking for some point of weakness that might mean escape. Freedom haunted his every thought. He repeatedly petitioned the government and demanded he be released on the grounds he was a journalist. Churchill made a point of stressing the fact that he was not armed when captured. This was true, but not because of any conscious decision on his part.

Over the course of one week—starting on November 18—Churchill wrote three letters to Louis de Souza, the Boer secretary of state, arguing his case. On November 19 General Joubert ordered that Churchill "be guarded and watched as he is dangerous for our war; otherwise he can still do us a lot of harm. In a word, he must not be released during the war. It is through his active part that one section of the armored train got away." Joubert ordered that Churchill remain imprisoned for the war's entirety. A Boer captain who had taken part in the capture of the armored train voiced a similar sentiment, writing in a letter, "In my view, Churchill is one of the most dangerous prisoners in our hands." Churchill spent his twenty-fifth birthday, November 30, in captivity. The following day Captain Aylmer Haldane pulled Churchill aside and said he and another man, Sergeant Major Brockie, planned to escape by climbing over the wall near the prison latrine when the sentries weren't watching. They planned to make their way by night to the border of Portuguese Mozambique, some three hundred miles away. Churchill asked if he could join the venture. Brockie vehemently opposed letting another person in on the scheme; the more were involved, the greater the risk of failure. Churchill's notoriety also made him an unwelcome presence, but Haldane could not refuse one who had served so well under his command.

Haldane decided on the morning of Monday, December 11, that they would attempt their escape that night—if Churchill didn't give it away first. "Churchill is in a great state of excitement and letting everyone know that he means going tonight," notes an entry in Haldane's diary that day. Churchill spent the day in a state of "positive terror," so nervous was he about breaking out. If he and his two cohorts managed to climb the wall without being detected, it would only be the start of their ordeal. Even an optimist like Churchill knew the chances of success were slim. He did his best throughout the day to keep his mind occupied by reading William Lecky's *The History of England*. Churchill had always enjoyed Lecky's writing, but under the present circumstances he found the man intolerable and tossed the book aside.

The hours passed slowly and only fueled Churchill's fear until, at last, the sky darkened. The trio planned to hop the fence while the other inmates ate dinner. Churchill, Haldane, and Brockie watched their fellow officers trudge off to eat at seven o'clock, when the dinner bell chimed. The three men made their way to the latrine out in the yard, only to discover a sentry standing fifteen yards away. It quickly became apparent the guard had no intention of moving, prompting the would-be escapers to abort the plan. Churchill went to bed that night relieved at not having gone through with the escape, yet equally frustrated for the very same reason.

They made another attempt the following night. After the seven o'clock dinner bell, Churchill and Haldane crossed the courtyard to the latrine and—once again—found a guard loitering nearby. They retreated back to the veranda, where Brockie mocked the two men for being cowardly. Haldane told Brockie to go and see for himself. Brockie went to inspect the scene, with Churchill following close behind. Satisfied that an escape attempt would be unwise, Brockie walked back and joined Haldane in the dining room for dinner. Churchill, meanwhile, lingered behind and kept his eye on things.

The guard momentarily diverted his gaze to light a pipe. Churchill, not wasting a second, scrambled up the wall, lowered himself into a garden, and hid behind some bushes. Twenty yards away sat a house with light spilling from the windows. Churchill and the others knew the house was there but believed it to be vacant. At this inopportune time, he discovered "it was full of people." One of the occupants opened the back door and wandered into the garden. The man stopped ten yards short of Churchill's hiding place. Fear, almost overwhelming in its gut-twisting intensity, gripped Churchill with an icy hand and squeezed hard. Surely, Churchill thought, he would be discovered. He closed his eyes and mentally willed his heart to not beat so loudly. He pushed himself further into the shadows. He dared not breathe, for he felt certain the dark figure was staring directly at him. He prayed his comrades did not choose this moment to come after him and climb the wall. The man stood there for an eternity before another individual joined him outside to smoke a cigar. A cold sweat clung to Churchill's back despite the warm night air. After exchanging a few words, the two men turned to leave. Churchill closed his eyes and sighed with relief, the rush of air from his lungs almost deafening in the silent garden. Just as he felt his body relax somewhat, a cat darted across the lawn and into the bushes with a dog in close pursuit. The cat ran full throttle into Churchill and released a terrified yowl before charging once more across the garden, allowing the dog to resume the chase. The two men turned and stared in Churchill's direction. For one horrible moment, he feared they would approach the bush to investigate the commotion. Instead, they shrugged off the noise and continued on their way. Churchill already felt spent, but his adventure had just begun. His body cramped, he remained hiding in the bushes for more than an hour, wondering where Brockie and Haldane could be.

He soon heard two officers talking on the other side of the prison wall and realized the conversation was nothing but a gibberish mix of English, Latin, and random laughter. In the middle of the nonsensical banter, one of the officers mentioned Churchill's name. Churchill coughed into his hand and heard one of the men whisper, "We can't get out and the sentry is suspicious. It's all over. Do you think you can climb back?"

Churchill balked. Climbing the wall had taken an extraordinary amount of courage. He was fully committed. His decision to go solo would not be without controversy. Some prisoners, the *Manchester Guardian* reported the following year, resented "Mr Winston Churchill's publication of the full details of his escape, as thereby others among the imprisoned officers who had hoped to avail themselves of the same means of escape were prevented from doing so by reason of the extra precautions taken." Others would accuse Churchill of abandoning his fellow officers.

While there is an element of truth to such criticisms, the man can hardly be blamed for seizing the opportunity when it presented itself. Climbing back over the fence would have no doubt alerted guards in the compound and exposed the blind spot in their security measures. Why risk the repercussions? What would Haldane and Brockie have done if they were in his position? It hardly mattered. Haldane, who escaped at a later date, carried a grudge against Churchill for a number of years. "Had Churchill," he later argued, "only possessed the moral courage to admit that, in the excitement of the moment, he saw a chance of escape and could not resist the temptation to take advantage of it, not realizing that it would compromise the escape of his companions, all would have been well." At the time, there was no doubt what Churchill's course of action would be. "I shall go on alone," he whispered to Haldane and Brockie.

Feeling surprisingly confident in this daring enterprise, Churchill emerged from the bushes and brushed himself off. He slapped his hat on his head and strolled through the garden toward the gate. He walked past the windows in full view of those inside without making any effort to hide. Making it through the gate struck him as a victory of sorts—the first milestone in a long and dangerous journey. He turned left without really giving much thought to the direction in which he was traveling and kept walking. Tempting fate, he passed within five yards of a sentry and the prison entrance. Churchill's slightly stooped posture meant most guards knew him by sight, but providence seemed to be on his side. The State Model School behind him, he had the town of Pretoria to get through.

Churchill hid in plain sight; to duck into the shadows or run through town would only arouse suspicion. Wanting to appear like a man without a care, he opted to walk in the middle of the street. No one paid him the least bit of attention, and soon the town proper was behind him. But what now? He still had vast miles of enemy territory to cross before reaching salvation. He had little money and did not speak the local language. In the dark, his options few and far between, Churchill felt very alone. Prison guards would discover his absence early the next morning. It was vital he put as many miles as possible between himself and Pretoria by daybreak—but in what direction?

Standing there in the pitch black, unsure where to turn, Churchill remembered the night he had spent lost in the Egyptian desert the year before. Then he had followed the constellation Orion to safety. He now opted to do the same. He looked skyward and saw the celestial hunter pointing the way. Trudging through dark, open country, he soon came to a set of railway tracks. Although unsure where they led, he decided to follow them. The night air smelled sweet, and he enjoyed the experience as only one who has known captivity can. A wild surge of excitement washed over him, for he was free—if only temporarily. No matter, he would take what he could get and pondered with fascination what might lie ahead.

After two hours of walking, he saw the "signal lights of a station" blinking in the distance. He realized the futility of trying to walk three hundred miles to safety. He gave the station a wide berth and continued some way down the tracks before taking cover in a ditch. It was time to hitch a ride. More than an hour passed before he heard the clatter of an approaching train, its whistle a desolate sound floating across the dark veldt. Churchill peered over the edge of the ditch and watched the train pull into the station. It stayed there for several minutes before a loud hiss of steam signaled its imminent departure. Slowly it pulled away from the platform. The large light at the front of the train looked not unlike a glaring yellow eye.

Two hundred yards out of the station, the engine passed Churchill's position. He emerged from the ditch, safe in the knowledge he would not be spotted by the engine driver. The ground shook beneath his feet as the train picked up speed. He ran hard and reached desperately for the side of a carriage. He just managed to grab a handhold, his feet dragging momentarily along the ground, as he slowly pulled himself up through the open siding. The train was hauling sacks of coal. Churchill, desperate for sleep, crawled atop the dust-covered sacks and discovered much to his delight that they were quite soft. He burrowed down among them and in less than five minutes had created a little warren for himself. He reveled in the warmth and comfort of these new surroundings. Whatever challenges still lay ahead were, for the moment, not a concern. Tired in mind and body—listening to the rhythmic clatter of the wheels on the tracks—Churchill drifted off to sleep.

He woke in darkness, oblivious to how much time had passed, and pondered his next move. He feared eventual recapture if he remained on the train too long. He crawled out from under the sacks and stood at the truck's open siding, feeling the warm rush of wind and watching the black landscape pass at a steady clip. There was only one way off. Not wanting to give it too much thought, he flung himself into the night. The ground met his feet with a hard thud and sent him sprawling. He got up slowly, shaken and bruised, but with no major injuries, and watched the train continue on its way. The moon and stars, still out, cast a million points of light on the tall, dew-soaked grass around him. In the near distance he could just make out the dark rise of low hills. All was silent save the fading clatter of the train as it disappeared into the night. Churchill turned away from the tracks and began walking through the wet grass, desperate to soothe his parched throat and get the taste of coal dust out of his mouth. He soon came to a gully with a clear pool. Churchill dropped to his knees, drank deeply, and splashed the cold water on his blackened face. When he could drink no more, he moved on in search of a hiding place.

A ribbon of light began to reveal itself in the east above the hills. Climbing a steep ravine, he discovered a grove of trees that seemed an adequate place to wait out the daylight hours. It being four o'clock in the morning, Churchill had a long wait ahead of him. It took tremendous willpower to resist the urge to keep moving. He struggled to keep warm in the frigid predawn air, but was soon sweating uncomfortably in the late-morning heat. A massive vulture, who wandered into the grove and seemed in no hurry to leave, added to Churchill's discomfort. Each kept a wary eye on the other. Through the trees Churchill saw the spread of a wide valley dotted with farms. To the west the sun glinted off the tin roofs of a small town. The railway, running west to east, cut the valley in two.

He bit into his meager ration of chocolate to quell his growing hunger, but the confection only aggravated his thirst. He considered making a run to the pool from which he had drunk the night before, but he feared such a move might result in his capture. The excitement he had felt the previous night slipped away, and hopelessness took its place. His stomach ached with a hunger no chocolate bar could possibly satisfy. Groggy with fatigue, he tried to sleep—but his overwrought nerves thwarted any attempt at rest. He dwelled on the futility of his situation. What chance did he really have of making it to safety? How many miles separated him from refuge? The harder he tried to distract his thoughts, the more depressing his ruminations grew—but not once did he consider surrendering. Death was almost a preferable alternative to being dragged back to Pretoria and locked away. Being deprived of freedom was to be deprived of life.

Four trains thundered by on the tracks that day; he assumed the same number would travel the route at night. He would break cover after dark, stow away on another train, and ride the rails as far as he could.

CHAPTER 11

Dead or Alive

Guards at the State Model School discovered they were short a prisoner at 10:30 on the morning of December 13. The previous evening, after Churchill had scrambled over the wall, Haldane and Brockie had arranged his bed with pillows under the sheets so it appeared to be occupied. When one of the soldier servants charged with waking up the officers made the rounds that morning, he left a steaming cup of coffee at Churchill's bedside after failing to wake the apparently deeply sleeping occupant. As other officer inmates began to stir and start their day, it became evident to prison officials that something was amiss. When guards finally disturbed the blankets on Churchill's bed, they found an envelope addressed to Boer Secretary of State de Souza. In the envelope was a letter. "Sir," it began:

> I have the honor to inform you that as I do not consider that your Government have any right to detain me as a military prisoner, I have decided to escape from your custody. I have every confidence in the arrangements I have made with my friends outside, and I do not therefore expect to have another opportunity of seeing you. I therefore take this occasion to observe that I consider your treatment of prisoners is correct and humane, and that I see no grounds for complaint. When

I return to the British lines, I will make a public statement to this effect. I have also to thank you personally for your civility to me, and to
express the hope that we may meet again at Pretoria before very long,
and under different circumstances. Regretting that I am unable to bid
you a more ceremonious or personal farewell,

I have the honor, to be, sir

Your most humble and obedient servant,

Winston Churchill

A room-by-room search turned up nothing, even as frantic guards
were threatened with hanging if Churchill was not found. The prison
commandant ordered everyone into the courtyard for roll call. Heads
were counted and rosters checked, but nothing changed the incontro-
vertible fact that Winston Churchill had got away—but how? His letter
to de Souza referenced arrangements with "friends outside," prompting
officials to believe someone in Pretoria had offered assistance.

It fell on the commandant to inform de Souza of Churchill's escape. In a report that morning, he wrote that Churchill's behavior the
previous week had caused some concern among prison officials. He
claimed Churchill had become unnaturally silent, almost reclusive,
and shunned the company and conversation of his fellow prisoners.
Instead, he preferred to wander the prison courtyard on his own for
hours at a time, as if lost in some reverie—or hatching some nefarious
scheme. It was the commandant's view that only with inside help had
Churchill escaped. In all likelihood, he had befriended and ultimately
bribed a guard, for it would have been impossible for Churchill to
break out and not be caught in the act.

It's difficult to believe Churchill, a social animal who thrived on being the center of attention, would keep to himself for four or five days.
No one would ever accuse him of possessing a retiring disposition.
Haldane suggested the exact opposite in his diary entry the day before
the escape. The commandant's belief that Churchill had bribed a guard
was most likely an effort to shift the blame to his underlings.

Operating on the assumption Churchill had received outside assistance, a massive search of homes and businesses in Pretoria was begun that day. A wanted poster quickly went up, describing Churchill as an "Englishman 25 years old, about 5 ft 8 in tall, average build, walks with a slight stoop, pale appearance, red brown hair, almost invisible small mustache, speaks through the nose, cannot pronounce the letter 'S', cannot speak Dutch, during long conversations occasionally makes a rattling noise in his throat, was last seen in a brown suit of clothes." Officials slapped a £25 bounty on Churchill's head, payable on delivery: dead or alive.

Miles removed from the panic in Pretoria, Churchill passed the endless hours watching small figures work the distant farms. At one point a Boer approached Churchill's hiding place with a rifle and tried his luck shooting at several birds, but he did not see the fugitive hiding among the trees. The sun soon began its merciful descent. An eternity, one plagued by unceasing restlessness, thirst, and hunger, had now passed. Churchill watched shadows lengthen across the valley and the warm glow of lights appear in the scattered farmhouses and town. When the daylight had nearly faded, he emerged from the trees and made his way toward the tracks, pausing once to drink from a stream. The nocturnal silence unsettled him, and it took a moment to realize why. He could not hear, even in the distance, the sound of any approaching train. With a full moon casting the tracks and valley in pallid light, Churchill resigned himself to a long journey on foot and began to follow the railway. He hoped to cover at least twenty miles before sunrise, but he soon discovered plenty of obstacles in his path. Occasionally he would come to a small town—or a guarded bridge—that forced him to abandon the tracks and make a "wide circuit" to avoid detection. Several times this entailed working his way through tall, wet grass and rancid swamps. The going proved tough. Having spent the past month confined behind prison walls with minimal physical activity, Churchill soon found himself struggling to continue. His clothes, drenched through up to the waist, added to his burden. Starved, parched, and tired, he wondered how much ground he could cover. He felt utterly miserable when he spied soft yellow light spilling from the window of a house. He imagined the occupants, reveling in its warmth and comfort and perhaps taking such luxuries for granted. Never had he felt so helpless.

He approached a railroad station, a single platform with a few tin-roofed huts thrown up around it in the middle of the veldt and three cargo trains sitting idle nearby. He considered stowing away in one of the carriages and traveling come morning to the train's mystery desti-nation. It seemed like a good idea in his worn-out state, until he imag-ined the indignity of being unloaded with the goods they carried and dragged back into captivity. He retreated once more into the high veldt grass and, on aching legs, continued his endless trek.

The flicker of several distant fires soon caught his eye. Out of des-peration, he convinced himself it was a Bantu kraal, for he had heard the Bantus were loyal to the British. He walked toward the light and what he hoped to be salvation. Thoughts of food, sleep, and warmth urged him on—but he soon began to second-guess himself. What if Bantus weren't tending the fires? What if he emerged from the tall grass to discover Boers gathered around the flames? Churchill dropped to the cold earth, in desperate need of an idea. The harder he thought, the more hopeless his situation seemed. It was a rare, fleeting state of mind. He soon felt confident, for no particular reason, that safety lay in the direction of the fires. In later years he attributed his certainty to a psychic premonition.

Churchill forced himself to keep moving. He at first believed the flickering light to be only a couple of miles away, yet after walking for nearly two hours, it appeared to be no closer. He pushed his way through thick grass, traversed a cold stream, and climbed a slope before his ultimate goal presented itself in greater detail. What he saw was not the tents and wagons of an encampment, but the tin-roofed buildings of a coal mine. The flames Churchill believed to be campfires were actually the mine's burning furnaces. He crouched in the grass and pondered his next move. A bungalow made of stone sat atop a slight hill and overlooked the quiet grounds. Glancing over his shoulder, he considered retreating back to the railway line and following wherever it led—but in his weakened state he knew that would result in unavoidable capture. He emerged from the grass, approached the bungalow, and listened at the front door. He heard nothing from within, but why would he at 1:30 in the morning? His knock received no answer. When he banged on the door again, light spilled from a window. A voice, in Dutch, inquired who was there. Churchill, having hoped the mine was an English operation, cursed his luck. Desperate, he called out that he'd been in an accident and needed help.

Someone turned a lock on the other side of the door. When it opened, Churchill saw a stern-looking man who appeared less than thrilled with the late-night intrusion. The inside of the house remained in total darkness behind him. He appraised Churchill with tired eyes and, in the Queen's English, asked him what he wanted. Relieved at hearing a friendly accent, Churchill spun a story out of nothing. He claimed to be a citizen of the Transvaal Republic who, while en route to join his commando unit at Komati Poort, fell off a train during some rough horseplay and dislocated his shoulder. Churchill had no idea where the story came from nor where it was going; the words simply spilled out of his mouth as if he were recounting an actual experience. The man listened to the tale with a blank expression before inviting Churchill to come in out of the cold. They walked a short distance down a dark passageway before entering a door off to one side. The man fumbled in the darkness and lit a lamp, which cast a yellow circle of light around what appeared to be a dining room and office space.

The man was John Howard, manager of the Transvaal and Delagoa Bay Collieries. Churchill had made it as far as Witbank, a little under seventy miles from Pretoria. Howard eyed the downtrodden specimen in front of him and made a point of displaying the revolver in his right hand. Churchill noticed the weapon for the first time. Howard did not buy Churchill's story and believed his midnight guest to be a Boer spy. Churchill, still maintaining the ruse, sank gratefully into a chair, oblivious to Howard's incredulous gaze. With the gun still in his hand, Howard told Churchill he knew the story to be an outright lie. Churchill feigned shock and indignation, but Howard would have none of it. Waving the gun for emphasis, he strongly suggested Churchill come clean. Churchill hesitated; he could maintain the charade or simply tell the truth. He put faith in a fellow Englishman and opted for the latter.

Howard flashed Churchill a knowing grin and said he thought it a wise decision. He sat and listened as Churchill came clean, detailing his role in South Africa as a correspondent and recounting his capture and subsequent escape. When Churchill had finished, Howard moved to the door and slid the deadbolt home—a move that made Churchill nervous. His worry, however, proved short lived. Howard shook Churchill's hand and declared he had come to the right place. At any other house for miles around, he surely would have been turned in. Howard formally introduced himself and offered to help. Churchill said he merely needed some rest, food, and—if possible—a revolver, before continuing on his way. Although assisting a fugitive would mean death for Howard if the Boers found out, he insisted on providing more than just provisions. He offered Churchill a bottle of whisky and brought from the kitchen a cold leg of mutton. While Churchill dined, Howard went off and informed his two miners, secretary, and engine-man, all of whom were British and loyal to the empire. They decided to hide Churchill in the mine's pit, where he could stay until they hatched a plan to get him out of the country.

In the predawn hours of December 14, Howard led Churchill from the house and across a dirt yard to the entrance of a mine shaft. Here Churchill met a man who introduced himself as colliery engineer Dan Dewsnap from Oldham. He shook Churchill's hand with great enthusiasm and promised everyone would vote for him come the next election. With that, Churchill and Howard were ushered into the lift cage and lowered underground. They dropped for what seemed an eternity, the world around them growing increasingly dark. Above, the patch of faintly colored sky visible through the mouth of the pit grew smaller and smaller. The cage touched down with a thump and was met by two Scottish miners, who offered Churchill a mattress and blankets. With lanterns lit, the men traversed a network of tunnels before reaching what looked like a cave. A cool breeze blew from somewhere and kept the space free of stagnant air. Churchill's hosts left him with a box of cigars, a bottle of whisky, a candle, and instructions not to move until they came back for him. Churchill watched Howard and the two miners retreat back into the tunnel, the glow of their lanterns quickly fading from view. Compared to all he had recently endured, his new surroundings were luxurious. He made himself comfortable on the mattress and dreamed in the total darkness of his triumphant return to British lines with a remarkable story to tell.

His thoughts soon surrendered to a deep sleep. When he woke up, he had no way of knowing how long he'd been out. He groped in the darkness for his candle but couldn't find it. He briefly considered exploring the mine, but with nothing to light his way he feared he might fall down a shaft or get hopelessly lost. In the end, he followed Howard's sage advice and stayed put. Several hours passed before Howard returned, lantern in hand, with a chicken dinner and a stack of books. Why, Howard wanted to know, hadn't Churchill lit his candle? When Churchill said he couldn't find it, Howard explained rats must have taken it; the mine was infested with them. He passed Churchill the chicken and said he had gotten it from a doctor who lived twenty miles away. Howard employed two Dutch servants, who carefully monitored the food stock, and he did not want to arouse their suspicions. When Churchill again volunteered to leave, Howard refused and said only here would Churchill be safe from recapture. He left six extra candles and told Churchill to keep them under his pillow or mattress to prevent rats from once more absconding with them. Full of chicken and whisky, Churchill again dozed off, only to wake up to something tugging at his pillow. When he reached out in the darkness to investigate, the sound of scurrying erupted around him. He seized a candle from under his pillow and lit one. The flame threw a small circle of light, beyond which Churchill sensed constant movement and countless eyes peering at him. He eventually fell back to sleep, only to wake up to something clambering over his body. He shot up on his mattress, beating at his torso. Once more he lit a candle, only to find himself visibly alone in the dark.

Occasional visits by Howard and the two Scottish miners, who took him on a tour of the subterranean labyrinth, relieved the monotony. In hiding, Churchill did not go completely unnoticed. Bored at one point, with nothing better to do, he surrendered to his favorite vice, lit a cigar, and enjoyed a smoke. The smell of tobacco wafted up from underground and caught the attention of a young mine boy, who went to investigate. The young lad entered the cavern in which Churchill was hiding and saw a dirty, disheveled entity with a flaming mouth. The boy screamed and ran for the surface, where he informed the other mine boys of his horrific discovery. It would take many weeks for Howard to convince them the mine was not haunted.

Word soon reached Howard that Boer authorities were still searching homes in Pretoria, believing Churchill to be in the city. After three days of subterranean seclusion, Churchill returned to Howard's house and hid in a back room behind a pile of crates. The troglodytic existence had left him feeling unwell. He enjoyed a walk outside late that night, the cold air invigorating against his hot skin.

Meanwhile, Howard busied himself laying the groundwork for smuggling Churchill out of the country. The plan, much to Churchill's consternation, rested on the dependability of a local Dutchman, Charles Burnham, who was sympathetic to the British. Burnham planned to ship a consignment of wool by rail to Delagoa. The wool would be loaded onto a carriage at Howard's mine, which connected via branch line to the main railway. The bales of wool would be loaded in such a fashion that Churchill could hide among them. It was an incredibly risky plan, and Churchill had his doubts. He had come to take his freedom for granted, certain he would make it back to British lines. But his fate now lay in the hands of another—a Dutchman of all people. Concealed in the carriage, he would have no control over his fate; he was at the mercy of circumstances and the trustworthiness of an enemy national. But what choice did he have? His chances would prove equally slim if he tried to make his escape on foot.

Churchill reluctantly acquiesced to the scheme. The plan was set for December 19. He spent the day before his departure reading Robert Louis Stevenson's *Kidnapped* and found comfort in the adventures of David Balfour and Alan Breck Stewart. The fear that his pursuers might at any moment knock on Howard's door and search the premises kept him in a constant state of dread. Although frightened of what lay ahead, the mere act of waiting proved just as torturous. The sound of gunfire late that night pushed his nerves to the limit. Fearful the Boers had discovered his hiding place, he was immensely relieved to learn the noise was only Howard and a local official shooting at bottles.

On one occasion Churchill nearly blew his own cover. After finishing his cleaning duties one morning, the office boy placed his broom against the door to the room in which Churchill hid. Churchill, believing the tapping sound to be some sort of signal and thinking Howard wanted to chat, opened the door and found himself face-to-face with the terrified youth. For what seemed a lifetime, Churchill and the boy stared wide-eyed at one another, both rendered motionless by absolute shock. The boy, however, quickly regained his senses and took off to alert others. Howard, hearing of this, intervened and swore the boy to secrecy by bribing him with a new set of clothes.

At two o'clock on the morning of December 19, Howard entered Churchill's room and beckoned him to follow. The two men walked in silence to the colliery siding and the waiting railway cars. Howard motioned to one truck in particular. Churchill climbed in and saw a space between the stack of wool bales and the back wall of the carriage. He squeezed himself into the space and saw the bales had been arranged to form a narrow tunnel. Churchill shimmied the tunnel's length to the center of the truck and came to a space with just enough room to lie down and sit up. He was thankful for the limited movement the space afforded, for the journey was expected to last sixteen hours if there were no delays. All Churchill could do was sit in the darkness and wait. Smoking cigars was not an option. Several hours passed before he heard the rumble of an approaching engine. His carriage was coupled up to the train and soon was on its way.

As the sun came up, pale morning light spilled through the slats in the carriage walls and filled the spaces between the stacked wool bales, providing Churchill with some illumination. He saw Howard had left him a revolver, some bread, a couple of cooked chickens, some slabs of meat, and cold tea to wash it down. The miles passed one after the other, the train rhythmically rocking from side to side. Churchill lay on his back, hands behind his head, with only his thoughts to keep him occupied. All he had to do was make it over the border into Portuguese Mozambique—but the inevitable frontier checkpoint loomed large in his mind like an oncoming terror. Through the slats, daylight began to fade. That night the train pulled into a station. Churchill knew, having memorized the route beforehand, that he was halfway to the checkpoint at Komati Poort. He was desperate for sleep, but he feared he might snore and give himself away. Exhaustion, however, soon got the better of him. He slept without incident and awoke the next morning to the train's gentle rocking.

The train pulled into Komati Poort late that afternoon. He buried himself deeper beneath the sacks, his heart hammering against his ribs. He lay there for several hours and listened to men walking up and down the length of the train, conversing in Dutch. Someone eventually opened the carriage siding and began searching the cargo. Churchill pushed himself against the floorboards, in his nervous state his every breath amplified to a hideous volume. The inspector, much to Churchill's good fortune, proved less than thorough and concluded his efforts without discovering anything amiss.

The train remained in the station overnight and did not resume its journey until 11:00 the following morning. Knowing he was in Portuguese territory thrilled Churchill, which temporarily got the better of him. Without much thought or care, he crawled from his hiding place and fired his revolver three times in the air. The rumbling and clatter of the train drowned out the sound of gunfire and his celebratory cries.

Wanting to ensure Churchill's safe journey, Burnham had traveled with the train under the guise of keeping an eye on his wool shipment. Transporting wool was not a priority for the railway in a time of war, meaning Burnham had to bribe several officials to guarantee his shipment reached Lourenco Marques as soon as possible. A bottle of whisky to a guard at the first station where the train stopped for the night ensured the carriages would not be subjected to any surprise searches. At another station the following day, he distracted one curious guard with a hot cup of coffee.

It was with considerable relief that Burnham saw the train across the frontier at Komati Poort. He disembarked when it arrived at Lourenco

Marques at four in the afternoon and hovered about the carriages, waiting for Churchill. His behavior drew the attention of an observant police officer, who arrested Burnham for loitering but released him shortly thereafter. Burnham returned to the train in time to see a number of black laborers unloading the wool carriages. Still in his hiding place, Churchill decided to make his exit, having rid the carriage of all leftover food prior to the train's arrival. He crawled to the end of the carriage and lowered himself out near the couplings, emerging into daylight covered in coal dust and black as night. Railway workers and the manual laborers unloading the train walked past without paying him the least bit of attention. Churchill walked toward the station gates, doing his best to maintain a casual pace. He saw Burnham waiting for him. The two men briefly made eye contact before Burnham turned and started walking through the crowded Lourenco Marques streets. Churchill trailed at a close distance and followed Burnham to the British Consul Office, the Union Jack flapping atop the building as if in triumphant welcome.

When Churchill strolled inside, the consul secretary took one look at the filthy specimen before him and told him to leave. After all he had endured, Churchill threw a fit and demanded to see the consul immediately. The temper tantrum did the trick. The consul emerged from his office to investigate the commotion and asked the disgruntled gentleman his name. No sooner had Churchill uttered it than every accommodation was made for his comfort. A telegram arrived at Howard's home that afternoon. It simply read: "Goods arrived safely." In the evening, after the pleasures of a hot bath, Churchill sat down "to dinner with a real table cloth and real glasses." He caught up on the latest war news, which made for grim reading. Between December 10 and 15, the British had suffered bitter defeats at Stormberg and Methuen. The third and final drubbing of what the press dubbed "Black Week" took place at Colenso, where the Boers had dug themselves in north of the Tugela River and blocked direct passage to Ladymsith, which remained under siege. A disastrous frontal assault on the town cost the British nearly twelve hundred men; Boer losses proved negligible.

Britain was at war with a modern enemy—one who employed Gatling guns, barbed wire, trenches, sandbags, and heavy artillery—not the tribesmen of some barren, far-flung land. Realizing a change in command might be prudent, London had dispatched Field Marshal Lord Roberts to replace Sir Redvers Buller as commander in chief, though Buller maintained overall command of the Natal front. Churchill was desperate to get back in the game. Clean and well fed, he purchased some new clothes—including a slouch hat—and arranged passage on the small steamer *Induna*, bound that night for Durban. Before saying farewell to the comforts of the consul's office, he penned a brief telegram to the *Standard and Diggers' News* in Pretoria:

From: Churchill

To: Editor, *Standard and Diggers' News*

Am now writing "How I Escaped From the Boers"; but regret cannot, for obvious reasons, disclose many interesting details. Shall be happy to give you any you may require when next I visit Pretoria, probably third week in March.

That evening, Churchill—accompanied by an armed escort—went to the dock and boarded the boat. He was already back with the British Army when the newspaper in Pretoria responded to his letter:

The "Standard and Diggers' News" has been honored by Mr. Winston Churchill's evident desire to become a contributor to its columns, where, in about the third week of March, he would relate his experiences under the title "How I Escaped from the Boers." We are sorry indeed to have to disappoint so promising a youth; but unless Mr. Churchill can offer something much more interesting to the general public, we must decline the promised contribution. Mr. Churchill is a very young man who has his way to make in the world, and we would, from our maturer experience, venture to suggest that it would be advisable to bear in mind the old adages, "A still tongue makes a wise head," "Least said, soonest mended." And to demonstrate to our journalistic fledgling the true appreciation of his particular desire we would recommend that he alter the title of his lubrication to "How I Was Allowed to Escape from the Boers," a précis of which would read: A moonlight night, easy-going guards, Netherlands Railway Station. A coal truck. Ressano Garcia Station. Begrimed and miserable object. Arrived at Lourenzo Marquez. Admittance to British Consulate. Departure by French Steamer.

Churchill was never one to take advice.

CHAPTER 12

Back in the Fray

C hurchill reached the port of Durban on the afternoon of December 23, having spent the night at sea in his cabin, detailing his escape for the *Morning Post*. Very much aware that Howard and Burnham could face death if he exposed them in print, he omitted from his account any mention of their names or the fact that he had received help at all. He promised his readers to reveal the full details of his escape after the war. So extraordinary was the tale, he boasted, that they would find it well worth the wait. As the steamer chugged toward the jetty, Churchill stepped out on deck and saw a large crowd awaiting the ship's arrival. Not until he disembarked did he realize he was the object of their interest. The people cheered, waved hats and flags, and chanted his name. Escaping the Boers had elevated Churchill to the lofty heights of colonial hero—and a national one back home.

They followed him to the city hall, where he mounted the steps and addressed the adoring masses. He thanked them profusely for the flattering welcome and their support of the British cause. "With the determination of a great Empire surrounded by colonies of unprecedented loyalty," he bellowed, "we shall carry our policy to a successful conclusion, and under the old Union Jack there will be an era of peace, purity, liberty, equality, and good government in South Africa."

And so Winston Churchill delivered his first war speech. In a subsequent dispatch he described his reception as "an hour of turmoil, which I frankly admit I enjoyed extremely." He soon made his way to the local station and boarded a train for Pietermaritzburg. He spent a day resting at the house of the governor of Natal and traveled the next day, Christmas Eve, by rail to Frere to join up once more with British forces. Before departing he visited a local hospital to observe the wounded. Everywhere he looked was the grim aftermath of battle. Several men—their bodies wrapped almost entirely in bandages—lay on reclining chairs out on the veranda; the sun and fresh air seemed to afford them little comfort. Inside, behind closed doors, could be heard the ministrations of doctors and the complaints of the wounded. Men, some with missing limbs and newly bandaged stumps, hobbled along the hallways on crutches. Nurses quietly pushed stretchers—the occupants of some motionless beneath a white blanket—from one room to another.

Churchill was glad to leave the morbid scene behind and return to the British lines, where he received a warm welcome from Sir Redvers Buller. "Winston Churchill turned up here yesterday escaped from Pretoria," the general wrote a friend. "He really is a fine fellow and I must say I admire him greatly. I wish he was leading irregular troops instead of writing for a rotten paper. We are very short of good men, as he appears to be out here." When shown to his tent, Churchill was amused to find it was just fifty yards from the scene of his capture. "So after much trouble and adventure," he wrote, "I came safely home again to the wars." He could see the hill from which the Boers had fired upon the armored train. It now lay in British hands. Thousands of white tents covered the plain below, creating a makeshift city. Trains rolled in and out of the station around the clock, providing a steady stream of supplies. The last time he surveyed the landscape had been under blistering enemy fire and the real prospect of death. Now he was safe amid his own army—but some things had not changed. He could still hear the distant thunder of Boer guns blasting Ladysmith. The town, noted Churchill, "has stood two months' siege and bombardment."

How much longer could its beleaguered residents and garrison endure such torment? Disease was reportedly running rampant through civilians and soldiers alike; ammunition stores were dwindling; and food was in short supply. Men, pushed to starvation, will eat anything—and Churchill pondered the horrific scenes that might follow should all rations be exhausted. Rats and horses, cats and dogs—and whatever else people could get their hands on—would become the primary means of sustenance. No one could hold out indefinitely under such conditions.

The town sat in a valley surrounded by hills, upon which the Boers were firmly entrenched. From their elevated position they could easily repulse an advancing army and prevent the beleaguered British garrison from escaping. Wanting to observe the situation for himself, Churchill rode to Chieveley, where British naval guns were trained on the occupied heights. He arrived in the early evening just before the British began their nightly bombardment. Churchill could see through his looking glass the network of Boer trenches snaking along the hillsides. He saw figures in the gathering gloom: some were deepening trenches with shovels, others sat idly and enjoyed the evening's serenity; two men sparred in a friendly boxing match. The British gunners trained their artillery on an encampment of six or seven men. Range and trajectory calculated, the barrel of the 4.7-inch cannons pointed skyward. The guns roared, belching smoke and flame. The noise enthralled Churchill. "The desire of murder," he wrote, "rose in my heart."

He turned back to his looking glass. On the hill, some five miles away, the Boers—startled by the noise—ceased their activities. They seemed momentarily incapable of movement before they came to their senses and ran, diving into trenches and flattening themselves against the ground. A massive flash of flame and broken earth obscured Churchill's field of vision as the shell struck home. The guns boomed for thirty minutes. Churchill watched, with satisfaction, the fire wreak havoc across the Boer positions. When the sun at last set, the firing ceased and Churchill returned to camp. The next day was Christmas, prompting each side to leave the other in peace. Churchill attended a prayer service in the morning and spent the afternoon participating in various sporting events. The men enjoyed a traditional feast of "roast beef, plum pudding, a quart of beer for everyone, and various smoking concerts afterwards." In the days that followed, the British resumed their heavy bombardment. The Boers responded with sniper fire and small-scale attacks along the British lines. Such encounters, though insignificant in the larger context of things, eased the boredom of camp life.

Churchill woke to the sound of heavy artillery at two in the morning of January 6, 1900. Surely, he thought, the forlorn garrison at Ladysmith could not withstand much more. He imagined the starving, wretched men clinging to sanity and the dying vestiges of hope. The sound of Ladysmith under fire was not unusual, but this particular barrage seemed different. The booming rhythm of the guns gradually picked up pace until it coalesced into one long, thunderous drone. Despite all Churchill had heard up to this point, the intensity of this bombardment was something new. How, he wondered, could anyone survive such a pummeling? And still it grew in volume until it completely drowned out all other noise. Fascinated, he lay in his tent listening and contemplating what might necessitate such a fury.

The barrage continued into the afternoon. Speculation in the camp about what was happening ran wild. They found out when a message arrived via heliograph. The Boers, emboldened by the withering state of the town's garrison, had attacked Ladysmith's defensive outposts. Fighting at close quarters, the British waged a desperate defense that ultimately pushed the Boers back. Orders to prepare for combat rippled through the camp at one o'clock. In a frenzy of excitement, men debated the nature of the pending action. Surely, some opined, it must be a full assault on Colenso and then a push through to Ladysmith. Nonsense, others chimed in, it would most likely be a nighttime bayonet charge against the Boer lines. All this was mere speculation, but it did nothing to dampen the men's enthusiasm.

If Churchill and the others were spoiling for a fight, they were to be disappointed. Buller instead dispatched a large diversionary force to Colenso to draw the Boers away from Ladysmith and relieve the wilting garrison. Churchill, attached at his request to the South African Light Horse, watched the exercise atop a hill in the rear. His vantage point allowed him to view the entire scene. Across brown and parched country, infantry, cavalry, and artillery spread along the Colenso front. Through his field glasses he could see Boers running to their trenches on the outskirts of town. Dark thunderclouds rolled across the field of battle as the British artillery began blasting the enemy's front. As the cannonade echoed off the hills, the clouds burst in a torrential downpour. All along the British line the big guns threw tongues of red flame into the air. The shells landed in the streets and yards of Colenso, detonating in vibrant stabs of white and yellow. It made for spectacular viewing. As thunder battered the heavens, the crash of cannons drifted back to Churchill's position, which remained in warm sunlight. In the near distance lightning flashed in bolts of dazzling white and blue, as heavy British fire continued sending flame and smoke skyward. The barrage eventually ended, and the men withdrew back to camp. News from Ladysmith that evening confirmed the diversionary tactic had done the trick.

That evening Churchill put pen to paper in a letter home. He confessed there was anxiety among the ranks, for the Boers were a strong and resolute enemy. But although British victory remained a distant concept, he did not doubt it would ultimately be achieved. He felt secure in his belief that he was where he should be and was content to let things play out. This was the time for calm nerves and resolve and to mine strength in the righteousness of the cause. Never, he told his mother, would he return to England until the war reached a favorable conclusion.

In her latest correspondence Jennie had included published reviews of *The River War*, which Churchill found "satisfactory—though there is an undercurrent of envy in some of them." He added, somewhat prophetically, "One creates unknown enemies at every onward step." Later that night the British and Boers again faced off—but in a different kind of battle. Hoping to bolster the morale of the Ladysmith garrison, the men at Chieveley began using the camp searchlight to flash encouraging messages in Morse code off the low-hanging clouds. The Boers, quick to catch on, used their own searchlight to thwart the effort. Men on both sides gathered to watch the opposing beams of light dart about the sky in a weird game of cat and mouse. The next morning Churchill busied himself with a *Morning Post* dispatch and gave voice to what he considered the means to victory:

> Battles now-a-days are fought mainly with firearms, but no troops, however brave, however well directed, can enjoy the full advantage of their success if they exclude the possibilities of cold steel and are not prepared to maintain what they have won, if necessary with their fists. The moral strength of an army which welcomes the closest personal encounter must exceed that of an army which depends for its victories only on being able to kill its foes at a distance. The bayonet is the most powerful weapon we possess out here. Firearms kill many of the enemy, but it is the white weapon that makes them run away. Rifles can inflict the loss, but victory depends, for us at least, on the bayonets.

The bayonet would be put to plenty of use in the days ahead.

The British prepared for a new offensive to relieve Ladysmith. Hospitals in Pietermaritzburg and Frere moved their patients elsewhere to make room for new casualties. Churchill could see through the opening of his tent distant clouds of smoke from the shelling of Ladysmith blotting the sky. As he put the finishing touches on his article, some seven hundred civilians who had volunteered as stretcher bearers—or "body-snatchers," as the soldiers morbidly called them—arrived in the camp. Preparations for battle were fully evident even to the untrained eye, as ammunition, artillery, and the more basic necessities of food, water, and alcohol were loaded onto carts and wagons, which were hitched to mules, oxen, and horses. The mountain of supplies amazed and concerned Churchill in equal measure. Never before had he seen an army in the field encumbered by so much baggage. Not only did it place severe limits on the agility of its men, it also removed from its arsenal the element of surprise. The Boers would see a vast convoy of trunks and suitcases approaching long before the army ever had a chance to attack. Neither on the North-West Frontier nor in the Sudan—where the heat put South African temperatures to shame—had Churchill seen officers on the march sleeping in tents. In contrast, every soldier in South Africa had one. It seemed a waste of resources, Churchill opined, to "let a soldier live well for three days at the price of killing him on the fourth."

At daybreak on January 11 the army began to move out in long columns of wagons and khaki-clad soldiers. The clomping of countless hooves thickened the air with choking clouds of yellow dust. Buller had no intention of attempting another frontal assault on Colenso. Instead, he hoped to outflank the enemy and cross the Tugela River at two points west of the town. To achieve this aim he had under his command a considerable force of "19,000 infantry, 8,000 cavalry, and 60 guns."

Although the grateful Buller commissioned him to the South African Light Horse without making him resign as a correspondent, Churchill by this point had little faith in the general's abilities. An effort by a smaller force to cross the river on January 10 had ended in failure, prompting Churchill to write to Pamela Plowden, the woman who had captured his heart in India four years earlier, "Buller started out full of determination to do or die but his courage soon ebbed and we stood still and watched while one poor wretched brigade was pounded and hammered and we were not allowed to help them." In Churchill's opinion there was only one man suitable for the job, Sir Bindon Blood, but he doubted the opinion of a *Morning Post* correspondent would carry much weight with the War Office. Buller's present plan called for one-third of his force to cross at Potgieter's Drift, where seven thousand Boers under the command of General Louis Botha were dug in. The main bulk of the British army—handed to Lieutenant General Charles Warren—would cross further upstream at Trichardt's Drift, where Boer defenses were less formidable. Once the enemy had been shoved aside, the two British prongs would traverse the hills beyond the river, unite on the plain below, and march on Ladysmith.

With so much baggage to contend with, it took Warren and his men a week to cross the river, giving Botha plenty of time to strengthen his line. Each passing day was an opportunity wasted—a fact that caused disgruntlement among the fighting men. Each night the cavalry retired strong in the belief they would see action the next morning, yet day after day they awoke to disappointment. When the men finally did hit the Boer entrenchments, the generals would have much to answer for. The success of an offensive at Potgieter's depended on Warren's attack at Trichardt—but not until January 20 did Warren strike. With British artillery slugging away at the Boer entrenchments, Warren's infantry made little progress and suffered four hundred casualties. The next day saw more of the same, despite the enemy being pummeled by three thousand British shells. Although the gun crews claimed to have caused the enemy considerable grief, Churchill observed that the Boers still put up a spirited defense. Certainly the British had failed to knock out the other side's artillery and obliterate its trenches.

The British stayed put on January 22 and 23 and held onto their slight gains, all the while suffering ceaseless enemy shelling. Buller, desperate for something to happen, met with his commanders. His options were few. He could attack the Boer line head-on, a move Churchill thought would entail unnecessary risk and horrendous losses. Conversely, retreating back across the river would constitute "a moral defeat." The final, and agreed upon, option was to seize Spion Kop—or Spy Hill—which lay at the center of the Boer front. Taking the hill would give the British command of the Boer defenses and the surrounding country. Buller and his commanders devised a plan "to attack Spion Kop by night, rush the Boer trenches with Bayonet, entrench as far as possible before dawn, hold on during the day, drag guns up at night, and thus dominate the Boer lines."

At one o'clock in the morning on January 24 an attack force composed of the Lancashire Fusiliers, the Royal Lancaster Regiment, and elements of the South Lancashires and Mounted Infantry moved out under heavy darkness and began their ascent. The climb over steep and rocky ground proved slow and grueling. Surprise was paramount. Should the Boers open fire from their elevated position, the British assault would end before it even began. After a two-hour climb the British reached the top of the hill and caught the Boers unaware. The sharp stutter of gunfire and the angry cries of men drifted off the hill and floated over the pitch-black plain below. Churchill listened to the frantic sounds of battle until, at last, all was silent. Three celebratory cheers from the summit signaled to British commanders that all was well.

At daybreak the Boers began reclaiming what they had lost. Buller's men now had little to cheer about. Realizing the hilltop's strategic importance, the enemy aimed every gun they had at the summit and threw every man up the slopes, resulting in a ferocious struggle. The British were exposed and vulnerable, as the hard ground atop the hill was impervious to pick axes, shovels, and other tools used to dig trenches. Artillery fire killed most of the senior officers and left little in the way of leadership. As the men suffered under relentless shelling, Boer infantry began scrambling up the hill. Bullets and bayonets wreaked havoc on both sides. A British colonel named Thorneycroft was put in charge on the beleaguered summit. Not a man of timid demeanor, he showed little concern for his own safety as he struggled to rally his troops. The sight of one group of British soldiers hoisting a white flag sent him into a rage. As Boer riflemen led the capitulators off the hill, Thorneycroft approached them in fighting spirit. One Boer later recalled: "We should have had the whole hill. The English were about to surrender and we were all coming up, when a great big, angry-faced soldier ran out of the trench on our right and shouted, 'I'm in command here. Take your men back to hell, sir. I allow no surrender.'" The fighting, savage and without mercy, continued. As the sun blazed its arc across the sky and the temperature climbed, bodies began to bake in the unforgiving heat. Churchill later wrote:

> No words in these days of extravagant expression can do justice to the glorious endurance which the English regiments—for they were all English—displayed through the long dragging hours of hell fire. Between three and four o'clock the shells were falling on the hill from both sides, as I counted, at the rate of seven a minute, and the strange discharges of the Maxim shells guns—the "pom-poms" as these terrible engines are called for want of a correct name—lacerated the hillsides with dotted chains of smoke and dust.

Ambulance wagons began to gather at the base of the hill to cart off the bloody wrecks who came stumbling down or were carried or crawled. Hospital tents went up to shelter those undergoing slaughter-house surgery. Spion Kop was an abattoir—a horrific prologue to the carnage of the Western Front and the horrors of twentieth-century war-fare. Churchill and his regiment, frustrated by their exclusion from the battle, watched from a distance. In the afternoon, Churchill mounted his horse and rode to Warren's headquarters at Three Tree Hill, to the west of Spion Kop, where six batteries of British artillery and howitzers sat with barrels pointing silently skyward. Why, he asked, were they not firing?

The answer proved frustrating. The Boer guns hammering the sum-mit were too well concealed. The British crews had nothing to aim at. Churchill could no longer tolerate inaction. He and others witnessing the massacre from below were infuriated by the one-sidedness of it. At four o'clock he and a fellow cavalryman—Captain Brooke of the 7th Hussars—mounted their horses and took off for Spion Kop to assess the situation for themselves. They passed ambulance wagons and blood-spattered surgical tents and heard the screams of the wounded, before dismounting at the base of the embattled hill. The abysmal state of affairs became apparent the moment they started climbing and saw the wounded coming down. Bodies lay everywhere. The nature of the wounds spoke to the ferocity of the struggle. Many no longer possessed a human form, their bodies mutilated by shrapnel and clobbered by shells. Churchill counted at least two hundred corpses on his way up the slope. All the while the wounded continued their descent. Some simply collapsed from exhaustion and moved no more, while others cursed their luck and the war in general.

The fighting on the summit continued. Bullets and shells churning up earth and rock around them, Churchill and Brooke continued their ascent. The top of the hill was a nightmare landscape of gore and suffer-ing. "The dead and injured, smashed and broken by the shells, littered the summit till it was a bloody, reeking shambles," Churchill reported. "Thirst tormented the soldiers, for though water was at hand the fight was too close and furious to give even a moment's breathing space."

Churchill was no stranger to combat, but Spion Kop surpassed anything he had witnessed up to this point. In his dispatches he spared the readers back home nothing. Always a gifted writer, his reporting skills were at their zenith. He painted pictures both vivid and horrific. Although a staunch patriot and a true believer in the supremacy of empire, he did not soften his words, criticizing military leaders in whom he saw faults. He excelled not only at conveying the soldier's plight, but also at portraying the strategic complexities of the whole enterprise.

Having seen the extent of the carnage, Churchill and Brooke scurried back down the hill to present a full report to Warren. Night had fallen by the time they returned to camp. The fighting had severed communications with the summit, leaving Warren and his senior officers in the dark. Churchill found the general in a grim mood and did nothing to bolster his spirits when he detailed the situation. Warren's staff officer told Churchill reinforcements would be sent in at first light. He put the message in writing and asked Churchill to deliver it to Thorneycroft. Once again, Churchill returned to Spion Kop and made for the summit. The going proved slow in the total darkness. The path, plagued by uneven ground and sharp rocks, did not help matters—nor did the heavy traffic. Ambulance wagons and the walking wounded all jostled for space along the route. The congestion soon forced Churchill to dismount his horse and proceed on foot, but his pace hardly quickened. All over the slope men staggered around in varying degrees of shock and incapacity. Finally, Churchill reached the crest of the hill.

He found Thorneycroft barking commands at the bloodied remains of his men, who, Churchill noted, "had fought for him like lions and followed him like dogs." Churchill identified himself and handed Thorneycroft Warren's message. Thorneycroft, exhausted in body and spirit, told Churchill he had ordered his men to retreat an hour earlier. Reinforcements were unnecessary; the cause was lost. Churchill urged Thorneycroft to reconsider—or at least allow him to inform Warren before any firm decision was made. Thorneycroft shook his head. Hours of ceaseless bombardment and fighting at close quarters had pushed his men beyond their breaking point. "Better six good battalions safely down the hill than a mop up in the morning," he said, discarding Warren's note.

Churchill remained at Thorneycroft's side as they withdrew down the slope. The trek was made mostly in silence. At one point the two men pulled their revolvers when they noticed shadowy figures moving among some scorched trees. It came as a considerable relief to discover the shadows were merely those of British soldiers making their way down to safety. Weapons holstered, they made an uneventful journey back to Warren's headquarters. The sight of approaching reinforcements did, for one brief moment, cause Thorneycroft to second-guess his decision. But any doubt he may have had proved fleeting, and he continued on his course. They arrived at camp to find General Warren asleep but woke him up with the bad news. The general, much to Churchill's surprise, maintained an outwardly calm demeanor. The battle was over. "We have approached, tested, and assailed the Boer positions beyond the Tugela, fighting more or less continuously for five days," Churchill wrote later, on January 25, "and the result is that we find they cannot be pierced from the direction of Trichardt's Drift any more than at Colenso." The battle of Spion Kop proved to be an unmitigated disaster, costing the British fifteen hundred men, nearly three hundred of whom died on the summit. Boer casualties numbered less than four hundred. As he would do following the evacuation of Dunkirk in 1940, Churchill distilled some triumph from defeat. "It is an event which the British people may regard with feelings of equal pride and sadness," he wrote in his *Morning Post* dispatch. "It redounds to the honor of the soldiers, though not greatly to that of the generals. . . . We will have another try, and, if it pleases God, do better next time."

Daybreak on January 25 did nothing to alleviate the previous night's gloom. Churchill stirred under his blanket and sat up on the hard ground. His mood heavy, he listened to the camp slowly coming to life around him. Fires were lit and kettles filled. As men cooked their breakfast in tin pans and cast their gaze on the dark mass of Spion Kop, a senior officer stomped through the camp bellowing orders. "All baggage to move east of Venter's Spruit immediately," he shouted. "Troops ready to be turned out at thirty minutes' notice." Buller was pulling his army back across the Tugela. Retreating did not sit well with the men, and grumblings of disapproval rippled through the ranks. The horrendous sacrifice on Spion Kop had been for nothing. The British withdrawal from the summit not only left it open for the Boers to reclaim, but gave the enemy free rein—should they choose—to bombard Buller's retreating men.

Churchill and his comrades anticipated a bloody, fighting withdrawal across the river. They had no way of knowing the Boers had considered the battle lost the day before. So stubborn had British resistance been, the majority of Boers had staggered away in the heat of battle, leaving only a nominal force to carry on the struggle. By nightfall Boer commanders saw no hope in their situation. When Boer scouts discovered the summit deserted on the morning of January 25, they couldn't believe their luck—nor could they believe the human detritus littering the battleground. They allowed the British to retrieve their dead and wounded. A Boer surgeon watching the casualties being hauled off acknowledged British fortitude. "We Boers," he said, "would not, could not suffer like this."

On the night of January 26 the infantry began their retreat in pouring rain across the river. The ground did not favor swift movement and rendered the British slow-moving targets for the nearby Boer guns—but the Dutch showed their beleaguered opponent a modicum of mercy. Supply wagons, carts, and artillery crossed the river on January 25 and 26 without major incident, despite the closest enemy line being a mere thousand yards from the British position.

In the days that followed, the army established a camp behind Spearman's Hill, named for a nearby farm. Buller addressed the men and told them reinforcements and more artillery would soon replenish the ranks. They would, he promised, be in Ladysmith before too long. On January 28 Churchill wrote to Pamela Plowden and caught her up on recent events. In typical fashion, he thought little of how his words might worry his true love at home. He told her the past five days had been spent under continual fire—an enemy round even knocked the feather from his hat. But as always seemed to be the case, fate or destiny had seen him through. He may have been okay, but he worried about his brother, for whom he had secured a commission in the South African Light Horse. Churchill had hoped the siege of Ladysmith would be over by the time Jack arrived, sparing his brother the ordeal of fighting in what he anticipated to be the war's bloodiest battle. But fretting would not alter the course of bullets. Before he saw further action, he planned to take three days' leave and meet his mother and brother on the hospital ship *Maine*—for which Jennie had led the fund-raising effort back home—due to arrive that day in Durban. He kept the details about Spion Kop brief, saying only that the battle ranked as one of the most awful things he had ever witnessed.

In Durban he spent his three days living on board the *Maine* as one might enjoy a pleasure cruise. He and Jennie were invited to tour the British cruiser *Terrible*, also anchored in Durban. The vessel's captain, Percy Scott, having taken a liking to Jennie, named the ship's 4.7-inch gun in her honor. When Churchill's leave ended, he returned to the front with Jack, who was now a lieutenant.

Two days later, on February 5, Buller ordered his troops once more across the Tugela to seize Vaal Krantz, a ridge of small hills east of Spion Kop. The battle commenced shortly after 7:00 that morning with a blistering bombardment of the ridgeline that "the Boers had fortified by four tiers of trenches, with bombproof casemates, barbed-wire entanglements, and a line of redoubts." As shells soared overhead, the infantry began their forward march. The cavalry, ready to join the attack, took up position near a pontoon bridge constructed a mile south of Potgieter's. For three hours the firing remained one sided, the British gun crews working at a feverish pace. In the near distance, along the ridge, plumes of earth mushroomed skyward.

Then the Boers responded in kind, lobbing shells along the army's artillery line. Flaming rock and debris pelted the British gun crews. The men—choking and partially blinded by dust—maintained their steady rate of fire, as the two sides hammered each other and littered the plain with shrapnel. British troops, having crossed the river, advanced on the enemy ridge and stormed the Boer trenches, putting their bayonets to bloody use. Churchill and Jack watched the spectacle from the cavalry's staging area. The British captured five prisoners and horses at a loss, according to Churchill, of "seven officers and sixty or seventy men." The big guns, however, had done the trick, for the majority of Boers "had retired before the attack, unable to endure the appalling concentration of artillery which had prepared it."

With the infantry making strong gains, word passed down the line that the cavalry would not be needed until the next day. The British firmly held Vaal Krantz by nightfall. Churchill and his fellow cavalrymen dismounted and prepared for a long night in the open. Frigid temperatures forced Churchill to share a blanket with his regiment's colonel. The night seemed interminable. Whenever one man rolled over, he pulled the blanket off the other. Churchill endured the suffering in silence, but the colonel did not—he was, after all, the superior officer. Morning could not come fast enough, but it brought another setback. Reports from the Vaal Krantz ridge said it was too steep and rocky to support British artillery. Strangely, the Boers seemed to have no problem hauling their big guns up and down hills. This wiped out any strategic value the ridge may have had.

The Boers made life miserable for the defenseless British entrenched atop the ridge, lobbing artillery shells in their direction and harassing the line with long-range rifle fire. Boer forces made two attempts to reclaim their lost ground, one at 4:00 on the afternoon of February 6 and the other at midnight. The British repulsed both efforts, the first attack being fought at close quarters. The situation was hardly improved by daybreak on February 7, when the Boers resumed their bombardment. It soon became apparent to Buller and his staff that there was little more they could do. If field guns could not be hauled to the top of Vaal Krantz (and no attempt was made to see if this could be done), the infantry would have no artillery support going forward. Once again Buller called it a day. Late on the evening of February 7 he ordered his men to withdraw. A retreat back across the Tugela soon followed and once more rankled the army.

No more than two infantry brigades had engaged the enemy. Anger, more than disappointment, infected the men. One bloody sacrifice after another was being made, with no discernible gains. Behind the infantry followed the cavalry, with the artillery bringing up the rear. All along the retreating column the mood remained grim. Four attempts had been made to relieve Ladysmith, and all of them had ended in rout and ruin. How much more could Buller's men take?

The string of defeats notwithstanding, Churchill enjoyed the rough-shod existence of a soldier in the field. He found the fighting to relieve Ladysmith as enjoyable as his time on the North-West Frontier. Predictability and the monotony of routine did not exist on the battle-field—consequently, the dawn of each new day promised something different. "One lived in the present with something happening all the time," he wrote. "Care-free, no regrets for the past, no fears for the future; no expenses, no duns, no complications, and all the time my salary was safely piling up at home!" That his brother now served along-side him only added to Churchill's enjoyment.

Jack had yet to see any action, but that would soon change. Buller busied himself planning yet another attempt to relieve Ladysmith. Vi-tal to the Boers' strong hold on Colenso, which had so thwarted the general back in December, was a series of hills to the east of town, the highest being Hlangwani, at five hundred feet, on the south bank of the river. If the British could place artillery atop the "rocky scrub-cov-ered hill," it would, Churchill told his *Morning Post* readers, obliterate the Boers' hold on the town and allow Buller to cross the Tugela there on a direct route to Ladysmith. The plan's success lay in capturing the neighboring hills. At 8:00 on the morning of February 12 Buller dis-patched a small force—including the Churchill brothers in the South African Light Horse—to seize nearby Hussar Hill to the southeast of Colenso. The force did so with ease, for the Boer defenses proved rela-tively light. Buller scrambled up the hill and arrived on the summit at noon to survey the area and familiarize himself with the battlefield's ge-ography. He departed an hour later and ordered his men to withdraw.

Seeing the British abandon the rise for no apparent reason prompted the Boers to give chase. As the cavalry trotted down the hill, a fusil-lade of shots rang out behind them. Churchill estimated some three hundred rifles blazed from above; the sound proved deafening. The enemy barrage kicked up so much dust and dirt between the horses, Churchill felt sure it was only a matter of time before men started falling from their saddles—yet not one shot found its mark. The cavalry broke into a gallop and spread out to thin their ranks. The crack of enemy musketry could still be heard over the thundering of hooves. Churchill shot a glance over his shoulder and discovered, much to his relief, the majority of Boer shots were falling short and tearing up the ground two hundred yards back. The cavalry soon reached the safety of their own lines and watched British artillery blast the hill.

Churchill and the others leapt from their horses, unslung their carbines, and fired away. Both sides shot blind, as neither could see the other. The hot exchange would have been a savage melee if not for the considerable distance between friend and enemy, and the effective cover available to both. In typical fashion, Churchill walked along the firing line with little thought for his own well-being. In the distance, beyond a smattering of trees and above the tall grass, he could see smudges of black smoke rising from the enemy's guns.

Neither side inflicted much damage. Churchill saw a couple of men fall, but their wounds did not appear serious. As he watched the action and took mental notes for his next dispatch, he noticed a young soldier lying in the grass, rapidly squeezing off rounds. It was, Churchill realized, his brother. He approached and saw Jack convulse. "Are you hurt?" he asked, feeling a pang of guilt. Jack uttered something through clenched teeth, as Churchill knelt beside him. A quick examination revealed a bullet hole in Jack's calf. Churchill helped his brother to an ambulance wagon, which promptly wheeled him off to a field hospital. Not long thereafter, both sides tired of the skirmish and broke off the engagement. The whole thing had lasted no more than ten minutes. Casualties in the South African Light Horse were negligible, with several men and horses wounded and only one man killed. Churchill paid a visit to his brother later that day. The doctors told him it would take a month for Jack to make a full recovery. Churchill had to break the news to his mother. "It is a coincidence," he wrote Jennie, "that one of the first patients on board the *Maine* should be your own son . . . but you may be glad with me that he is out of harm's way for a month. There will be a great battle in a few days and his presence—though I would not lift a finger to prevent him—adds much to my anxiety when there is fighting." In one dispatch he could not help but ponder war's random selection. How strange that one man should be struck down his first time in battle, yet another could pass through one maelstrom after another and come out safe on the other side. Fate was a fickle thing.

As Churchill wrote his articles, Buller surveyed maps at his headquarters. Having acquired a good lay of the land from atop Hussar Hill, he realized the successful seizure of Hlangwani depended on capturing two heavily wooded mountain ridges to the east called Cingolo and Monte Cristo, which, joined by a stretch of land, formed the Monte Cristo Range. Artillery placed on this ridge would support the attack on Hlangwani, which the Boers had been fortifying heavily since December. With a strategy in place, Buller launched his new offensive. It began with an assault on February 14 against Hussar Hill. The summit fell with minimal resistance, allowing the British to finally haul up their artillery and pound enemy positions on neighboring slopes. The South African Light Horse then began to push east toward the Monte Cristo Range. The terrain—"all rock, high grass, and dense thickets"—made the going slow. The regiment eventually had to dismount and lead the horses over the sharp, uneven ground. The animals, Churchill reported, struggled to navigate through the trees and boulders. They eventually reached the base of Cingolo and waited thirty minutes to see if the enemy would present themselves. After an uneventful half hour the men commenced their climb up the hill through nearly impenetrable forest. Branches snagged clothing and tore skin, forcing the regiment to hack its way upward with swords. Bleeding and exhausted, they reached the summit by eleven that morning. Here the forest surrendered to areas of open space littered with large rocks—big enough for men to hide behind. As Churchill and the others moved cautiously forward, the Boers, hidden in positions at the top, revealed themselves with a volley of rifle fire.

The defenders proved to be few in number and were quickly overwhelmed. The British held firm to Cingolo by the time Churchill and his comrades bivouacked for the night on February 17. The following morning Buller's men charged across the strip of land that joined Cingolo and Monte Cristo. The Boers had dug themselves in halfway across the ridge and fired over the top of their trench. The British met the onslaught head-on. They blasted their way through the defensive line and shoved the Boers aside, leaving one hundred of their own bleeding on the ground. Once across, they scrambled up the slopes of Monte Cristo, enraged by past defeats yet pushed on by the sense of pending victory. They climbed over boulders and ducked in and out of trees, firing at a frenzied rate and stabbing with their bayonets. The defending Boers began melting away and by midafternoon had abandoned Monte Cristo. Buller's blood-toll was relatively light, at fewer than two hundred casualties. From the summit they could see Ladysmith in the distance. Churchill ascended the hill later that day and cast his gaze on the army's ultimate objective. It lay eight miles away, shimmering in the mid-distance like some oasis. But it was more than that for Churchill. It was a memorial to the fallen who had died pursuing its rescue and a symbol of British determination. It was an unsightly town of gum trees and simple tin houses "but famous to the uttermost ends of the earth."

CHAPTER 13

Blood and Fury

It rained during the night, but Buller's army slept "the restless sleep of men who had done great things." Two miles of Boer fortifications and trench line lay in British hands. More important, they had set the stage for the relief of Ladysmith. On the morning of February 19, as early sunlight touched the battle-scarred hills, Churchill woke with a sense of optimism. The tide, at long last, had turned—or so he hoped. Although this was not a time for celebration, Churchill's optimism was not misplaced.

With Monte Cristo conquered, the British next seized Green Hill, which lay between the Monte Cristo Range and Hlangwani. Their position rapidly deteriorating, the Boers abandoned Hlangwani without much fight and fled the Tugela's south bank, crossing to the other side. "So it came to pass," noted one account, "that [when] two battalions of infantry went swinging up the side of the coveted hill they met with no resistance." British artillery placed atop Hlangwani punished Colenso that same day and battered the Boer entrenchments in and around the town. Buller's men watched and cheered from their hilltop positions as the Boers fled and left the British to claim their prize.

With Colenso finally in their possession, the British threw a pontoon bridge across the river to the north of town. Confident the Boers were on the run, Buller abandoned the high ground his men had only just conquered. Churchill thought the move a monumental blunder, a blatant shunning of hard lessons learned in recent fighting. Buller's forces began crossing the river on the afternoon of February 21. That morning Churchill took a moment to write to Pamela.

He told her, in typical fashion, that he lived a dangerous life—one in which a day was not complete without someone shooting at him. When not charging along the front with his cavalry regiment, he was fulfilling his duties to the *Morning Post*. It was imperative, as a war correspondent, that he have a front-row seat to the action at all times. To convey the true nature of combat, one must smell the gunpowder, feel the concussion of artillery, and hear the angry buzz of bullets. And yet, through it all, he remained safe and free from serious harm—despite having tempted fate more times than he could count. The same could not be said of poor Jack. Churchill's luck, where so many suffered misfortune, only underscored the belief he had in his own destiny. "Perhaps," he wrote, "I am to be of use."

He folded the letter and placed it in his saddlebag to finish another time, for things were heating up across the river. Buller's first brigade to cross soon found itself entangled in a nightmare landscape of boulders and kopjes—small hills that littered the veldt and made maneuvering all but impossible. The Boers, having claimed a series of summits after watching Buller's men vacate the high ground and remove the threat of artillery, pummeled the brigade with blistering fire.

Lacking artillery support and cramped among the cluttered landscape, the brigade took heavy casualties, including its general. By sunset nearly two hundred men had fallen. A plan to send the cavalry across the river on the morning of February 22 was scrapped in favor of hurling every infantryman and a number of field guns into the fray. Buller, believing he was up against a rearguard protecting the Boer retreat, thought overwhelming force would see the day through. Churchill and other members of his regiment returned to the top of Hlangwani and watched the roiling scene as darkness began to settle. One by one his companions retreated down the slope to their camp for the night, until only Churchill remained. He stood there for some time, listening to the symphony of battle and watching its attendant light show. It was beautiful in its own strange way. Then, all at once, there rose above the din the ear-splitting clatter "of a tremendous fusillade" that carried on unabated for several hours. Great white flashes illuminated the scene in strobe-like fashion. The heavy percussion of big guns rolled across the river and echoed off the hills recently vacated by the British. It was impossible to tell what side the battle favored. Churchill, unable to make anything out in the dark, soon climbed down and joined his comrades in camp, where he fell asleep to the sound of gunfire.

The battle raged through the night on the opposite shore, but the British maintained a firm grip on their hard-fought gains, primarily two summits they had christened Wynne Hill and Horseshoe Hill. Gunfire still crackled when Churchill woke on the morning of February 23. An order quickly passed through the ranks: "Push for Ladysmith today, horse, foot, and artillery! Both cavalry brigades to cross the river at once!"

The cavalry began crossing the bridge at 8:00 under heavy bombardment, with great plumes of water erupting on either side of the expanse. The infantry followed. "Each man was forced to run the gauntlet himself," one rifleman later remembered, "and had to [run] as hard as he could." Churchill rode to a nearby kopje to watch the action alongside Buller. On the other side of the bridge Buller's army sought cover behind rocks and small hills as the Boers smothered the line of advance with steady fire. Stretcher-bearers worked frantically, struggling to keep pace with the bloodletting as they hauled an escalating number of wounded from the front.

The prime objective this day was a hill, soon to be dubbed Hart Hill after the general who led the assault. Major General Fitzroy Hart ordered his men forward at half past twelve. Churchill left his place alongside Buller and, following the bedraggled stream of casualties that flowed from the fighting line, rode to a hill further along to get a better view of the action. The three thousand men of Hart's four Irish battalions—"the Dublin Fusiliers, the Inniskilling Fusiliers, the Connaught Fusiliers, and the Imperial Light Infantry"—marched toward their ultimate objective. Churchill tracked their path through his field glasses. In the near distance, he reported, the hill, "crowned with sangers and entrenchments, rose up gloomy and, as yet, silent." Before reaching the hill's lower slopes the men had to cross a railway bridge that traversed a gorge. The bridge gave way to flat, open land that would make the infantry easy targets for the Boer guns. As the men took their first steps onto the plain, the enemy's armaments came to life with a startling roar.

Rounds clanged and sparked off the railway bridge, as men still making the crossing fell lifeless onto the tracks. The plain, which only moments ago had been quiet, now seemed to boil as bullets hammered the dusty ground. The infantry charged through the fusillade at a bloody cost toward the slopes. Churchill reported seeing at least sixty men gunned down. He almost forgot how close he was to the action until an artillery shell landed nearby and sent him scurrying partway down the hill for better cover. By 4:00 two of Hart's battalions had reached the base of the hill. The general, without waiting for the remainder of his force, ordered his men up the slopes.

Hart's men began their frantic climb against heavy fire from above. Churchill marveled at their courage—but bravery was not enough. Rushing headlong into the murderous barrage, they fell like dominoes. British artillery pounded the enemy entrenchments but failed to silence the guns. C. F. Romer, a major in the Second Battalion Royal Dublin Fusiliers who took part in the attack, witnessed the slaughter up close. "In the gathering darkness the Boer trenches quivered with the rifle-flashes, and the bullets struck out sparks as they hit the rocks," he later wrote. "At such a short range the enemy's marksmen could hardly miss, and the line of charging infantry was almost mowed down. The assault was checked, and the attackers flung themselves on the ground and sought what little cover there was." "It was," Churchill noted, "a frantic scene of blood and fury." Hart's brigade faced the real danger of bleeding to death. Reinforcements provided fresh gristle for the Boer guns but did nothing to advance the desperate cause on the bloodied slopes. The attackers, not wanting to abandon their gains, stayed put on the hill and built makeshift cover out of earth and rock. From behind these hastily constructed walls, they returned fire.

Shattered bodies littered the hillside. Two colonels, three majors, and twenty officers lay among the dead. Out of roughly twelve hundred men who took part in the attack, some six hundred were killed or wounded. Darkness bestowed a small mercy and brought the struggle to a temporary close. On the morning of February 24 Churchill and a companion—Captain Brooke—mounted their horses and rode back to the tortured scene. They passed the hill from which Churchill had watched the battle the day before and took up position in a hollow. The men had no sooner settled down than the sky above them exploded. A deafening roar clobbered their senses when a shrapnel shell detonated overhead.

Hot metal decimated the side of the hill, cutting through a number of men and horses on the slope. The concussion rattled Churchill and Brook to the core; the detonation consumed everything in a blinding white flash. It took Churchill a moment to process what, exactly, had happened. The first thing he realized was that he remained upright in his saddle. Thick clouds of dust rose up around his horse, which seemed only mildly disturbed by the event. Having regained his equilibrium, Churchill let go of the reins and carefully ran his hands up and down his torso and along his arms. Much to his amazement, he had suffered not a single scratch. Reveling in his good fortune, he turned to Brooke to utter a pithy comment regarding the ineffectiveness of Boer shrapnel, but stopped when he saw the writhing figures on the hillside. The blast had killed or wounded eight men. Providence, it seemed, had intervened once again on Churchill's behalf.

Two more shells followed in quick succession, killing and maiming more men and horses. Churchill and Brooke abandoned the hollow and climbed up the hill. From the summit they could see the slopes of Hart Hill. Only a few hundred yards separated Hart's men from the Boer trenches. Both sides appeared locked in a bloody stalemate, as they hammered one another with continual rifle fire. The infantry made no attempt to storm the summit and remained behind their earthen cover. The scene's carnage took Churchill's mind back to the

Dervish slaughter at Omdurman and the countless enemy wounded left to die in the desert. On Hart Hill the wounded still littered the slopes; their cries for help and desperate pleas for water drifted on the wind. Churchill watched British artillery again target the Boer trenches. The shells blasted away great swaths of hillside. Those that fell short of their targets obliterated the wounded sprawled near the enemy lines. During all this, Churchill found a moment to take his unfinished letter to Pamela out of his saddlebag and scribble a few more lines:

> We have advanced, crossed the Tugela and are struggling towards Lady-smith. Very fierce and bloody fighting all day and night. Progress very slow and the danger to the whole army is great. I would write more my dearest Pamela, but here I sit on a rocky hill without any conveniences for writing and with all manner of work for the *Morning Post*—which I am paid to do—claiming my attention. Moreover they have begun shelling us again which is a nuisance. I was vy nearly killed two hours ago by a shrapnel shell. But though I was in the full burst of it God preserved me. . . . I wonder whether we shall get through and whether I shall live to see the end.

He concluded with a bit of bravado, telling her his nerves remained steady and bullets became less of a bother with each passing day. Such talk from Churchill hardly qualified as empty boasting. He remained a creature of war, fixated on its complexities and scope and riveted by its human drama. It was the ultimate test of one's courage and spirit. Although he fully acknowledged the horrors of the battlefield, the heroes and tales of daring forged in its blast furnace never ceased to enthrall him.

A sudden flash of red drew Churchill's attention back to the embattled slope. A large Red Cross flag fluttered above the Boer lines. Gunfire surrendered to an eerie silence as the enemy scrambled out of their trenches to drag their wounded to safety. Some Boers knelt alongside their stricken opponents and offered water from their canteens. As the British waited for stretcher-bearers from their side to climb the hill, they saw a number of Boers, reported Churchill, "despoil the dead and wounded, taking off their boots and turning out their pockets." The enraged British resumed firing and sent the Boers scurrying. The day passed with both sides exchanging volleys in what one soldier called "a ceaseless rifle-duel." When the sun came up on February 25, the Boers still held the hill. Shortly after daybreak both sides negotiated a cease-fire to retrieve their dead and wounded. Recovery teams moved up the slope to collect their grisly cargo. For two days the wounded had suffered without food or water, while the dead were left to rot.

The bodies of those slain on Hart Hill brought back to Churchill's mind the Dervish dead at Omdurman. Black and swollen, their grotesque condition was rendered all the more disturbing by the raw, gaping wounds inflicted by the expanding ammunition routinely used by the Boers. In some areas the dead covered the ground completely. On one particular bloody patch of slope only three survivors were found among eighty twisted corpses. The recovery operation continued until nine that evening. All the while, Buller ordered a number of brigades back to the south side of the river. Throughout the day the Boers, behind their silent guns, had seen men, horses, wagons, and guns returning to the opposite shore. British battlefield reconnaissance had revealed a blind spot in the Boer defenses, which Buller hoped to exploit and break through to Ladysmith. Two miles downstream, to the right of the Boer positions, the Tugela flowed through a gorge. Here the British could throw a bridge across and pass once more to the south side unseen. The pontoon bridge was relocated to its new position just below a waterfall on the night of February 26. The stage was set for yet another attempt, though it seemed obvious to men of all ranks that for Ladysmith this would be the last chance.

The attack commenced at first light, the taste of breakfast and the morning's cup of coffee still fresh in the men's mouths. Buller had repositioned his artillery atop the Monte Cristo ridge and Hlangwani, and now the big guns threw shells into a patchy sky. Churchill and the rest of the South African Light Horse took up positions at the top of Monte Cristo with rifles at the ready. They had a clear view of the bridge and could support the infantry with "long-range rifle fire" if necessary. As the artillery thundered, British Maxim guns strafed the north bank of the river. "We soon had a capital loud noise," Churchill told his London readers, "which I think is a most invigorating element in an attack." The gunners fired in advance of the infantry moving across the bridge to clear the opposing shore and keep enemy snipers at bay.

Churchill enjoyed the grand spectacle. "It was," he wrote, "like a stage scene viewed from the dress circle." Two hills—Railway and Pieters—still blocked Buller's path to Ladysmith and would have to be taken. Infantry began swarming up the slopes of Pieters Hill shortly after nine o'clock; the attack on Railway Hill began a few hours later. "From the distance," notes one contemporary account, "it looked like one long line of moving khaki, two miles in extent." One by one the hills fell to the British: Pieters, Railway, and—finally—Hart, which was taken in fierce hand-to-hand fighting. Churchill watched the Boer defenders abandon the last ridge. One Dutchman leapt from his trench and tried to thwart the inevitable British victory with a few shots from his rifle. Somewhere behind Churchill a big gun lobbed a fifty-pound shell skyward. The lone defender disappeared seconds later in a violent flash.

The sun's last light was beginning to fade, turning the sky a deep magenta. At last came the moment Churchill had long awaited: the order for the cavalry to mount and pursue the retreating enemy. The men of the South African Light Horse—still atop Monte Cristo—mounted their steeds and galloped down to the pontoon bridge, where, to their surprise, they found General Buller blocking their path. Worried the cavalry might suffer heavy losses giving chase, he ordered the men back to the summit. The decision rankled Churchill, who thought it a strategic blunder. Why not pursue the enemy and inflict as much damage as possible?

That night, still annoyed, Churchill watched British soldiers rounding up a number of Boer prisoners. Studying the captives up close, Churchill saw nothing to suggest their proficiency on the battlefield. The Boers did not wear uniforms and fought in their everyday clothing, much of it threadbare after the exertions of combat. They appeared to be a slovenly lot, like "loafers round a public house," which—in Churchill's mind—cast a great shadow of mystery over the whole lot: What, exactly, made these simple-looking men such a ferocious adversary?

On the morning of Wednesday, February 28, Captain W. A. Tilney flew above Ladysmith in his observation balloon, his face creased with worry. The near-distant rumbling of artillery over the preceding days had offered a small measure of comfort to the besieged inhabitants, as it meant their would-be rescuers were attempting a breakthrough. Now, at daybreak, it remained silent, prompting speculation that Buller had been defeated once again. A thick ribbon of mist obscured the horizon, but a spectacular scene gradually took shape as the sun burned the vapor away. Tilney stared, at first unsure of the sight framed in his looking glass; then the realization struck home. He landed the balloon and spread the word. Soldiers and civilians, not quite believing the news, scrambled up a ridge dubbed Observation Hill and stared across the veldt. One witness remembered the glorious sight of the retreating Boer army: "Waggons were crowded together by the hundreds. If one could not go fast enough it had to fall out of the road, making way for others. Above them hung dense dust clouds. Elsewhere in the open, dust whirled in thinner, higher wreaths above groups of horsemen hurrying off in confusion, and paying no heed to the straights of their transport. A beaten army in full retreat if I have ever seen one! Still people doubted and grew uneasy, because of General Buller's silence." Buller's silence did not last long. In the early afternoon he sent Ladysmith a message via heliograph: "I beat the enemy thoroughly yesterday, and am sending my cavalry on as fast as very bad roads will admit to ascertain where they are going. I believe the enemy to be in full retreat."

Churchill spent part of that morning with his regiment, watching Buller's army cross the pontoon bridge to the north side of the river. At the same time, stretcher-bearers continued the task of bringing the dead and wounded back from the battlefield. He eyed each passing casualty from atop his horse. One particular officer—a captain with bandaged eyes—made an impression, for although incapacitated, he still seemed to be in fine fighting spirit. "Yes, but what I want to know is this," Churchill heard the captain demand of his rescuers, "did they get into them with the bayonet?" The two men hauling the wounded captain exchanged a quizzical glance and shrugged. "Yes," one of them replied, "they gave 'em 'ell, sir." That was the kind of doggedness Churchill appreciated. Boer casualties soon followed. "Most of these poor creatures," wrote Churchill, expressing an empathetic note, "were fearfully shattered." He respected the bravery of fighting men regardless of their side. The order finally arrived for the cavalry to cross the river. For Churchill it was long overdue; he still bristled at being denied a chance to engage the enemy. As his regiment crossed the pontoon bridge to the Tugela's north bank, Churchill was amused to see a signpost shaped like a finger pointing into the distance. "To Ladysmith," it read.

The cavalry negotiated the ridges beyond the riverbank and emerged onto the veldt. The ride to Ladysmith could begin at last—but Churchill first made a quick detour. He was eager to see the enemy entrenchments atop Hart's Hill, which had caused so much grief. At the summit a young soldier hopping with excitement led him to a "bloke . . . without a head." A gore-stained blanket covered the corpse, which the soldier offered to remove with all the excitement of a child anxious to show off a toy. Churchill's insistence that viewing the body was unnecessary left the soldier "mightily disappointed." Having seen enough, Churchill returned to his regiment and resumed the ride.

Although the Boers were in full retreat, the gallop across the veldt did not pass without incident. A few brave Dutchmen opened fire on the cavalry from a nearby hill. The riders came to a halt and had to wait for the horse-drawn artillery to pull up. The big guns duly blasted the hilltop and brought the enemy fire to an abrupt halt. The cavalry continued on its way—but at a cautious pace. The ride exhilarated Churchill. His horse, sturdy and strong beneath him, handled the sharp, uneven ground with grace. The landscape teased the men's expectations, for beyond the next hill or undulation, would they finally catch a glimpse of Ladysmith—the cause for which they had endured and suffered so much?

As night fell the inhabitants of Ladysmith heard a faint noise outside the town. It grew louder with each passing second until the nature of the noise became evident: it was wild cheering; the celebratory cries of the approaching cavalry. Men, women, and children rushed to greet their saviors and gathered on the banks of the nearby Klip River. "The voices of strong men break into childish treble as they try to cheer," noted *Daily News* correspondent Henry Pearse. It was not long before "a horseman, weather-stained and begrimed by days of bivouacking, floundered from deep water onto the slippery bank." The sight sent a roar of jubilation through the crowd. "Women laugh and cry by turns, and all crowd about the troopers, giving them such a welcome as few victors from the battlefield have ever known," wrote Pearse. "The hour of our deliverance has come. After a hundred and twenty-two days of bombardment—a hundred and nineteen of close investment—the siege of Ladysmith is at an end." Someone started singing "God Save the Queen." Hundreds of voices belted the words into the star-filled sky.

Churchill dined with Sir George White, the garrison's commander, that evening. Although the town had no more than four days' worth of rations left, Churchill and company enjoyed a surprisingly decent meal. Bottles of champagne preserved for the occasion were opened and quickly emptied. Churchill scanned the feast with a wary eye open for horsemeat. To his relief, he saw none; the last ox in Ladysmith had been butchered for the meal.

At the table was General Ian Hamilton, who, as a colonel in charge of musketry training in India, had befriended Churchill four years earlier. For Churchill the evening was a thrill. With his love of history, he reveled in being part of a momentous occasion. Ever the journalist, he spent the next day exploring the town in search of a story. Soldiers and citizens devastated by dysentery and enteric fever crowded the hospital. A medical camp set up in the town helped to deal with the overflow. Churchill interviewed doctors and patients and heard one story after another of men who, having survived a combat wound, died of starvation. All being gaunt and pallid in appearance, it was difficult to discern the caregivers from the sick. Six hundred white crosses behind the medical camp spoke of Ladysmith's long misery. Churchill summed it up in a simple sentence: "Sun, stink, and sickness harassed the beleaguered." And what of the relieving army? It too had been ravaged in its attempts to reach the town. In the course of ten weeks and twenty-five days of grueling battle, out of twenty-three thousand men, the British had lost more than five thousand. The relief of Ladysmith meant much-needed food and supplies for the town—and desperate rest for the army.

But Churchill never took it easy. He busied himself with his dispatches and personal correspondence. Always with an eye on the future and his public profile, he negotiated a book deal with Longmans for his *Morning Post* articles, which rightly irked his occasional literary agent, A. P. Watt. Although Watt did not know the terms of the deal, he was sure the young author—ignorant of the vagaries of the marketplace— had sold himself short. He was no longer a literary lightweight. The success of his Malakand book and certainly *The River War*, with three thousand copies sold so far, had drastically raised Churchill's stock. Even had he not published these previous titles, his escape from the Boers guaranteed the success of any future work. It would be in Churchill's best interest, Watt advised, if he allowed a professional to handle such deals in the future.

In other book news, Watt informed Churchill that the recent publication of *Savrola*—Churchill's seventy-thousand-word novel, which he had somehow managed to finish in between *Malakand* and *The River War*—had met with relatively kind reviews in England. One write-up, which appeared in the *Star*, complimented the book in a backhanded manner: "It will not add to the reputation gained by *The River War*, compared with which it is in many respects crude and immature; but it is, nevertheless, a brilliant, witty, and exciting political tale. Mr. Churchill follows the Disraelian tradition. He is ambitious; he is a perfect poseur; and he is adept at the arts of notoriety. He has turned war correspondence into a gigantic advertisement of his modest personality. The novel is a sideshow which, as Dizzy knew, is an excellent means of keeping up public interest." Since Churchill's escape, public interest in his books had earned him £1,500 in royalties. Pondering another creative outlet, Churchill considered writing a play about the war. But journalism, which served his literary and personal reputations well, remained his top priority for the moment. One army officer, in a personal letter, singled Churchill out among the many correspondents covering the war. "Winston Churchill is the one exception to the lot—he does go and see things with his own eyes and not through a long-range telescope, or through his ears."

The day after the cavalry entered Ladysmith, "the garrison reverted to a full half-ration of biscuits and horseflesh." Two days later, on March 3, Buller arrived with the rest of his army. A seemingly endless column of men, wagons, and guns paraded down the town's main thoroughfare beneath tattered Union Jacks hauled out for the occasion. Churchill, overcome by the scene and stirred by patriotic fervor, struggled to keep his emotions in check. The men looked worn and battered, their uniforms threadbare and their faces smeared with blood and dirt, but they marched with their heads high. "It was," Churchill noted, "a procession of lions." Lions with a grievance. In the wake of Ladysmith's deliverance, residents and soldiers expressed a strong hatred of the Dutch. Churchill railed against such attitudes in a letter that ran in both the *Natal Witness* and the *Morning Post*.

A wounded animal will still fight—and often pose a greater risk—when cornered. Men, Churchill opined, were no exception. While Britain was right to wage war with all its might and "remorsel[essl]y beat" those who stood against it, steps had to be taken to ensure the Boers could easily accept defeat. Only then would the struggle come to a timely end. The Boers were fighting in defense of their families and homeland—the strongest motivation for war that exists—and should not, Churchill warned, be pushed to desperation. The threat of punitive sanctions or a difficult peace would only convince the Boers they had nothing to lose by continuing the fight. Was the prospect of a bloody guerrilla war worth it to those in London demanding "an eye for an eye and a tooth for a tooth"? It would be a shame, he wrote, after all that had transpired in this corner of the world, for the ensuing peace to bear the ugly stain of racial hatred. A global audience focused its attention on South Africa. Churchill urged the Natal colonists and the soldiers of Her Majesty's Army not to let animosity and pettiness in victory overshadow the glory with which they had fought.

Here we see a glimmer of Churchill the future war leader, who, in victory, urged magnanimity toward Germany. At Casablanca in 1943, he would privately oppose President Roosevelt's proclamation that the Allies would accept nothing short of Germany's unconditional surrender. Churchill believed in 1900 that humiliating a defeated enemy only bred vengeance, as Versailles would prove in the not-too-distant future. In war he was a fierce opponent, but in its smoldering and desolate aftermath, he was a strong advocate of building the peace. "I have always urged fighting wars and other contentions with might and main till overwhelming victory, and then offering the hand of friendship to the vanquished," he later wrote. "Thus, I have always been against the Pacifists during the quarrel, and against the Jingoes at its close." The moral of his Second World War memoirs could easily have applied to the Boer conflict:

IN WAR: RESOLUTION
IN DEFEAT: DEFIANCE
IN VICTORY: MAGNANIMITY
IN PEACE: GOODWILL

Even as a young man Churchill was forward thinking and able to conceptualize the big picture. But just as his warnings about Germany were ignored in the 1930s, his calls to treat the Boers fairly met with widespread disapproval. The message did not go down well in England, where the Boers found little sympathy among an outraged public. Even the *Morning Post* distanced itself from its star correspondent's opinion. "From the military point of view, Mr. Churchill's opinion carries great weight," the paper opined, but

[w]e do not think the time has yet come to offer terms to the rebels. When the armies of the Republics have surrendered absolutely, rebels and belligerents alike will know what awaits them. There will be

nothing vindictive in the treatment they will receive. They will not even suffer the just punishment of their deeds. But at this moment to endorse the impudent and disloyal prophecy of Mr. Sauer* that the rebels would not be unkindly treated, would be to alienate, not only the allegiance of the loyalists in South Africa, but to strike with dismay the colonies which have with such splendid devotion stood by the Mother Country in her hour of need.

The response proved no better in Natal. The Boers had gone to war against Britain and invaded the Natal colony of their own free will, public opinion decreed. To show them mercy or extend the hand of friendship simply to end the war would only reward them for their treachery. Jack, also in Ladysmith after having recovered from his wound, wrote Jennie to let her know that Winston's views were proving to be less than popular. Many feared the Boers would simply keep fighting if they knew defeat would bring with it no punitive measures. If they had nothing to lose; they might as well continue to the bitter end. Churchill stood by his opinion, arguing, "Those who can win a war well can rarely make a good peace, and those who could make a good peace would never have won the war." Lifting the siege on Ladysmith effectively brought the conflict in Natal to an end. The Boers, busy retreating from the colony, fell back into their own territories. Churchill set his sights on joining the army of commander in chief Field Marshal Lord Roberts as it prepared to march through the Orange Free State, into the Transvaal ("the heart of the Boer territory"), and on to Pretoria. Desperate to witness what he believed would be the war's final and decisive campaign, he fired off a telegram seeking the necessary permission and hoped for the best.

Having secured a leave of absence from the South African Light Horse—but still holding onto his commission—he traveled by rail to Durban, the journey taking him past places forever burned into his memory. Staring out the window, Churchill realized he knew every

---

*Jacobus Wilhelmus Sauer was a liberal member of the Cape Parliament accused of supporting the Boer cause.

undulation and stream, every kopje and boulder. Only weeks before, men had died and bled in vast numbers on this ground, yet nothing remained to memorialize the struggle. How mundane these scenes of past battles looked—a deserted stage that had once played host to a great drama.

He boarded a boat at Durban called the *Guelph*, bound for East London. From there it was a two-day, seven-hundred-mile journey by rail to Cape Town, where he checked into the Mount Nelson Hotel. He thought the establishment possessed "all the luxuries of a first-class European Hotel without the resulting comfort." The food was subpar and the service lacking. The fact that no message from Lord Roberts awaited Churchill on his arrival only made matters worse. As each passing day failed to bring a response from the field marshal, Churchill's anxiety grew. Lord Roberts and Churchill's father had been very close friends until Randolph's death—a fact Winston hoped would serve him well. He began to wonder whether he had done something to offend Roberts or some other high-ranking official. In the days when newspapers provided the only means of informing the public at home of conflicts abroad, war correspondents enjoyed a certain status. Churchill, in the wake of his great escape, was one of the most prominent journalists in South Africa. It seemed strange that Roberts would not want someone of his caliber tagging along.

It was Churchill's good fortune to have two friends posted to Lord Roberts's headquarters in Bloemfontein. Generals Sir William Nicholson and Ian Hamilton informed him by telegraph that the obstacle to his plans was Roberts's chief of staff. This, most unfortunately, happened to be Lord Kitchener, not a great fan of Churchill's since the publication of *The River War*. Lord Roberts did not want to antagonize a senior member of his staff by bringing Churchill on board. Kitchener aside, Roberts had taken issue with a dispatch Churchill wrote on February 4, in which he blasted a lackluster sermon by an army chaplain the night before the battle of Vaal Krantz. Why was it, Churchill reported one soldier asking, that the medical profession will send its best men to the front to care for the wounded—but the wounded souls of men were left in the hands "of a village practitioner?" The church seemed to care more about converting savages in the distant corners of empire than tending to the spiritual needs of fighting men.

Churchill shrugged off Kitchener's sensitive nature and Roberts's desire to coddle the Church of England. What Churchill wanted, Churchill got. His two friends lobbied vigorously on his behalf. The result of their efforts was evident in a telegram Churchill received at the Mount Nelson Hotel on April 11 from Military Secretary Neville Chamberlain.* "Lord Roberts desires me to say that he is willing to permit you to accompany this force as a correspondent—for your father's sake." It was all Churchill needed, though he remained nonplussed. He had every right as a journalist to accompany Roberts's army. For the War Office to invoke Lord Randolph's memory and act as if some great favor had been bestowed showed a certain lack of class, to Churchill's mind.

He packed his bags, purchased a railway ticket, and was soon heading back to the front line.

---

*Not the future prime minister.

CHAPTER 14

Adventures and Escapes

Bloemfontein, Churchill wrote, was "a town of brick and tin" on the "apparent edge of a vast plain of withered grass." He arrived persona non grata in the eyes of Lord Roberts. Although Nicholson and Hamilton extended a warm welcome, Roberts maintained a cool distance. The close bond the field marshal had once enjoyed with Lord Randolph did not extend to the son. Churchill thought this petty behavior for a man of Roberts's stature.

He spent his first afternoon in town milling about the market square, "crowded with officers and soldiers listening to the band of the Buffs." Everywhere Churchill looked bustled with activity as men from every regiment and—seemingly—colony in Britain's empire enjoyed a brief respite from the slow grind of war. Soldiers haggled with vendors for a fair price, while the higher ranks milled outside the nearby officer's club and watched proceedings over the rims of their half-filled glasses. "One cannot see any gaps in the crowd," Churchill noted. "It is so full of animation that the spaces where Death has put his hand are not to be seen. The strong surges of life have swept across them as a sunny sea closes over the foundered ship." As he pushed his way through the packed square, a murmur of excitement rippled through the crowd. He turned and saw Roberts—a gray-haired man of diminutive stature with broad shoulders almost too wide for his frame and a back so ramrod straight it seemed infused with iron—strolling through the parting masses. Churchill snapped to attention but was annoyed when Roberts walked past, saluting by rote and paying him no more attention than a stranger. He did not waste time worrying about it; there was still a war to cover.

Churchill left Bloemfontein by train in the early morning hours of April 17 to join the British 8th Division, some eleven miles from the Boer-held town of Dewetsdorp. He reached his destination on the night of April 19 and joined a brigade led by his old 4th Hussar commander, Brigadier-General John Brabazon, charged with scouting the approaches to the town. On the afternoon of April 21, beneath a gunmetal gray sky, Churchill sat on horseback alongside Brabazon and watched the brigade fire on an enemy position. As the sound of rifle fire drifted across the veldt, Churchill and the general saw two hundred Boer horsemen racing toward a nearby hill. The sight riled up Captain Angus McNeil, commander of a scouting party, who approached Brabazon and asked permission to head the enemy off. "All right," the general replied, "you may try." McNeil, in a thunderous voice, ordered his men to mount and turned to Churchill. "Come with us," he said. "We'll give you a show—first class."

Several days before, over drinks and cigars, Churchill had promised the scouts that he would accompany them on one of their forays. At the time he thought of it as a throwaway comment—something said in the course of idle banter. McNeil obviously thought otherwise. Since a good reporter always goes in search of his stories, Churchill agreed to tag along. With a quick jab of spurs, the horses took off. As the party galloped across the plain, Churchill shot a glance in the enemy's direction and saw they were almost at the hill, their hard-pressed horses frothing at the mouth. There was no way, he thought, McNeil and his men would beat them to the summit. Churchill yelled as much to the scout leader, but McNeil simply urged his horse on.

The party charged up the slope and stopped 120 yards short of the summit, their progress blocked by a wire fence. Two scouts dismounted and started hacking away at the obstacle, desperate to make the crest before the Boers arrived. Churchill saw two Dutchmen materialize seemingly out of nowhere and take aim with their rifles. McNeil turned on his horse and ordered his men to make a hasty retreat. Bullets began to fly. Churchill, who had dismounted to watch the fence-cutting operation, reached for his horse.

The scouting party was well down the hill before Churchill even got his foot in a stirrup. His steed, skittish from the gunfire, did not wait for its rider and bolted. Churchill grasped at the animal, but to no avail. The horse left him in a swirling cloud of dust with no cover and no means of escape. Churchill, cursing his luck and his blasted horse, turned and ran for his life. In that desperate moment, his mind flashed back to the armored train and thoughts of captivity. He could hear the Boers behind him yelling, perhaps telling him to stop. He had always believed he was destined for greatness and that fate would see him through—but now he wasn't so sure. How many times could one man cheat death?

He had with him a pistol and would stand and fight as a last resort, but escape remained his primary aim. Rifles clattered behind him as he beat a furious retreat down the hill. At such close range, the best he could hope for was "a disabling wound." In an act of sudden deliverance, a scout on a pale horse—"Death in Revelations, but life to me"— galloped across Churchill's path. The man, trooper Clement Roberts, stopped and allowed Churchill to scramble onto the saddle behind him. Churchill reached around Roberts's waist and held tight to the horse's mane. Doing so, he felt something wet. He pulled his hands away and saw his palms glistening with blood. A round had struck the horse—but the animal carried on undaunted, the thundering of its hooves soon overpowering the sound of gunfire as the enemy receded in the distance. "Don't be frightened," Roberts told Churchill. "They won't hit you." No sooner had the words escaped his mouth, than he realized his horse had been struck. "The devils!" he roared. "But their hour will come. Oh, my poor horse!" The two men made the cover of another hill; Churchill grateful he "had thrown double sixes again." He turned to thank Roberts but found the man grieving for his injured horse. Churchill tried to console the fellow by pointing out that he had saved the life of another soldier. Roberts shrugged. "Ah," he said, "but it's the horse I'm thinking about." The next day, Churchill opined in a dispatch: "Whether I am to see the White Cliffs of Dover again I know not, nor will I attempt to predict. But it seems that my fortunes in this land are to be a succession of adventures and escapes, any of which would suffice for a personal experience of the campaign." Then, perhaps disingenuously, he added: "I acquit myself of all desire to seek for these. Indeed, I have zealously tried to avoid all danger except what must attend a War Correspondent's precarious existence. This I recognize as a necessary evil, for the lot of the writer in the field is a hard . and heavy one."

There were still several adventures to come.

On May 1, 1900, Churchill sent his mother a lengthy update from Bloemfontein on his recent escapades. "I had another disagreeable adventure near Dewetsdorp," he wrote, "indeed I do not think I have ever been so near destruction." He informed her he was joining General Ian Hamilton's eleven-thousand-man column, responsible for guarding the right flank of Lord Roberts's main army. Accompanying Churchill would be his cousin Sunny, the 9th Duke of Marlborough, a member of Lord Roberts's staff. As it so happened, Roberts had two other dukes on his staff—the Duke of Westminster and the Duke of Norfolk—prompting some snide comments in the press. By diluting Roberts's aristocratic burden, Churchill had done the field marshal a favor, resulting in a slight thaw in relations.

The long march to Pretoria began on May 1. Churchill equipped himself well for the adventure with a four-horse wagon boasting a hidden compartment beneath the floorboards. Into this space he crammed as many bottles of whisky and wine as he could, along with some tinned meat and other dry goods. The wide, open veldt still had the power to awe Churchill, who marveled at the endless sky and the dry, sunbaked landscape that stretched away to eternity. The plain was not immune to the ravages of war. An errant soldier, discarding a match or tossing aside a smoldering cigarette, on more than one occasion ignited a massive conflagration. Wind fanned the flames in a matter of seconds, smudging the sky with thick, black smoke; at night, everything glowed a pulsating red.

Wildfires and the possibility of a Boer attack notwithstanding, the column moved quickly across the veldt and seized one town after another. Through it all, Churchill began to think more frequently of home. "I have had so many adventures that I shall be glad of a little peace and security," he wrote his Aunt Leonie. "I have been under fire now in forty separate affairs, in this country alone and one cannot help wondering how long good luck will hold. . . . I stand the wear and tear pretty well and indeed my health, nerve and spirits were never better than now at the end of seven months of war." He was eager to ascertain public sentiment regarding his literary output and political aspirations. His writings had certainly bolstered his profile. A number of constituencies wanted him to stand in the next general election, including Oldham, scene of his first electoral defeat.

On May 12 Kroonstad, which the Boers had only recently established as their Free State capital, fell without a fight. They set up a new capital in the town of Lindley, which fell to Hamilton's men after a quick skirmish on May 18. Churchill rode into town with a taste for potatoes and sought out the general store. There were two such businesses—the biggest buildings in town, at which one could buy anything from a bottle of shampoo to a piano. Alas, they did not sell potatoes. A store clerk directed Churchill to the home of a local Englishman who might be willing to part with some from his own private stash. The gentleman, thrilled by the British Army's arrival, was more than willing to share his bounty. The town had long been awaiting its liberation from the Dutch. The man said the Boers had confiscated property, horses, food, and clothing for the war effort. They spread terrible lies about British barbarity, but no one in town dared argue the point out of fear of retribution. Expressing little enthusiasm for the other side, his allegiance to queen and country was underscored by the Union Jack flapping outside the front of his small-framed house. Churchill eyed the flag and wondered what the Boers might do should they return to Lindley and see it. He urged the man to take it down immediately, explaining that British troops would not be staying in town—they were merely passing through on their way to seize Johannesburg and Pretoria. The man appeared crestfallen, but there was little Churchill could do other than thank him for the potatoes.

Hamilton's column resumed its march in the predawn hours of May 20. In the morning's gathering light the Boers—observing from the hills around Lindley—watched the serpentine line of men, horses, guns, and wagons move out. The Boers stormed back into the town. They took cover in a number of houses and began blasting away at Hamilton's rear flank. Kindly old men who had welcomed the British as liberating heroes the day before took to their front porches with rifles in hand and fired with great enthusiasm. One of Churchill's colleagues, the war correspondent for the *Times*, had arrived in Lindley late the previous night and checked into the town's only hotel. He was asleep in his room when the manager barged in and alerted him to the fighting. The *Times* man wasted not a moment clambering into his saddle and beating a hasty retreat out of town. "History," Churchill dryly noted, "does not record whether among such disturbing events he retained his presence of mind sufficiently to settle his hotel bill."

The fighting continued throughout the day but did nothing to impede the army's progress. Six days later, on May 26, the army crossed the Vaal, the last natural barrier before Johannesburg. Roberts ordered Hamilton to cut off the main road to the west of the town. Along this road the Boers had entrenched themselves on a rocky ridge called Doornkop. On May 29 Hamilton threw two infantry brigades against the hill in a full frontal assault. That afternoon, before the attack commenced, Churchill lunched with Hamilton and the Duke of Marlborough. As the men ate their dwindling rations, Churchill pondered the ridge in the near distance and thought of Spion Kop, Hart Hill, and other recent bloodlettings of a similar nature. Although he would not actively be taking part in the battle, he was surprised to find his stomach twisted by nerves. At 3:00 the infantry marched forward to the sound of Hamilton's booming artillery. The Boers, sheltered among the rocks, survived the shelling relatively unscathed and set the tall grass on the slopes on fire. Churchill rode close enough to watch one brigade—the Gordon Highlanders—begin their climb.

Flames crisscrossed the brigade's path, choking and blinding the men with acrid smoke. Against the fires, the kilted Highlanders stood out in sharp silhouette. They looked, to Churchill, like phantom figures in a dream. The men slowly picked their way across the burning ground and soon reached a spot where the torched slope gave way to sharp, jutting rocks. It was here the Boers had entrenched themselves, holding their fire until they were sure of their targets. They allowed the Gordons to close within eight hundred yards before the shooting began. From where he sat Churchill could see the scene, illuminated as it was by fire and the flash of enemy rifles. Highlanders began to drop, but their advance continued. "Some troops might have checked," noted one witness, "might have, at least, thrown themselves down under for a few minutes . . . but this was not the fashion of the 1st Highlanders." The men pushed on, oblivious to their falling comrades, until they were fifty yards shy of the Boers' firing line. Here they fixed bayonets— the gleaming blades reflecting the colors of the burning hillside—and charged forward, eager to avenge their dead. The Boers fired frantically to try to stem the onslaught, but their efforts achieved little. The Gordons stormed the trench "shouting as only Highlanders can shout when the steel goes red."

The battle raged at close quarters until after sunset. The infantry, exhausted and with bayonets bloodied, dislodged the defenders from their rocky entrenchments and sent them reeling down the hill in a blaze of rifle fire. One of Hamilton's commanders decided to move his artillery to the captured ridge and invited Churchill to join him. The two men rode forward on their horses in search of a suitable place to position the guns. Smoke from the grassfire stung their eyes and veiled their surroundings, making it hard to see where they were going. Without knowing it, they rode straight past the Gordons and came within yards of the retreating enemy. Only when the smoke temporarily cleared did they realize their mistake. They were easy targets, as the sudden roar of gunfire seemed to attest. Bullets whistled past them with only inches to spare, prompting Churchill and his companion to retreat into the smoke and abandon their task. The *Morning Post*'s correspondent had survived yet another close call.

The sounds of battle gradually died away until "the chill and silence of the night succeeded the hot tumult of the day." Hamilton climbed the hill to address his men against the slope's fiery backdrop. "Men of the Gordons, officers of the Gordons," he bellowed, "I want to tell you how proud I am of you; of my father's old regiment, and of the regiment I was born in. You have done splendidly." One hundred Gordons lay dead on the slopes. The stretcher-bearers began their grim work. Churchill could see from his vantage point the flicker of lanterns moving about the rocks as the "body-snatchers" searched for the dead and wounded. He climbed the hill the next morning to observe the site of battle and jot down some notes for his dispatch. He stopped when he came to an outcropping of rocks beside which lay the bodies of eighteen Gordon Highlanders, arranged neatly in a row. Blankets covered their faces; their boots had been removed, exposing feet in gray socks. Churchill was accustomed to seeing the dead, but something about the scene struck him as particularly tragic and stirred in him a sudden flash of anger. He did not want to believe the war was being fought solely for control of South Africa's gold mines, but the idea seemed overpowering when—from where he stood—he could see chimney stacks belching smoke into the skies above the Rand, the gold-rich region of the Transvaal.

Hamilton's men buried their dead that morning to a slow dirge on bagpipes. Later that afternoon they captured a Boer train carrying troops and supplies. Churchill, curious, went to have a look at the prisoners. As he observed the men under guard, one captive approached and, in surprisingly good English, told Churchill he had taken part in the attack on the armored train that had resulted in Churchill's captivity. He knew how Churchill must have felt. Churchill smiled and said it was much better to be taken prisoner at the end of a war than at the beginning.

As the day progressed, Churchill began wondering how he would file his latest reports. Only a few correspondents had been present at the battle of Doornkop, and he wanted to get his copy to London and beat the competition. Reaching the nearest telegraph wires would entail passing through Johannesburg, still held by the Boers. The alternative was making an eighty-mile trek around the city. This also posed a problem for Hamilton, who was anxious to relay recent events to Lord Roberts. As the two men considered the issue, two cyclists pedaled by from the direction of Johannesburg. One of them—a French mining official named Lautré—stopped and chatted with Churchill. After a friendly exchange, in which Churchill explained his predicament, Lautré offered to escort Churchill through the city. The Boers, Lautré said, would most likely think nothing of two civilians on bikes. Churchill considered the Frenchman's offer and decided, with slight trepidation, to accept. Lautré's companion kindly surrendered his bike.

Churchill swapped his khaki uniform and slouch hat for a suit and cap from his travel case. Hamilton handed Churchill a dispatch to pass along to Roberts and wished him luck. Churchill and his escort set off. They avoided the main road into the city, which made the going tough. They traversed steep, rocky hills and patches of soft, sandy ground. If they were stopped for questioning, Lautré said, it would be best to address their inquisitor in French. It was Churchill's luck that he spoke the language, but he did so with a deplorable accent. Surely a Dutchman wouldn't notice. They entered Johannesburg, a dead city, at sunset. The place had the makings of a ghost town: deserted storefronts and houses with doors and windows boarded up. Fading daylight and lengthening shadows lent an extra weight to the grim atmosphere and magnified the city's despair.

The Boers, although evacuating, still lingered in considerable numbers. The situation wreaked havoc on Churchill's nerves. He was still an escaped prisoner of war with a price on his head. Now here he was, a commissioned officer in the British Army, dressed in civilian clothing while riding a bike through the heart of Boer country. The enemy would not hesitate to put him in front of a firing squad if he were captured. An uncomfortable encounter ensued when a Dutchman on horseback pulled up alongside the two cyclists and kept pace with them for what, to Churchill, seemed an eternity. He felt the blood drain from his cheeks and thanked providence for the day's failing light. The horseman had an unpleasant look about him—at least in Churchill's opinion. His face was gaunt and pallid and all sharp angles; his eyes looked cold and lifeless beneath the wide brim of a slouch hat. Churchill did his utmost not to pedal any faster and felt self-conscious in his effort to appear normal. The horseman continued to shadow the two men until he abruptly turned down a side street. Churchill and Lautré soon reached the British lines on the southern edge of town and refreshed themselves with whisky and water before resuming their ride.

They stopped briefly in the town of Germiston, downed a quick meal, and sent off Churchill's dispatches before arriving at Roberts's camp two miles out. The general had just finished dinner when Churchill made his appearance and presented Hamilton's report. Roberts read it with interest and eyed the dusty, disheveled figure in front of him. How, Roberts wanted to know, had Churchill made it through Johannesburg? When Churchill finished telling him, Roberts flashed an approving smile.

Churchill and Lautré spent the night at headquarters before parting ways the next day, May 31. Johannesburg officially surrendered at 11:00 that morning. The Boers sought a twenty-four-hour armistice to withdraw their army in exchange for leaving the region's gold mines in working order. Roberts, seeing no reason why not, consented. "It was probably," notes one historian, "the most serious strategic mistake of his career." It allowed the Boers to hold on to their vital implements of war: artillery, wagons, horses, ammunition, and currency. The local bank was emptied of all its gold. Roberts could have brought the war to a close then and there, but his concern for the mines would "extend the fighting by nearly two years of dismal guerilla warfare."

By June 4 the British had reached the outskirts of Pretoria. Roberts's artillery bombarded the Boer forts on the fringes of the city. The rumbling of big guns rolled across the veldt, but the enemy armaments remained silent. As in Johannesburg, the Boers had little intention of putting up any stiff resistance. The British Army marching on Pretoria numbered some 200,000 men—a numerical superiority the Boers could not hope to match. Churchill, anticipating a tough battle, was let down by the anticlimax but set about creating his own excitement. He wanted to be among the first to enter the city where, six months before, he had languished as a prisoner. At first light on June 5 he and Sunny rode to the front of the lines and marched into Pretoria with the advance guard. Churchill and his cousin galloped ahead of the army to see if the Boers had relocated their prisoners of war. In the course of their search they came across a Dutchman on horseback who agreed to lead them to the prison camp. A short ride brought them to "a long tin building surrounded by a dense wire entanglement." Churchill waved his hat in the air and let loose a celebratory yell. What happened next is captured in the journal entry of a prisoner:

> Presently, at about half-past eight, two figures in khaki came round the corner, crossed the little brook and galloped towards us. Were they Boers come to order our removal?—the advance scouts, perhaps, of a commando to enforce order!—or were they our friends at last? Yes, thank God! One of the horsemen raised his hat and cheered. There was a wild rush across the enclosure, hoarse discordant yells, and the prisoners tore like mad-men to welcome the first of their deliverers. Who should I see on reaching the gate but Churchill, who, with his cousin, the Duke of Marlborough, had galloped on in front of the army to bring us the good tidings. It is impossible to describe our feelings on being freed. I can scarcely believe it, after seven months' imprisonment, the joy nearly made up for all our former troubles, and, besides, the war is not yet over.

Some guards accepted defeat and dropped their weapons; others, who hesitated, had their rifles snatched away by jubilant prisoners. The Transvaal flag, flapping on a pole in the prison compound, was lowered, and a Union Jack—made by a British officer in captivity—took its place in the sharp morning breeze. The liberated men—all 168 of them—roared their approval. Churchill recorded the time in his *Morning Post* dispatch as 8:47. The camp's commandant surrendered himself and his fifty-two guards to the Duke of Marlborough, dressed splendidly—Churchill later recalled—and wearing red staff tabs. It all proved to be a civil affair, with the duke going so far as to give a receipt to the commandant for the confiscated rifles. The liberated took over the compound and marched their one-time overseers into a "wire cage." Some five hours later—at two o'clock—Lord Roberts entered Pretoria and hoisted the Union Jack above the town's main government building. "The victorious army then began to parade past it," Churchill reported. "For three hours the broad river of steel and khaki flowed unceasingly, and the townfolk gazed in awe and wonder at those majestic soldiers, whose discipline neither perils nor hardships had disturbed, whose relentless march no obstacles could prevent."

Churchill filed his article from Pretoria on June 8. The following day he sent a letter to his mother telling her of his intention to come home. The start of his journey would be delayed, however, as the Boers had severed the railway line out of the city. Nevertheless, he was most anxious to return to England, build upon his burgeoning literary career, and get back into politics. He also hoped to marry Pamela Plowden.

His new book, *From London to Ladysmith*, a collection of his first twenty-two South African dispatches for the *Morning Post*, had arrived in stores on May 15. By age twenty-five, Churchill had seen action in four military campaigns and published three best-selling works of nonfiction and a novel, an impressive feat by any standards, but one that for Churchill was simply a matter of course. His father's death at age forty-five had convinced Churchill that he, too, would die young. On the occasion of his twenty-fifth birthday the previous November, while still a prisoner, he had penned a letter to Bourke Cockran in New York. "I am 25 today," he wrote, "it is terrible to think how little time remains!" Certainly in South Africa he had experienced and endured more than most men do in a lifetime—but the continent was not done with him yet.

It became obvious to the British within days of capturing Pretoria that the Boers had no intention of surrendering. The immediate concern was whether they would attempt to retake the town. An army of four thousand Boers and twenty-five field guns entrenched "along a high line of steep and often precipitous hills" fifteen miles to the east caused Roberts considerable unease. It was therefore no surprise when he ordered his troops to rid the "Diamond Hill plateau"—bisected by the main railway line in and out of Pretoria—of the enemy scourge.

It was not a pleasant prospect. As many of Roberts's war-weary men knew, dislodging the Boers from a hilltop position would be a hellacious undertaking.

On the morning of June 11, fourteen thousand British soldiers marched once more into harm's way. Churchill rode with Ian Hamilton's men. In his dispatch dated June 14, Churchill provides a vivid account of the battle, noting how the Boer artillery began shelling the advancing British and how, over the next two days, through a grueling action, "the country round Pretoria for forty miles was cleared of the Boers." What he fails to mention is his own daring exploit, which helped secure victory. Not until 1944, when Ian Hamilton published his memoirs, *Listening for the Drums*, did Churchill's bravado become public knowledge. "Winston," Hamilton wrote, "gave the embattled hosts at Diamond Hill an exhibition of conspicuous gallantry (the phrase often used in recommendations for the [Victoria Cross]) for which he has never received full credit." Courage was the attribute Churchill most admired in men. "Men and kings must be judged in the testing moments of their lives," he would later write. "Courage is rightly esteemed the first of human qualities because, as has been said, it is the quality which guarantees all others." Churchill's legacy is rooted in his moral courage, but he was equally courageous in body and spirit.

Hamilton positioned his men and guns "opposite and below a grassy mound, bare of rocks or trees, not unlike our own South Downs where they meet the sea." The Boers occupied the crest of the mound. "The key to the battlefield," Hamilton noted, "lay on the summit but nobody knew it until Winston, who had been attached to my column by the high command, somehow managed to give me the slip and climb this mountain, most of it being dead ground to the Boers lining the crestline as they had to keep their heads down owing to our heavy gunfire." Hamilton's account continues:

> He climbed this mountain as our scouts were trained to climb on the Indian frontier and ensconced himself in a niche not much more than a pistol shot directly below the Boer commandos—no mean feat of

arms in broad daylight and showing a fine trust in the accuracy of our own guns. Had even half a dozen of the Burghers run twenty yards over the brow they could have knocked him off his perch with a volley of stones. Thus it was that from his lofty perch Winston had the nerve to signal me, if I remember right, with his handkerchief on a stick, that if I could only manage to gallop up at the head of my mounted infantry we ought to be able to rush this summit.

Hamilton's forces swarmed up the hill's southern slope. Churchill, perched in his crevice, had a front-row seat to the ensuing action. British artillery, dragged up the hill and placed less than two thousand yards from the fighting, roared to life and pummeled the summit. The onslaught prompted the Boers to vacate the hilltop and abandon the plateau in its entirety that night under the cover darkness. The British, having lost 180 men, proclaimed victory on the morning of the thirteenth.

In his memoirs Hamilton referred to Diamond Hill as "the turning point of the war." This is debatable. Certainly it prevented the Boers from retaking Pretoria—but not until May 1902 would the conflict come to an end. Hamilton, impressed by his friend's "initiative and daring," tried to convince military officials that Churchill deserved the Victoria Cross—something for which Churchill had been lusting since his days on the North-West Frontier. Roberts and Kitchener, both of whom considered the son of Lord Randolph a glory hound and strongly disapproved of his reporting duties, thought him worthy of no such honor. He was, they said, only a "press correspondent."

Churchill returned with Hamilton's men to Pretoria and began preparations for his journey home. With the fall of Pretoria, he had seen the war through its major campaigns. Although plenty of fighting still remained, Churchill was ready to focus on other things. Saying farewell to the men he had served alongside was bittersweet. He watched early one morning as they again marched south, off to another battle, until they faded from view between a gap in the hills. The rust-colored dust cloud marking the army's movement gradually vanished on the breeze until there was nothing but the empty veldt. Churchill turned away and made one simple wish: "May they all come safely home." Two days later he began his own long journey back to England. With the blessings of his superiors—who may have been happy to see him go—Churchill purchased a ticket for Cape Town, boarded a train at Pretoria Station, and bid farewell to the war. The first two days of travel passed without incident.

Early on the third morning Churchill was breakfasting in the dining car on "a suitable meal of sardines, pickles, and whisky" when the train suddenly came to a halt. A railway bridge up ahead, a waiter informed diners, was burning. Naturally, Churchill decided to investigate and stepped outside into the bright glare of morning. Lowering himself onto the tracks, he saw great tongues of red and orange flame rising up in front of the train. Other passengers, including nearly a hundred soldiers, also disembarked and hurried forward to get a better look. They seemed amused by the whole thing, like holidaymakers enjoying a tourist attraction, and laughed merrily as they approached the burning expanse. The thirty-foot-wide bridge was nearly fully engulfed; fire danced the length of its track and was slowly eating away the supports. Churchill, deciding he didn't have much luck when it came to trains, again reflected on past events. As a correspondent always on the lookout for a story, the conflagration did not necessarily bother him—but as a man trying to get home, it drove him mad.

Through the smoke he saw "two dark horsemen" fleeing the scene and "sixty or seventy more approaching along the railway from the north." Turning to climb into the carriage and retrieve his Mauser, he heard the loud crack of an artillery piece. A shell tore across the top of the train with inches to spare and slammed into the earth mere yards from where Churchill stood. The "sightseers" who had disembarked only moments before to survey the inferno came scurrying back. Their curiosity apparently satisfied, they appeared most eager to be on their way. The engine driver, of the same mind, pulled the whistle and released the brakes. The train began rolling back in the direction it had come. A loud boom signaled another incoming shell, but it fell wide of the mark.

As the train slowly picked up speed, the two fleeing horsemen took aim with their rifles and opened fire. Churchill and other armed passengers leaned out the carriage windows and did likewise. The distance was such that neither side was in danger of hitting the other, but the cacophony of gunfire coming from the train seemed to dissuade the large number of horsemen approaching from the north.

The train retreated to Kopjes Station, named for the surrounding fortified hills, and the protection of its five-inch gun. With the line severed, there was little Churchill and the others on board could do but wait until army engineers repaired the bridge. They spent a freezing night on the train, which "was shunted several times during the night." Not even several heavy blankets could keep the cold at bay. Churchill woke before sunrise and stepped outside. The chill took his breath away, and the frost-covered ground crunched beneath his feet. Rays of early sunlight, absent comforting warmth, soon palely lit the eastern sky. All he could do that day was bide his time. Work on the devastated bridge did not begin until the evening. The major in charge of the reconstruction effort had helped build the railway line that supplied Kitchener's army in the Sudan. He and Churchill dined together that night on the train and discussed past adventures. Afterward the major invited Churchill to view the bridge work.

A large bonfire feeding off a junked railway carriage—and assisted by two gas flares—cast light on the damaged expanse beneath a frigid sky resplendent with stars. British engineers stood off to the side, barking commands at native workers, who scrambled about the damaged framework like spiders. Everything was movement and noise, from the myriad sounds of construction to the varying dialects of the men.

Churchill watched in amazement as the scene changed before his very eyes. Fresh wood appeared where once there had been charred wreckage, as men hammered and sawed, hauled and lifted. "A loud monotonous chant" seemed to drift down the tracks. Going to investigate, Churchill came across eighty Bantus carrying a massive log, some eighty feet long and two feet thick, on their shoulders. Churchill could only guess the immensity of its weight and watched in shocked admiration as the men moved slowly forward. They looked, thought Churchill, like a massive caterpillar. Despite the night's considerable chill, the men's skin glistened with sweat. They stepped to a steady rhythm established by a fugleman who, following behind, chanted a song to set the pace. The native workmen echoed the melody—sung in a language Churchill did not recognize—"with the most extraordinary earnestness and conviction." They set the log down near the shattered section of track and went back for another. The bridge was repaired by morning.

Churchill made his way to Honing Spruit Station and caught a train to Cape Town, where he learned *From London to Ladysmith* had so far sold eleven thousand copies, earning him £720 in royalties. In high spirits, he bid farewell to South Africa on July 7 and boarded the *Dunottar Castle* for England. Doing his best to ignore the ocean's pitching, and putting his two weeks at sea to good use, he completed the follow-up volume, *Ian Hamilton's March*, a collection of his remaining *Morning Post* dispatches. Churchill's reputation as a man of words was firmly established, thanks to his capture and daring escape. He left South Africa as a correspondent of international repute, riding not on the coattails of his father's name, but on his own accomplishments. His bank account, frustratingly barren for so long, bore testament to his success. The *Morning Post* paid him £2050—"the highest sum yet paid to a journalist for such work"—for his dispatches, while royalties from his books continued to mount. "I have about £4,000 altogether," Churchill wrote Jack. "With judicious economy, I shall hope to make that carry me through the lean years."

Before setting sail from Cape Town on the very boat that had brought him to South Africa the previous October, Churchill filed his final article, on June 28. "I make my bow to the reader," he wrote, "and bring these letters to a conclusion." For nine months he had done his best to convey the full impact of war, often writing "under a waggon, in the shadow of a rock, by the uncertain light of a lantern, or even sitting on the ground in the rain." He hoped his readers had gained a deeper understanding, not so much of war, but of the human element involved. The glory of empire was, after all, built on a foundation of blood. "If in this fashion," he wrote, "it has helped bring those who have borne the long anxiety at home into closer sympathy with their soldiers at the wars, I shall be content, and even be bold enough to ask the reader to dismiss me with a smile."

Into History

The white cliffs of Dover greeted Churchill on Friday, July 20. The *Dunottar Castle* docked that afternoon in Southampton. Churchill disembarked to none of the revelry that had met him upon his arrival in Durban following his escape. Not even his mother made an appearance, busy as she was with last-minute preparations for her questionable marriage to George Cornwallis-West, an army captain only two weeks older than Churchill. Lady Randolph's affairs were her own business; Churchill's mind was focused on the immediate future and capitalizing on his success. He set foot on English soil—according to the *Morning Post*—"bronzed and healthy, as full of energy as ever . . . looking none the worse for the exciting personal experiences which have fallen his lot."

Two days after his homecoming he sat down with a *Morning Post* reporter for an interview that "was continually broken by the arrival of telegrams congratulating him on his return from the war." He voiced his opinion on various matters, including the effectiveness of the bayonet and the superiority of the Mauser to other firearms. British victory, he warned, remained in the distant future. Although "the great operations are over," one would be mistaken "to think the war has come to an end." The Boer was a resolute and worthy enemy. "He is essentially a cavalryman," Churchill said. "He is a beautiful horseman, with a graceful seat, his body sways with every movement, showing his complete sympathy with his mount. Then, too, he is a scout, trained by nature in matters of reconnaissance." The Boers would continue to "fight until they are either killed or placed in some position in which further resistance is hopeless."

Churchill's political fortunes were vastly different than they had been before he went to South Africa. Although "eleven Conservative constituencies" wanted him as their candidate, his loyalties lay with Oldham. He arrived in town on July 25 to a raucous welcome. More than ten thousand people crowded the streets, waving flags and chanting his name. He dined that night at the local Conservative Club and was surprised, upon leaving at midnight, to find supporters still out in large numbers. The next day he addressed a packed house at the Empire Theatre. He discussed in detail British setbacks and victories in South Africa and recalled the pride he had felt in seeing the Union Jack raised above the government buildings in Pretoria. "Surely," he proclaimed to the cheering audience, "the people of England will never allow it to be hauled down again." The biggest ovation came when he detailed his escape and mentioned Dan Dewsnap, the Oldham local who operated the lift at John Howard's mine. "His wife's in the gallery," the audience roared. Mrs. Dewsnap stood up and took a bow, to the great joy of everyone present.

He took a break from politicking on July 27 to attend his mother's wedding in Knightsbridge, then launched himself back into the fray. He spent August traveling about the country, addressing large crowds and establishing his platform, stressing—among other things—the need for a strong military to counter future threats on the European continent. Addressing a capacity crowd at the Plymouth Guildhall on Friday, August 17, Churchill struck a prophetic note, saying that someday, perhaps in the not-too-distant future, Great Britain would face the real threat of invasion. How and from where this danger might emerge was impossible to tell, but it was vital the British people acknowledge the strong possibility of such an eventuality and that the government take steps to ensure a vigorous response to any foreign aggressor. Invasions, he warned, unlike men dueling with pistols, were not a thing of the past. People might find it hard to imagine a foreign army marching through British towns and villages, stealing food and possessions, using the slightest provocation to imprison citizens, killing indiscriminately, ordering residents about, and laying claim to whatever they fancied. In a world of civilized nations, people did not want to believe—could not believe—one country would inflict that sort of misery on another. The prospect of such a nightmare becoming a reality seemed beyond the realm of possibility.

The country could not delude itself, Churchill said, by thinking aggressive foreign powers harbored any moral reservations about invading another nation. Nor should the public take false comfort in believing other countries would rise in the wake of such a crime and come to the defense of the beleaguered. Britain had only itself to depend on. With his military service and recent adventures in the field, Churchill said, he knew a little something about war. "Heaven forbid I should pose as an expert," he said, "but I know enough to tell you this—that there are very few things in military administration which a business man of commonsense and a little imagination cannot understand if he turns his attention to the subject; and anyone who comes along and tells you the contrary is nothing better than a humbug." The speech would not have seemed out of place among Churchill's countless warnings about the growing Nazi menace three decades later. For a man obsessed with history, he always had one eye on the future.

Voters in Oldham went to the polls on October 1 and sent Churchill to Parliament by a slim margin of 221 votes—but it was victory nonetheless. Eleven days later, on October 12, his second volume of *Morning Post* dispatches, *Ian Hamilton's March*, was published to favorable reviews. In less than two months it sold 8,000 copies, "with a further 1,500 copies in the United States." Churchill, still eager to milk his popularity for all it was worth, launched an extensive speaking tour of not only Britain, but also North America. He arrived in New York City on December 8 aboard the steamer *Lucania* and stayed once more with Bourke Cockran.

On the evening of Wednesday, December 12, a wealthy audience packed the ballroom of the Waldorf Astoria hotel to hear the young war hero speak of his South African adventures. Mark Twain introduced Churchill. A fan of Twain's, Churchill was thrilled by the honor but grimaced when the novelist used his introduction to criticize the British. "Mr. Clemens, introducing the speaker, said Mr. Churchill knew all about war and nothing about peace," reported the *New York Times*. "War might be very interesting to persons who like that sort of entertainment, but he had never enjoyed it himself. . . . Personally, he disapproved of the war in South Africa, and he thought England sinned when she interfered with the Boers as the United States is sinning in meddling in the affairs of the Filipinos." Twain did manage some kind words in welcoming Churchill to the stage: "Mr. Churchill by his father is an Englishman, by his mother is an American, no doubt a blend that makes the perfect man. England and America; we are kin. And now that we are also kin in sin, there is nothing more to be desired. The harmony is perfect—like Mr. Churchill himself, whom I now have the honor to present to you." Churchill took the stage to polite applause. Although "he showed nervousness at first," he soon found his stride. "After alluding to the fact that he had already written a book about his escape from Pretoria," noted the *New York Times*, "he said he trusted that everyone in the audience would purchase a copy."

In Albany he dined with Theodore Roosevelt, the newly elected vice president, who in less than a year would ascend to the presidency following the assassination of President William McKinley. Whatever happened at the dinner table did not bode well for future relations, as Roosevelt conceived a long-lasting dislike of Churchill. He made no secret of his feelings, writing to a British politician in 1914, "I have never liked Winston Churchill." As both men were historians, authors, and adventurers, this might seem strange, but Roosevelt's daughter would attribute her father's animosity to the fact that he and Churchill "were so alike."

If Churchill's New York speech was a success, other appearances left much to be desired. He found himself on many occasions addressing mostly empty benches or audiences not entirely sympathetic to the

British cause. His discontent peaked in one particular city upon discovering that his tour agent had booked him to speak at a private dinner party. The guests took more interest in their cocktails than in the eloquent young man orating in the parlor. Things improved in Canada, where audiences proved more attentive and appreciative.

In Ottawa he stayed over Christmas at Government House—as, by sheer coincidence, did Pamela Plowden, long the object of his affection. She had kept the candle burning for him during his South African adventures, but their relationship had quickly cooled upon his return to England. Although he still cared deeply for her, politics and books remained his primary loves. Pamela, naturally, did not want to be a runner-up to Churchill's other interests. Their split proved amicable and they remained friends, although Churchill still harbored feelings for her. From Ottawa he wrote his mother that Pamela was the only woman he could see himself spending the rest of his life with. She, however, had no shortage of other suitors and would soon become Lady Lytton. All things considered, it came as a relief when his speaking tour drew to a close.

Although his American visit was not the great success he had hoped it would be, it wasn't a complete failure, for he left £1,600 (about £80,000 today) richer. He boarded the SS *Etruria* in New York on February 2, 1901, for the voyage home. England was a country in transition following the death of Queen Victoria on January 22. The Victorian era, a booming age of science, progress, and prosperity, had officially drawn to a close. She was buried the same day Churchill sailed out of New York harbor. He was not that saddened by the news and wrote his mother a letter in which his greatest concern was whether he should pen a note of congratulations to Victoria's son, Albert, now King Edward VII. Perhaps this is not surprising. Churchill, like England, was also in a state of transition. Upon his return to England, he would launch his parliamentary career. His life, from this point on, "was to be spent before the public eye."

Churchill took his seat in Parliament on Thursday, February 14, pledged his oath of allegiance to the new king, and delivered his maiden speech four days later. He dressed for the occasion in a frock coat and enjoyed the support of his mother and a number of aunts on his father's side, who sat in the Ladies' Gallery. He spoke for half an hour, starting at 10:30 that evening to a full house—an honor not accorded many junior members of Parliament—on the ongoing South African conflict. Among his key arguments, he blasted a proposal to install a military government in Boer country after the war. While he professed his deep respect and admiration for British officers, regarding them as the best in the world not only in terms of their fighting ability but in how they handled "native races," he saw nothing in their skill set to suggest they knew how to govern "civil populations of European race."

He also renewed his call for the magnanimous treatment of the enemy in the wake of ultimate victory. He hoped the British would pursue a policy making it easy for the Boers to accept surrender and disastrous if they continued to fight. He urged His Majesty's government to do its utmost to ensure the Boers and Great Britain had no cause for further grievances. He continued: "If the Boers remain deaf to the voice of reason, and blind to the hand of friendship, if they refuse all overtures and disdain all terms, then, while we cannot help admiring their determination and endurance, we can only hope that our own race, in the pursuit of what they feel to be a righteous cause, will show determination as strong and endurance as lasting."

In conclusion, Churchill raised the specter of his father, thanking the House for its kindness and attributing its generosity to the fond memories many in the chamber must have had of Lord Randolph. Churchill, the eventual master of the spoken word, had spent days rehearsing the address in front of a mirror—and for the most part, it showed. The *Daily Express* proclaimed that he had "held a crowded House spellbound," while the *Daily Telegraph* decided the speech had "satisfied the highest expectations." Other publications were more lukewarm in their appraisal, including the *Manchester Guardian*, which proclaimed that Churchill's delivery "forcibly recalled his father, Lord Randolph Churchill, but the hon. Gentleman did not show much trace of his parent's brilliancy in debate." Nevertheless, the paper conceded that the young parliamentarian "may develop well, but to those who remember the electrical effect of the father's maiden speech, the son's first plunge into debate was nowhere so high a flight."

Whatever the final judgment regarding that first speech, Winston Churchill's long political hour had struck. His time on the front lines had equipped him well for the hard knocks of parliamentary life, for conflict would be a recurring—and certainly the defining—theme of his political career. Unlike politicians today, he did not pander to popular opinion and made decisions based solely on what he believed to be right—even if he was spectacularly wrong. Four years after entering Parliament as a Conservative, he crossed the floor and joined the Liberal Party following a dispute over tax reform. His political ascendancy nevertheless continued.

In 1910, following stints as Under Secretary for the Colonies and President of the Board of Trade, he was appointed Home Secretary. Shortly thereafter—in October 1911—he became First Lord of the Admiralty and readied the Royal Navy for the coming war with Germany. The bloody carnage at Gallipoli in 1915 brought his tenure at the Admiralty to a disastrous end. Denied any meaningful role in the government thereafter, he went to France in January 1916 as a lieutenant colonel in the British Army to command the 6th Battalion of the Royal Scots Fusiliers. Initially wary of their new commanding officer, the men of the Scottish battalion soon developed a deep admiration for Churchill and his apparent fearlessness in combat. The irresistible lure of politics, however, drew him back to England in May. The following year saw him appointed Minister of Munitions. In the years immediately following the war, 1919–1921, he served as Secretary of State for War and Air.

In 1924, uncomfortable with what he considered to be the Liberal Party's increasingly socialist agenda, he retreated back across the aisle to rejoin the Conservative Party and became Chancellor of the Exchequer in Prime Minister Stanley Baldwin's government. He held the office until 1929, when the Tories lost the general election. He spent the following decade wandering in the political wilderness, giving voice to unpopular points of view from the Tory backbenches. He argued passionately against Indian home rule and backed Edward VIII during the abdication crisis, none of which endeared him to his colleagues.

He kept himself busy writing articles and books. In September 1932, while visiting the continent to research a biography of his illustrious ancestor, the 1st Duke of Marlborough, he spent three days in Munich. Germany was a nation in chaos, rocked by the Great Depression and still reeling from the staggering punitive damages levied by the Allies after the war. With unemployment rampant and riots in the streets, a fringe political party—the National Socialist Workers Party—was rapidly becoming a force to be reckoned with. Only three months earlier the party had "won 37 percent of the poll in the General Election." An acquaintance in Munich offered to introduce Churchill to the party's leader, Adolph Hitler. Churchill, harboring a keen interest in Hitler's rising political star, agreed to the meeting. Hitler, however, did not. "What part does Churchill play?" he said when asked. "He is in opposition and no one pays any attention to him." The two men never met.

Returning to England, Churchill was not only concerned by what he had seen in Germany but troubled by the demands it was making for military parity with France. Armed with a new cause, he began arguing against German rearmament in newspapers, on the radio, and in the House of Commons. A rearmed Germany, he warned, would plunge Europe once more into the abyss of war. In opposition to defense cuts at home, he argued that a militarily strong Britain was vital for ensuring the peace. His stance proved unpopular with the public and members of his own party, many of whom still held a grudge for his earlier political defection. Critics dismissed him as an alarmist and warmonger, ignoring the fact that he was urging the country to take steps to prevent another war. His cause took on a greater urgency when Hitler became German chancellor on January 30, 1933. The ensuing years would see the reinstatement of compulsory military service in Germany and a radical expansion of the German air force, all while Britain pursued a policy of disarmament.

Churchill was publicly ridiculed, both in the press and in the House of Commons, for his paranoia, but he stayed on the offensive. Many people mellow with age, but not Churchill. He still held firm to the tenacity of his youth and argued his case against Germany with dogged determination, shrugging off the opposition and staying true to what he believed was right. Certainly in his long career Churchill was wrong about many things, but not when it came to German rearmament. He spoke from experience, knowing full well the horrors of war from his years spent as a correspondent and his brief time on the Western Front. He slowly began making inroads, changing minds in the government and among the public. Nevertheless, the primary decision makers still shunned his views, even while Hitler showed more outward signs of aggression.

In March 1936 the German leader reoccupied the Rhineland in a clear violation of the Treaty of Versailles. Britain and France did nothing, nor did they act in April 1938 when he announced the unification of Germany and Austria. One month later an emboldened Hitler amassed troops along Czechoslovakia's border, finally prompting Prime Minister Neville Chamberlain to do something. He flew to Germany and met Hitler in September. The resulting Munich Agreement ceded the Sudetenland—portions of Czechoslovakia inhabited primarily by German speakers—to Germany. Chamberlain returned to England on September 30 and addressed a jubilant crowd outside Downing Street later that day. "My good friends, for the second time in our history, a British prime minister has returned from Germany bringing peace with honor," he said. "I believe it is peace for our time."

Churchill blasted Chamberlain in the House of Commons. "Do not suppose this is the end," he said. "This is only the beginning of the reckoning." In March the following year Hitler sent his troops into Prague and annexed the rest of Czechoslovakia. Six months later, on September 1, 1939, he invaded Poland. Britain, having guaranteed Poland's sovereignty, declared war on September 3. That same day Chamberlain—a man ill suited for the rigors of war leadership—appointed Churchill First Lord of the Admiralty. He remained in that post until May 1940, when a parliamentary vote of no confidence ousted Chamberlain following the German invasion of Norway. Britain needed a new leader, and there was only one man for the job.

On May 13, 1940, Winston Churchill addressed the House of Commons for the first time as prime minister. His ascent to 10 Downing Street three days earlier had, perhaps fatefully, coincided with Hitler's invasion of Western Europe. Hours before Churchill received the king's prime ministerial commission, German ground and air forces assailed Belgium, Luxembourg, and the Netherlands. The armies of Britain and France moved to counter the German surge, but enemy armor had by now punched a fifty-mile hole in the Allied line. With the situation on the continent nearing catastrophe, Churchill did not mince words. As a journalist on the front line, he had penned articles in the heat of combat, honing his command of the English language. In the desperate years ahead, it would prove to be his greatest weapon. "We have before us many, many long months of struggle and suffering," he told the House:

> You ask, what is our policy? I will say: It is to wage war, by sea, land and air, with all our might and with all the strength that God can give us; to wage war against a monstrous tyranny, never surpassed in the dark, lamentable catalogue of human crime. That is our policy. You ask, what is our aim? I can answer in one word: victory, victory at all costs, victory in spite of all terror, victory, however long and hard the road may be; for without victory, there is no survival. Let that be realized; no survival for the British Empire, no survival for all that the British Empire has stood for, no survival for the urge and impulse of the ages, that mankind will move forward towards its goal.

The speech exemplified the man: direct and unyielding, enamored by the grand sweep of history, a true believer in the greatness of empire, and a champion of noble struggle. Churchill, besotted with romantic notions of valor but hardened by the true barbarity of conflict, was forged in war. War had long stirred his ambitions and fueled his passions. His experiences as a war correspondent, more than any others, helped shape his complex feelings on the subject. His reporting taught him how to relate the battlefield experience to everyday people. He would use to his advantage what he knew of war to convey to the British public in Shakespearean tones the horror and glory of their most desperate hour. He had told his mother in a letter from the North-West Frontier that he believed he was destined to save the empire. With Great Britain now fighting for its very survival, he found himself in his element. At long last, history met the man.

Acknowledgments

The writing of this book presented some challenges that weren't necessarily foreseen when I undertook the project. For his patience and guidance, I have to thank my phenomenal agent, Roger Williams. He has worked tirelessly on my behalf and has offered wise counsel on more than one occasion. At Da Capo Press, I am forever grateful to Robert Pigeon for his enthusiasm, support, and the time and energy he invested in the manuscript. Without these two gentlemen, there would be no book.

I owe many thanks to Amber Morris, who guided the book with care through the production process, and to Sharon Langworthy for her wonderful copyediting.

On the research front, I am indebted to researcher Ana Ramos at the British Library, who helped me track down Churchill's war reportage in the *Daily Graphic* and *Daily Telegraph*. At the online British Newspaper Archive, the source of the *Morning Post* columns referenced throughout the book, I want to thank Amy Sell for giving me a chance to blog about my research on the archive's Web site. I would certainly be remiss if I didn't thank the esteemed Allen Packwood, director of the Churchill Archives Centre at Churchill College, Cambridge, for his help and advice. His colleague Anne Woodman showed amazing patience in putting up with countless requests.

I am very grateful to Lee Pollock, executive director of the Churchill Centre, for his wonderful support and kind assistance. Likewise, many thanks go to Richard Langworth, CBE, editor of the Churchill journal *Finest Hour*, for his help when needed.

Anyone who writes about Sir Winston Churchill owes an amazing debt of gratitude to the man's official biographer, Sir Martin Gilbert, who sadly passed away during the writing of this book. His eight-volume biography—and its companion volumes of source documents—is a treasured resource. The thanks past and future Churchill biographers owe the man are beyond measure.

On the personal side of things, I want to thank all the usual suspects. My parents, Bill and Susan, have been tireless in their support over these many years. I am fully aware of how much I lucked out in the Mom-and-Dad Department. Love and thanks also go to my sister Sarah, a talented artist. I'm drinking a scotch as I write this and now hoist a glass to old friends—you know who you are. Sincere thanks go to Churchill's great-grandson, Jonathan Sandys, who offered very kind words of support during the writing of this book. And the same goes for Dean Karaynais, who cheered the project along with great enthusiasm.

Finally, it has to be said: I hit the mother of all jackpots when it comes to my wife. With unbelievable patience and understanding, Katie tolerated the long hours I spent locked away in my office. Countless evenings we could have spent drinking wine and watching reruns of *Breaking Bad* were sacrificed in the name of writing—or, as Katie calls it, "the other woman." As a partner, Katie is phenomenal in every way; as a mother to our two young sons, Spencer and Cameron, she is beyond extraordinary.

Katie, Spencer, and Cameron: I love you more than words on a page can convey.

Bibliography

Books

Best, Geoffrey. *Churchill and War*. London: Hambledom and Continuum, 2005.

Burleigh, Bennet. *Khartoum Campaign, 1898*. London: Chapman & Hall, 1899.

Churchill, Randolph S. *Winston Spencer Churchill*. Vol. 1, *Youth, 1874–1900*. Hillsdale, MI: Hillsdale College Press, 2006.

———. *Companion Volume 1, Part 1: 1874–1896*. London: William Heinemann, 1967.

———. *Companion Volume 1, Part 2: 1896–1900*. London: William Heinemann, 1967.

Churchill, Winston. *The Boer War*. New York: W.W. Norton, 1990.

———. *My Early Life*. London: Odhams Press Limited, 1949.

———. *The River War: An Account of the Reconquest of the Sudan*. New York: Skyshore Publishing, 2013.

———. *The Story of the Malakand Field Force*. Mineola, NY: Dover Publications, 2010.

Clarke, Peter. *Mr. Churchill's Profession: The Statesman as Author and the Book That Defined the "Special Relationship."* New York: Bloomsbury Press, 2012.

Coughlin, Con. *Churchill's First War: Young Winston at War with the Afghans*. New York: Thomas Dunne Books, 2013.

Danes, Richard. *Cassell's History of the Boer War, 1899–1901*. London: Cassell and Company, 1901.

Davitt, Michael. *The Boer Fight for Freedom*. New York: Funk & Wagnalls, 1902.

D'Este, Carlo. *Warlord: A Life of Churchill at War, 1874–1945*. London: Allen Lane, 2009.

Fincastle, Viscount, and P. C. Elliot-Lockhart. *A Frontier Campaign: A Narrative of the Operations of the Malakand and Buner Field Forces, 1897–1898*. London: Methuen, 1898.

Forbes, Archibald, G. A. Henty, and Arthur Griffiths. *Battles of the Nineteenth Century*. Vol. VI, *The Boer War of 1899–1900*. London: Cassell and Company, 1901.

Gilbert, Martin. *Churchill: A Life*. London: Pimlico, 2000.

———. *Churchill and America*. New York: Free Press, 2005.

———. *Churchill: The Power of Words; His Remarkable Life Recounted Through His Writings and Speeches*. New York: Da Capo, 2012.

Hamilton, Ian. *Listening for the Drums*. London: Faber and Faber, 1944.

Hastings, Max, ed. *The Oxford Book of Military Anecdotes*. New York: Oxford University Press, 1985.

Holmes, Richard. *In the Footsteps of Churchill*. London: BBC Books, 2005.

Jackson, Ashley. *Churchill*. London: Quercus, 2011.

Jenkins, Roy. *Churchill*. New York: Macmillan, 2001.

Johnson, Paul. *Churchill*. New York: Viking, 2009.

Jones, John Philip. *Johnny: The Legend and Tragedy of General Sir Ian Hamilton*. Barnsley, South Yorkshire: Pen and Sword Books, 2012.

Judd, Denis, and Keith Surridge. *The Boer War: A History*. London: I.B. Tauris, 2013.

Langworth, Richard, ed. *Churchill by Himself*. New York: PublicAffairs, 2008.

Lukacs, John. *Churchill: Visionary. Statesman. Historian*. New Haven, CT: Yale University Press, 2002.

Manchester, William. *The Last Lion: Alone, 1932–1940*. Boston: Little, Brown, 1988.

———. *The Last Lion: Visions of Glory, 1874–1932*. Boston: Little, Brown, 1983.

Martin, Ralph G., *Jennie: The Life of Lady Randolph Churchill*. Naperville, IL: Sourcebooks, 2007 (originally published by Prentice Hall, 1969).

McGinty, Stephen. *Churchill's Cigar*. New York: Macmillan, 2007.

Moorehead, Alan. *The White Nile*. New York: Harper Perennial, 2000.

Pakenham, Thomas. *The Boer War*. New York: Random House, 1979.

Paterson, Michael. *Winston Churchill: Personal Accounts of the Great Leader at War*. Cincinnati, OH: David & Charles, 2005.

Pearse, Henry H. S. *Four Months Besieged: The Story of Ladysmith*. New York: Macmillan, 1900.

Pemberton, W. Baring. *Battles of the Boer War*. London: Pan Books, 1969.

Raugh, Harold. *The Victorians at War: An Encyclopedia of British Military History*. Santa Barbara, CA: ABC-CLIO, 2004.

Romer C. F., and A. E. Mainwaring. *The Second Battalion Royal Dublin Fusiliers in the South African War: With a Description of the Operations in the Aden Hinterland*. London: A. L. Humphreys, 1908.

Royle, Trevor. *War Report: The War Correspondent's View of Battle from the Crimea to the Falklands*. Edinburgh: Mainstream Publishing, 1987.

Sandys, Celia. *Chasing Churchill: Travels with Winston Churchill*. New York: HarperCollins, 2003.

————. *Churchill: Wanted Dead or Alive.* New York: HarperCollins, 1999.

Singer, Barry. *Churchill Style: The Art of Being Winston Churchill.* New York: Abrams Image, 2012.

Thomson, Malcolm. *Churchill: His Life and Times.* London: Odhams Press Limited, 1954.

Toye, Richard. *Churchill's Empire: The World That Made Him and the World He Made.* New York: Henry Holt, 2010.

Woods, Frederick. *Artillery of Words: The Writings of Sir Winston Churchill.* London: Leo Cooper, 1992.

————, ed. *Winston Churchill: War Correspondent: 1895–1900.* London: Brassey's (UK), 1992.

Wrigley, Chris. *Churchill: A Biographical Companion.* Santa Barbara, CA: ABC-CLIO, 2002.

Wright, William. *Battle Story: Omdurman 1898.* Stroud, Gloucestershire: The History Press, 2012.

Newspaper Articles by Winston Churchill

Newspaper articles by and about Winston Churchill appearing in the *Daily Graphic, Daily Telegraph,* and *Morning Post* were collected from the British Library and the British Newspaper Archive. They are listed chronologically for each campaign.

The Cuban Campaign

"The Insurrection in Cuba: Letters from the Front—I." *Daily Graphic,* December 13, 1895.

"The Insurrection in Cuba: Letters from the Front—II." *Daily Graphic,* December 17, 1895.

"The Insurrection in Cuba: Letters from the Front—III." *Daily Graphic,* December 24, 1895.

"The Insurrection in Cuba: Letters from the Front—IV: The 'Battle' of La Reforma." *Daily Graphic,* December 27, 1895.

"The Cuban Insurrection: A Sombre Outlook—Fifth and Concluding Letter." *Daily Graphic,* January 13, 1896.

The Malakand Campaign

"On the Indian Frontier." *Daily Telegraph,* October 6, 1897.

"The War in the Indian Highlands." *Daily Telegraph,* October 7, 1897.

"The War in the Indian Highlands." *Daily Telegraph,* October 9, 1897.

"War in the Indian Highlands." *Daily Telegraph*, October 14, 1897.

"War in the Indian Highlands." *Daily Telegraph*, October 15, 1897.

"The War in the Indian Highlands." *Daily Telegraph*, October 26, 1897.

"The War in the Indian Highlands." *Daily Telegraph*, November 2, 1897.

"The War in the Indian Highlands: The Imperial Question." *Daily Telegraph*, November 6, 1897.

"The War in the Indian Highlands." *Daily Telegraph*, November 9, 1897.

The Sudan Campaign

"The Soudan Campaign: Anglo-Egyptian Force Nearing Khartoum." *Morning Post*, August 31, 1898.

"The Soudan Campaign: The War on the Nile." *Morning Post*, September 2, 1898.

"The Khalifa's Fight." *Morning Post*, September 5, 1898.

"The Fall of Omdurman." *Morning Post*, September 5, 1898.

"The Soudan Campaign: Khartoum Occupied." *Morning Post*, September 7, 1898.

"The Soudan Campaign: The War on the Nile." *Morning Post*, September 24, 1898.

"The Soudan Campaign: The War on the Nile." *Morning Post*, September 27, 1898.

"The Soudan Campaign: The War on the Nile." *Morning Post*, September 28, 1898.

"The Battle of Omdurman." *Morning Post*, September 29, 1898.

"The Entry into Omdurman." *Morning Post*, September 29, 1898.

"The Soudan Campaign: On the Road to Omdurman." *Morning Post*, October 3, 1898.

"The Reconnaissance of Kerreri." *Morning Post*, October 4, 1898.

"The Soudan Campaign: After the Victory." *Morning Post*, October 6, 1898.

"The Soudan Campaign: The Battlefield." *Morning Post*, October 6, 1898.

"Reflections of the Cavalry Charge." *Morning Post*, October 7, 1898.

"The Soudan Campaign: The City of Omdurman." *Morning Post*, October 8, 1898.

"The Soudan Campaign: Back from Omdurman." *Morning Post*, October 11, 1898.

"The Soudan Campaign: Civilisation Once More." October 13, 1898.

The Boer War

"Arrival and Situation: The Man Who Knew." *Morning Post*, November 27, 1899.

"With Headquarters: To Pietermaritzburg." *Morning Post*, December 6, 1899.

"With Headquarters: Cru[i]se in the Armoured Train." *Morning Post*, December 7, 1899.

"With Headquarters: Fate of the Armoured Train." *Morning Post*, January 1, 1900.

"The Invasion of Natal: A Time of Crisis." *Morning Post*, January 23, 1900.

"How I Escaped from Pretoria, and My Subsequent Adventures on the Road to Delagoa Bay." *Morning Post*, January 24, 1900.

"In the British Lines Again." *Morning Post*, January 27, 1900.

"With Headquarters: Christmas and New Year." *Morning Post*, February 5, 1900.

"With Headquarters: A Military Demonstration and Some Good News." *Morning Post*, February 6, 1900.

"The Dash for Potgieter's Ferry." *Morning Post*, February 13, 1900.

"The Passage of the Tugela." *Morning Post*, February 17, 1900.

"Five Days' Action at Spion Kop." *Morning Post*, February 17, 1900.

"A Week's Rest." *Morning Post*, March 5, 1900.

"The Combat of Vaal Krantz." *Morning Post*, March 10, 1900.

"On the Tugela." *Morning Post*, March 19, 1900.

"The Victory of Monte Cristo." *Morning Post*, March 27, 1900.

"Treatment of Rebels." *Morning Post*, March 31, 1900.

"The Battle of Pieters: The Passage of the River." *Morning Post*, April 7, 1900.

"The Third Day at Pieters: Attack of the Irish Brigade." *Morning Post*, April 10, 1900.

"The Anniversary of Majuba: Seventh Day's Action at Pieters." *Morning Post*, April 11, 1900.

"The Relief of Ladysmith." *Morning Post*, April 12, 1900.

"The Relief of Ladysmith: After the Siege." *Morning Post*, April 16, 1900.

"A Roving Commission." *Morning Post*, May 14, 1900.

"At Half-Way House." *Morning Post*, May 17, 1900.

"Exit General Gatacre." *Morning Post*, May 21, 1900.

"Two Days with Brabazon." *Morning Post*, May 28, 1900.

"Battle of Johannesburg." *Morning Post*, July 3, 1900.

"Concerning a Boer Convoy." *Morning Post*, July 12, 1900.

"The Capture of Pretoria." *Morning Post*, July 17, 1900.

"Action of Diamond Hill." *Morning Post*, July 20, 1900.

"Railway War." *Morning Post*, July 25, 1900.

Miscellaneous Articles

"She Is Now a Duchess." *New York Times*, November 7, 1895.

"Churchill on Cuba's War." *New York World*, December 15, 1895.

"The Burial of Hubert Howard." *New York Times*, September 9, 1898.

"The Battle of Omdurman." *Colonist*, October 21, 1898.

"Boers Wreck a Train: Churchill Is Missing." *Guardian*, November 16, 1899.

"Appreciation of Mr. Churchill's Services." *Pall Mall Gazette*, November 17, 1899.

"After the War: Mr. W. S. Churchill Interviewed." *Morning Post*, July 23, 1900.

"Mr. Winston S. Churchill at Oldham." *Morning Post*, July 26, 1900.

"Mr. Winston S. Churchill: Speech at Plymouth." *Morning Post*, August 18, 1900.

"How Lieut. Churchill Escaped from Boers." *New York Times*, December 13, 1900.

"Meanwhile: The Curious Case of the Severed Head." *New York Times*, April 3, 2007.

Other Sources

"Dr. Neufeld." *Appletons' Popular Science Monthly* 54 (November 1898–April 1899): 140–141.

Hansard Parliamentary Debates. H.C. 360 (May 13, 1940): 1501–1525.

"The Indian North-West Frontier Disturbances." *Dublin Journal of Medical Science* 106 (July–December 1898): 401–418.

Packwood, Allen. "How Young Winston Made and Wrote News." *Finest Hour* 152 (Autumn 2011): 16–21.

"The Reader: Winston Churchill, M.P., as a Man of Letters." *The Bookman* (July 1908): 133–138.

Online Sources

The Journals of the House of Commons 153 (February–August 1898). http://assets.parliament.uk/Journals/HCJ_volume_153.pdf.

"The Maiden Speech: February 18, 1901, House of Commons." The Churchill Centre. http://www.winstonchurchill.org/learn/speeches/speeches-of-winston-churchill/100-the-maiden-speech.

Russell, Douglas S. "Lt. Churchill, 4th Queen's Own Hussars." [Lecture presented in] Boston, October 28, 1995. The Churchill Centre. http://www.winstonchurchill.org/learn/biography/the-soldier/lt-churchill-4th-queens-own-hussars.

"The Second Anglo-Boer War, 9 October 1899–31 May 1902." South African History Online. http://www.sahistory.org.za/south-africa-1652–1806/south-african-war-1899–1902-second-anglo-boer-war.

Shonfield, David. "The Battle of Omdurman." *History Today Magazine* 48, no. 9 (September 1998). http://www.historytoday.com/david-shonfield /battle-omdurman.

Stott, Clement H. *The Boer Invasion of Natal: Being an Account of Natal's Share of the Boer War 1899–1900, as Viewed by a Natal Colonist.* S.W. Partridge, 1900.   http://www.angloboerwar.com/books/46-stott-the-boer-invasion -of-natal/1047-stott-chapter-viii-the-capture-of-pieters-hill.

"Whitehall, June 13, 1910." *London Gazette,* June 14, 1910. https://www .thegazette.co.uk/London/issue/28384/page/4172/data.pdf.

Notes

Sources are cited using the author's last name and the page number of the work in the bibliography that is being referenced. If an author has written multiple books, a short form of the title is included. Churchill's wonderful memoir, *My Early Life*, is abbreviated MEL. The official Winston Churchill biography—started by Winston's son, Randolph Spencer Churchill, and completed by Sir Martin Gilbert—is eight volumes long. Each main volume is paired with a companion volume(s) of primary source material, including letters, reports, memoranda, journal entries, and so forth. Letters referenced here were written by Churchill to family and friends and appear in the two companion volumes to volume 1 of the official biography. The main first volume of the official biography is cited as RSC. The companion volume 1, part 1, is cited as CV1/1-xxx; the companion volume 1, part 2, is cited as CV1/2-xxx (where xxx is the page number). References to letters include the date the letter was written. WSC stands for Winston Spencer Churchill. Citations to Churchill's published articles include newspaper title and date.

Prologue: History Calling

1 where the Hussars were barracked. RSC, p. 263.

2 ripe for the mining of gold and silver. *Daily Graphic*, December 17, 1895.

2 "The Pearl of the Antilles". MEL, p. 77.

2 given his rank . . . on February 12, 1895. CV1/1-557–558.

2 thrill of bullets missing him by inches. MEL, p. 76.

2 Cuba would be a dress rehearsal. MEL, p. 76.

3 "My dearest Mamma". Quoted in Martin, p. 339.

Chapter 1: In a Hurry

5 the baby was "wonderfully pretty". Manchester, *Visions of Glory*, pp. 107–108.

6 "part proprietor" of the *New York Times*. Jenkins, p. 6.

6 £50,000 dowry (roughly £3 million today). Coughlin, p. 6.

6 "the local parliamentary constituency for Blenheim". Coughlin, p. 6.

6 like a star, she remained distant. MEL, p. 5.

6 the defining influence of his early years. D'Este, p. 11.

6 in her that Winston confided. MEL, p. 5.

7 "to the delights of toy soldiers . . . ". D'Este, p. 14.

7 "the beautiful . . . Soldiers and Flags and Castle". Quoted in Gilbert, *Churchill: A Life*, p. 2.

7 "manly pursuits of riding, swimming . . . ". Russell lecture, 1995.

8 "He has no ambition". Quoted in Gilbert, *Churchill: A Life*, p. 6.

8 "Is a constant trouble to everybody . . . ". Quoted in Gilbert, *Churchill: A Life*, p. 6.

8 might prove beneficial to his son. D'Este, p. 19.

8 "His forgetfulness, carelessness . . . ". Quoted in Manchester, *Visions of Glory*, p. 158.

9 "defiant behavior, fights and disrespect . . . ". D'Este, p. 21.

9 "qualify him for a future commission in the infantry". D'Este, p. 36.

9 Randolph complained that Winston possessed. Lord Randolph to Frances, Duchess of Marlborough, July 5, 1893, in CVi/1-386.

10 cavalry were third-rate soldiers. Lord Randolph to WSC, August 9, 1893, CVi/1-390–391.

10 "I am certain that if you cannot prevent yourself . . . ". Lord Randolph to WSC, August 9, 1893, CVi/1-391.

10 He wanted to reduce military spending. Gilbert, *Churchill: A Life*, p. 12.

10 "I do not want to be wrangling . . . ". Quoted in Gilbert, *Churchill: A Life*, p. 12.

11 "He is so mad and odd . . . ". Quoted in Coughlin, p. 9.

11 imagined marching off to war against Napoleon. MEL, p. 44.

11 a most noble way to die. MEL, p. 45.

11 "eighth in a class of 150 cadets". D'Este, p. 41.

12 "one charger, three polo ponies . . . ". D'Este, p. 46.

12 seven months of summer training and five months of winter leave. MEL, 75.

12 with officers "receiving a solid block . . . ". MEL, p. 75.

12 the adventure would cost no more than £90. WSC to Lady Randolph, October 4, 1895, CVi/1-589.

12 were the only two people she had left. Martin, p. 339.

13 "little plans". Martin, p. 339.

13 "experience of life will in time teach you . . . ". Martin, p. 340.

13 founded the Primrose League. Martin, p. 147.

13 arranged for the Spanish minister of war. Sir H. Drummond Wolff to WSC, October 8, 1895, CVi/i-591.

13 provided maps and other useful information on Cuba. WSC to Lady Randolph, October 21, 1895, CVi/i-593.

13 He contacted Thomas Heath Joyce. Wrigley, p. 147.

13 Churchill and . . . Barnes set sail. WSC to Jack, November 2, 1895, CVi/i-595.

Chapter 2: Havana via New York

15 Waves pummeled the *Etruria*. WSC to Lady Randolph, November 8, 1895, CVi/i-595.

15 proud of being among the sturdy few. WSC to Lady Randolph, November 8, 1895, CVi/i-595.

15 fellow travelers . . . an utter bore. WSC to Lady Randolph, November 8, 1895, CVi/i-596.

15–16 "There is to be a concert on board tonight . . . ". WSC to Lady Randolph, November 8, 1895, CVi/i-596.

16 could not fathom ever wanting to travel by sea again. WSC to Lady Randolph, November 8, 1895, CVi/i-595.

16 invited Churchill and Barnes . . . to visit his courtroom. WSC to Lady Randolph, November 10, 1895, CVi/i-596.

16 treated the two young subalterns like royalty. WSC to Lady Randolph, November 10, 1895, CVi/i-597.

17 That both . . . classes could indulge. WSC to Mrs. John Leslie, November 12, 1895, CVi/i-598.

17 struck the Victorian Churchill as remarkable. WSC to Mrs. John Leslie, November 12, 1895, CVi/i-598.

17 pay his way across the Brooklyn Bridge. WSC to Mrs. John Leslie, November 12, 1895, CVi/i-598.

17 a cheap and unseemly form of currency. WSC to Mrs. John Leslie, November 12, 1895, CVi/i-598.

17 sharpest minds were in business. WSC to Mrs. John Leslie, November 12, 1895, CVi/i-598.

17 discussing . . . Cockran's enthusiasm for yachting. Martin, pp. 345-346.

17 did not admire . . . West Point. WSC to Jack, November 15, 1895, CVi/i-599.

18 tour several fire stations. WSC to Jack, November 15, 1895, CVi/i-599.

18 reminded Churchill of a rambunctious minor. WSC to Jack, November 15, 1895, CV1/1-600.

18 "without exception, the most magnificent . . .". *New York Times*, November 7, 1895.

18 cared little for American journalism. WSC to Jack, November 15, 1895, CV1/1-599.

19 found the food barely edible. WSC to Bourke Cockran, November 20, 1895, CV1/1-600.

19 a cramped carriage with the traveling masses. WSC to Lady Randolph, November 20, 1895, CV1/1-601.

20 killed by a firing squad. *Daily Graphic*, December 13, 1895.

20 encountered no signs of a rebellion. *Daily Graphic*, December 13, 1895.

20 insurgents exaggerated their gains. *Daily Graphic*, December 13, 1895.

20 puffed their way through several cigars. MEL, p. 77.

20 "not understand the delicious and tremulous sensations". MEL, p. 77.

21 through the towns of Matanzas and Cienfuegos. WSC to Lady Randolph, November 20, 1895, CV1/1-601–602.

21 concrete blockhouse guarded passage across every bridge. *Daily Graphic*, December 13, 1895.

21 the journey passed without incident. *Daily Graphic*, December 13, 1895.

22 would get no more than a few miles into the jungle. MEL, pp. 78–79.

23 "a process of deduction Sherlock Holmes might envy". *Daily Graphic*, December 17, 1895.

23 "an establishment more homely than pretentious". *Daily Graphic*, December 17, 1895.

23 the journey from Tunas to Sancti Spiritus. *Daily Graphic*, December 17, 1895.

24 a dismal slum overwhelmed by filth. *Daily Graphic*, December 17, 1895.

24 lurked some twenty thousand rebels. *Daily Graphic*, December 17, 1895.

24 admired the rebels' cunning. *Daily Graphic*, December 17, 1895.

25 They looked surprisingly fit. MEL, p. 79.

25 prove to be "awfully jolly". MEL, p. 79.

25   thrilled to be leaving Sancti Spiritus. WSC to Lady Randolph, December 6, 1895, CVi/1-603.

Chapter 3: Churchill Under Fire

27   could not think of one fellow. MEL, p. 80.

27–28   "I find the chief difficulty . . . ". *Daily Graphic*, December 24, 1895.

28   nearly two hundred rounds of ball ammunition. *Daily Graphic*, December 24, 1895.

28   be impressed by Spanish fortitude. *Daily Graphic*, December 24, 1895.

28   their morning siesta. MEL, p. 81.

29   he could extend his workday by two hours. MEL, p. 82.

29   the approach to the town . . . more exciting. *Daily Graphic*, December 24, 1895.

29   a smattering of houses and barns. *Daily Graphic*, December 24, 1895.

29   supplies to last them the next two months. *Daily Graphic*, December 24, 1895.

30   attached a similar value to their imperial holdings. MEL, p. 82.

30   smoldering campfires betrayed the rebels' movements. *Daily Graphic*, December 24, 1895.

30   Spanish troops attacked members of a Cuban reconnaissance party. *Daily Graphic*, December 24, 1895.

30   "destitute of floors". *Daily Graphic*, December 24, 1895.

30   no more than three rounds allocated to each man. *Daily Graphic*, December 24, 1895.

31   machete could easily . . . cut a rifle in half. *Daily Graphic*, December 24, 1895.

31   a relief to reach the town in one piece. *Daily Graphic*, December 24, 1895.

32   an outcome Churchill considered highly unlikely. *Daily Graphic*, December 24, 1895.

32   organized into the artillery and two squadrons of cavalry. *Daily Graphic*, December 27, 1895.

32   some measure of false comfort. MEL, p. 84.

33   reached the town of Lagitas. *Daily Graphic*, December 27, 1895.

33   four infantry companies were placed on guard duty. *Daily Graphic*, December 27, 1895.

33   fared no better in penetrating the blackness. *Daily Graphic*, December 27, 1895.

34 battling its way through thick vines and creepers. *Daily Graphic*, December 27, 1895.

34 biting into a bony chicken. MEL, p. 84.

34 missing Churchill's head by no more than a foot. MEL, p. 84.

34 the real dangers of his adventure. MEL, p. 84.

34 the massive palm trees that towered overhead. *Daily Graphic*, December 27, 1895.

35 bordered on three sides by the river. *Daily Graphic*, December 27, 1895.

35 "Of course . . . they had their rifles". *Daily Graphic*, December 27, 1895.

35 "shrill rattle" of the Spanish armaments. *Daily Graphic*, December 27, 1895.

35 vanished into the brush with their dead and wounded. *Daily Graphic*, December 27, 1895.

36 a measure of comfort in the rotund Spanish officer. MEL, p. 85.

36 laughing and mimicking the sound of gunshots. *Daily Graphic*, December 27, 1895.

36 "very lively for everybody". *Daily Graphic*, December 27, 1895.

36 a wide grass incline a mile in length. *Daily Graphic*, December 27, 1895.

37 above the rebel-occupied crest-line. *Daily Graphic*, December 27, 1895.

37 "out of all proportion . . . ". *Daily Graphic*, December 27, 1895.

37 "There was a sound in the air". *Daily Graphic*, December 27, 1895.

37 Spanish had merely seized a hill. *Daily Graphic*, December 27, 1895.

37 "It seems a strange and unaccountable thing . . . ". *Daily Graphic*, December 27, 1895.

38 It presented a delightful scene. *Daily Graphic*, January 13, 1896.

38 troops sat around several large bonfires. *Daily Graphic*, January 13, 1896.

38 "They were . . . fine infantry". *Daily Graphic*, January 13, 1896.

38 They rode small ponies. *Daily Graphic*, January 13, 1896.

38 "surrounded by palisades . . . ". *Daily Graphic*, January 13, 1896.

38 grateful for their kindness and hospitality. *Daily Graphic*, January 13, 1896.

38 After an adventurous two weeks. WSC to Lady Randolph, December 6, 1895, CVi/1-602.

39 adventure might have been reckless. WSC to Lady Randolph, December 6, 1895, CVi/1-603.

39 "a rough insurgent bullet". *New York World*, December 15, 1895.

39 watching Cuba fade from view. *Daily Graphic*, January 13, 1896.

39 Crippling taxes levied by Spain. *Daily Graphic*, January 13, 1896.

39 displayed true audacity on the battlefield. *Daily Graphic*, January 13, 1896.

40 viewed the rebels as thugs. *Daily Graphic*, January 13, 1896.

40 believed the island had a bright future. *Daily Graphic*, January 13, 1896.

40 "baptism of fire". *New York World*, December 15, 1895.

40 "trying to learn the name of the house . . . ". *New York World*, December 15, 1895.

40 "Of course the war isn't . . . ". *New York World*, December 15, 1895.

41 "how to whip the secessionists". *New York World*, December 15, 1895.

41 political intrigue as "nonsense". *New York World*, December 15, 1895.

41 "Churchill is not yet twenty-one years old". *New York World*, December 15, 1895.

41 "Rot!" *New York World*, December 15, 1895.

41 the rebellion would collapse by spring. *New York Herald*, December 19, 1895, CVi/1-621.

41 mass slaughter and total anarchy. *New York Herald*, December 19, 1895, CVi/1-621.

41 incapable of imagining colonies as sovereign states. Manchester, *Visions of Glory*, p. 231.

42 was most pleased with Churchill's work. Thomas Heath Joyce to WSC, January 10, 1896, CVi/1-623.

42 "Mr. Churchill was supposed to have gone . . . ". Sandys, *Chasing Churchill*, p. 28.

42 made no secret of his displeasure. Sir H. Drummond Wolff to WSC, February 17, 1896, CVi/1-664–665.

42 "revolutions would be periodic . . . ". Quoted in Manchester, *Visions of Glory*, p. 230.

42 "created much enthusiasm". Sir H. Drummond Wolff to WSC, February 24, 1896, CVi/1-665.

Chapter 4: Letters and Books

43 Churchill was allowed to live at his mother's house. MEL, p. 88.

43 Churchill enjoyed the festivities. MEL, p. 88.

44 "ten guineas a letter". Henry Norman to WSC, June 21, 1896, CVi/1-673.

44 Stories of . . . conflict saturated the newspapers. WSC to Lady Randolph, April 5, 1896, CV1/1-667.

44 Churchill decided he wanted to go there. WSC to Lady Randolph, August 4, 1896, CV1/1-676.

44 to pull some strings in his favor. WSC to Lady Randolph, August 4, 1896, CV1/1-676.

45 Lansdowne . . . said there was nothing he could do. Lord Lansdowne to Lady Randolph, August 11, 1896, CV1/1-674.

45 the voyage was much to his liking. WSC to Lady Randolph, September 18, 1896, CV1/2-679.

45 The food . . . didn't hurt, either. WSC to Lady Randolph, September 18, 1896, CV1/2-680.

45 awestruck by the canal's massive scope. WSC to Lady Randolph, September 30, 1896, CV1/2-682.

45 Men crowded the decks and gazed upon an exotic scene. MEL, p. 99.

46 they spent their second night roasting in tents. MEL, p. 100

46 Churchill hired a servant. WSC to Lady Randolph, October 4, 1896, CV1/2-684.

46 paradise for anyone who cared to be served. MEL, p. 101.

46 "nasty—vulgar creatures . . . ". Quoted in Coughlin, p. 106.

47 It was not a pleasant experience. WSC to Lady Randolph, October 14, 1896, CV1/2-688.

47 the temperatures were relatively mild. WSC to Lady Randolph, October 14, 1896, CV1/2-688.

47 installed in a pink-and-white stucco bungalow. WSC to Lady Randolph, October 14, 1896, CV1/2-688.

47 his surroundings now imbued him with the hope. WSC to Lady Randolph, October 14, 1896, CV1/2-688.

47 a few things to help him. WSC to Lady Randolph, October 14, 1896, CV1/2-689.

48 stalking the garden with a giant butterfly net. WSC to Lady Randolph, October 14, 1896, CV1/2-689.

48 "the serious purpose of life". Quoted in Martin, p. 362.

49 trotting about the place on horseback. MEL, p. 105.

49 "Now the station begins to live again". MEL, p. 105.

49 They played until sunset. MEL, p. 106.

49 and the efforts of the regimental band. MEL, p. 106.

49 in contrast to the United States. WSC to Jack, October 15, 1896, CV1/2-690.

49 dead specimens gave the place an unsettling atmosphere. WSC to Lady Randolph, October 26, 1896, CVi/2-695.

49 a nicer bungalow in camp. WSC to Lady Randolph, October 26, 1896, CVi/2-696.

50 hoped for a letter from home. WSC to Lady Randolph, October 26, 1896, CVi/2-696.

50 devoting up to five hours a day to reading. MEL, p. 110.

50 tackled four books simultaneously. WSC to Lady Randolph, March 31, 1897, CVi/2-746.

50 read to satisfy his intellectual curiosity. MEL, p. 107.

50 studying the quotations of educated men imparted wisdom. WSC to Lady Randolph, March 31, 1897, CVi/2-746; MEL, p. 114.

51 "to murder, mutiny, or rebellion". MEL, p. 112.

51 "Few writers stand the test of success". WSC to Jack, January 7, 1897, CVi/2-721, 722.

51 journeys of such length were the norm. WSC to Lady Randolph, October 26, 1896, CVi/2-696.

51 regiment played well . . . and . . . won the tournament. WSC to Lady Randolph, November 12, 1896, CVi/2-701.

52 the first English regiment to win a championship tournament. WSC to Lady Randolph, November 12, 1896, CVi/2-701.

52 the most stunning woman. WSC to Lady Randolph, November 4, 1896, CVi/2-697.

52 India was quickly losing its luster. WSC to Lady Randolph, November 4, 1896, CVi/2-697–698.

52 officers were told they could take three months' leave. MEL, p. 118.

52 every creditor in England would pounce on him. Lady Randolph to WSC, March 18, 1897, CVi/2-747.

52 would receive him with a warm and enthusiastic welcome. WSC to Lady Randolph, April 14, 1897, CVi/2-752.

53 India now failed to charm in every conceivable way. WSC to Lady Randolph, March 17, 1897, CVi/2-742.

53 he proposed traveling to the war zone. WSC to Lady Randolph, April 21, 1897, CVi/2-754–755.

53 He wanted £10 to £15 an article. WSC to Lady Randolph, April 21, 1897, CVi/2-755.

53 he received the disheartening news. WSC to Lady Randolph, May 26, 1897, CVi/2-768.

Chapter 5: The Theater of War

55 "Every influence, every motive . . . ". Churchill, *Malakand Field Force*, p. 4.

56 "giving out that he had been inspired . . . ". Fincastle and Elliot-Lockhart, pp. 28–29.

56 "in a storm of fanaticism". Fincastle and Elliot-Lockhart, p. 11.

56 "and they had hardly occupied . . . ". Fincastle and Elliot-Lockhart, p. 31.

56 "mostly Indian army troops". D'Este, p. 71.

57 "I hope so". MEL, p. 120.

57–58 air in the dining saloon . . . thick with heat. WSC to Lady Randolph, August 7, 1897, CV1/2-775.

58 contain himself as the steward distributed the mail. MEL, p. 121.

58 Churched watched with growing dismay. WSC to Lady Randolph, August 7, 1897 [footnote dated August 8], CV1/2-776.

58 life in the military would only mean disappointment. WSC to Lady Randolph, August 17, 1897, CV1/2-777.

58 as well as his dog. WSC to Lady Randolph, August 17, 1897, CV1/2-777.

58 "had a liking for words . . . ". Quoted in Manchester, p. 242.

58 The story, a political thriller. WSC to Lady Randolph, August 24, 1897, CV1/2-779.

58 "'Vehement, high, and daring' . . . ". "The Reader." *The Bookman* (July 1908): 136.

59 the greatest thing he had yet put to paper. WSC to Lady Randolph, August 24, 1897, CV1/2-779.

59 remained bitter about Blood's flagrant slight. WSC to Lady Randolph, August 24, 1897, CV1/2-779.

59 was disgusted at the general. Coughlin, pp. 120–121.

59 Blood said the only way possible. Sir Bindon Blood to WSC, August 22, 1897, CV1/2-780.

59 convinced his superiors to grant him a month's leave. WSC to Lady Randolph, August 29, 1897, CV1/2-780.

59 "situated on the India side of the Cabul River". Churchill, *Malakand Field Force*, p. 11.

59 "How far is it to Nowshera?" *Daily Telegraph*, October 6, 1897.

60 a testament to Britain's greatness. WSC to Jack, August 31, 1897, CV1/2-783.

60 the only way to build his political credibility. WSC to Lady Randolph, August 29, 1897, CV1/2-781.

61 British prestige was at stake. WSC to Jack, August 31, 1897, CVı/2-783.

61 "It is impossible for the British Government . . . ". Quoted in D'Este, p. 73.

61 with headless camels among its cargo. *Daily Telegraph*, October 6, 1897.

61 He caught a tonga. *Daily Telegraph*, October 6, 1897.

62 hard-hitting letters that painted in words. Lady Randolph to WSC, September 9, 1897, CVı/2-785.

63 tents on wooden platforms built into the hillside. *Daily Telegraph*, October 6, 1897.

63 the Bunerwals, a fierce Pashtun tribe. MEL, p. 124.

63 "Rumors run through the camp . . . ". *Daily Telegraph*, October 6, 1897.

63 possessions were auctioned off. MEL, p. 126.

63 Churchill found the whole thing quite morbid. MEL, p. 126.

63 acquire the necessary clothing and equipment. MEL, p. 126.

64 whisky had never been to his liking. MEL, p. 124.

64 a rough-and-tumble drink. MEL, p. 125.

64 no fleeting infatuation. MEL, p. 125.

64 an imposing figure against the mountainous backdrop. MEL, p. 128.

64 a fierce and fearless people. Churchill, *Malakand Field Force*, p. 5.

65 marching into "an unknown country . . . ". WSC to Lady Randolph, September 5, 1897, CVı/2-785.

65 might be dead by the time she read his words. WSC to Lady Randolph, September 5, 1897, CVı/2-784–785.

65 he wanted his name on each piece. WSC to Lady Randolph, September 5, 1897, CVı/2-784.

65 ("about £300 today"). Coughlin, p. 123.

65 "fertile plain" of the Lower Swat valley. *Daily Telegraph*, October 7, 1897.

65 "In spite of the shortness of the way . . . ". *Daily Telegraph*, October 7, 1897.

66 "The tribesmen cut through the walls . . . ". "*Daily Telegraph*, October 7, 1897.

66 including the Swatis, Bunerwals, and Mohmands. *Daily Telegraph*, October 7, 1897.

67 "Successful murder . . . ". *Daily Telegraph*, October 7, 1897.

67 "in a land of fanatics . . . ". *Daily Telegraph*, October 7, 1897.

67 He imagined them back home. *Daily Telegraph*, October 7, 1897.

67 "with firmness and without reserve . . . ". *Daily Telegraph*, October 7, 1897.

67 found it stark and depressing. Churchill, *Malakand Field Force*, p. 106.

67 the history of countless barbaric acts. Churchill, *Malakand Field Force*, p. 106.

67 "The dominant race". Coughlin, p. 178.

67 "cheery and good-humored" at the prospect. *Daily Telegraph*, October 9, 1897.

67 appeared "strained and weary". *Daily Telegraph*, October 9, 1897.

68 the stuff upon which empires were built. *Daily Telegraph*, October 9, 1897.

68 Sniper fire routinely pierced the nocturnal silence. MEL, p. 135.

68 let her know all was well. WSC to Lady Randolph, September 12, 1897, CV1/2-786.

68 Churchill saw a dozen tribesmen. WSC to Lieutenant R. Barnes, September 14, 1897, CV1/2-787.

68 Stanton demanded the natives stand up and salute. WSC to Lieutenant R. Barnes, September 14, 1897, CV1/2-787.

69 British troops considered the . . . sniping. WSC to Lieutenant R. Barnes, September 14, 1897, CV1/2-787.

69 would soon be escalating. WSC to Lieutenant R. Barnes, September 14, 1897, CV1/2-787–788.

69 and avenge their losses. Churchill, *Malakand Field Force*, p. 135.

69 join Jeffreys if he wished to see action. MEL, p. 136.

69 He rummaged through his trunk. *Daily Telegraph*, October 14, 1897.

69 "picked their way with care and caution". *Daily Telegraph*, October 14, 1897.

70 Churchill noticed "native beds". Churchill, *Malakand Field Force*, p. 135.

70 to catch up and take safety in larger numbers. *Daily Telegraph*, October 14, 1897.

70 "but they are still game". *Daily Telegraph*, October 14, 1897.

70 "You were lucky to be out of it last night". *Daily Telegraph*, October 14, 1897.

71 firing continued unabated for several hours. *Daily Telegraph*, October 14, 1897.

72 "long lines" of tribesmen. *Daily Telegraph*, October 15, 1897.

72　they began to descend the hills. *Daily Telegraph*, October 15, 1897.

72　Churchill could see puffs of gun smoke. *Daily Telegraph*, October 15, 1897.

73　"impelled by fanaticism". *Daily Telegraph*, November 6, 1897.

73　"Well-aimed volleys". *Daily Telegraph*, October 15, 1897.

73　surprised to find the place strangely quiet. *Daily Telegraph*, October 15, 1897.

73　scattered villages built of mud and stone. MEL, pp. 137–138.

74　"Like most young fools . . . ". Quoted in Coughlin, p. 186.

74　A withdrawal had been ordered. MEL, p. 138.

74　closed to almost spitting distance. WSC to Lord William Beresford, October 2, 1897, CVi/2-799.

74　Finding something to shoot at. MEL, p. 139.

75　the tribesmen did not take prisoners. MEL, pp. 139–140.

75　"utterly out of hand". WSC to Lord William Beresford, October 2, 1897, CVi/2-799.

75　grimy white bed sheets. *Daily Telegraph*, October 15, 1897.

75　overwhelmed by a strong and sudden bloodlust. MEL, p. 140.

76　drag a wounded man down the hill. MEL, p. 142.

76　Thirteen men . . . were sliced. MEL, p. 142.

76　continued to fall back under heavy fire. *Daily Telegraph*, October 15, 1897.

77　"the camp had been reduced to half its size". *Daily Telegraph*, October 15, 1897.

77　tents lay in discarded heaps. *Daily Telegraph*, October 15, 1897.

77　"two companies and the battery". *Daily Telegraph*, October 15, 1897.

77　their efforts only went so far. Churchill, *Malakand Field Force*, p. 151.

78　"their faces, drawn by pain and anxiety . . . ". *Daily Telegraph*, November 2, 1897.

78　"unsubstantiated fabrics of a dream". *Daily Telegraph*, November 2, 1897.

Chapter 6: Once More Unto the Breach

79　"vigorously continue operations . . . ". *Daily Telegraph*, November 2, 1897.

80　draped against a stone near a shallow pool. Churchill, *Malakand Field Force*, p. 161.

80 push forward with a new attack. *Daily Telegraph*, November 9, 1897.

81 nearly four hours of relentless enemy fire. *Daily Telegraph*, November 9, 1897.

81 writing such long pieces exhausted him. WSC to Lady Randolph, September 19, 1897, CV1/2-792.

81 trotting along the firing line. WSC to Lady Randolph, September 19, 1897, CV1/2-193.

81 England seemed a remote and distant concept. WSC to Lady Randolph, September 19, 1897, CV1/2-793.

81 admitted to feeling lonely. WSC to Lady Randolph, September 19, 1897, CV1/2-793.

81 ominous sound of drumming. Churchill, *Malakand Field Force*, pp. 162, 163.

82 Pashtuns . . . firing with impunity. *Daily Telegraph*, November 9, 1897.

82 with a wet smack. *Daily Telegraph*, November 9, 1897.

82 "the strength and majesty". *Daily Telegraph*, November 9, 1897.

82 the brigade lost sixteen men. *Daily Telegraph*, November 9, 1897.

83 a sight that was "horrible and revolting". *Daily Telegraph*, November 9, 1897.

83 spared his readers the gory details. *Daily Telegraph*, November 9, 1897.

83 "These tribesmen are among the most miserable and brutal . . . ". *Daily Telegraph*, November 9, 1897.

83 "badly mauled" in recent combat. Gilbert, *Churchill: A Life*, p. 78.

83 "I have put him in". Gilbert, *Churchill: A Life*, p. 78.

84 "'Maro' (kill), 'Chalo' (get on) . . . ". Coughlin, p. 203.

84 he mourned the loss of an exemplary character. Churchill, *Malakand Field Force*, p. 191.

85 The shells burst low above the village. *Daily Telegraph*, October 26, 1897.

85 from stretchers and blankets to mules and wagons. *Daily Telegraph*, October 26, 1897.

85 Their hair . . . dragged along the ground. Churchill, *Malakand Field Force*, p. 192.

86 "quite a formidable defense". *Daily Telegraph*, October 26, 1897.

86 light of the sun seemed to magnify. *Daily Telegraph*, October 26, 1897.

86 proving to be worthy adversaries. WSC to Lady Randolph, October 2, 1897, CV1/2-797.

86 he was enjoying himself. WSC to Lady Randolph, October 2, 1897, CV1/2-797.

87 "courage and resolution". Manchester, *Visions of Glory*, p. 258.

87 for every twenty tribesmen killed. MEL, p. 146.

87 Malakand Field Force never exceeded 1,200 men. Coughlin, p. 211.

87 "the Tirah region east of the Kyber Pass". Jackson, p. 60.

88 his time on the frontier qualified. WSC to Lady Randolph, October 21, 1897, CV1/2-805–806.

88 the excitement of life on the precipice. WSC to Lady Randolph, October 21, 1897, CV1/2-806.

88 dismayed to find his byline missing. WSC to Lady Randolph, October 25, 1898, CV1/2-811.

88 and "another stupid misprint". WSC to Lady Randolph, November 24, 1897, CV1/2-829.

88 Of his writing abilities, Churchill . . . had few doubts. WSC to Lady Randolph, October 25, 1897, CV1/2-813.

88 he decided to write a book on the campaign. WSC to Lady Randolph, November 10, 1897, CV1/2-824.

89 ready for publication by Christmas. WSC to Lady Randolph, November 10, 1897, CV1/2-824.

89 would rank as a great piece of literature. WSC to Lady Randolph, December 2, 1897, CV1/2-834.

89 dedicated at least five hours a day. WSC to Lady Randolph, December 22, 1897, CV1/2-839.

89 "Bullets—to a philosopher . . . ". WSC to Lady Randolph, December 22, 1897, CV1/2-839.

89 tired of writing. WSC to Lady Randolph, December 22, 1897, CV1/2-841.

90 agreeing to represent the work. A. P. Watt to Lady Randolph, January 7, 1898, CV1/2-852.

90 asked an uncle . . . to review the proofs. MEL, p. 153.

90 spent one horror-filled afternoon flipping. WSC to Lady Randolph, March 22, 1898, CV1/2-893.

90 an "idiot in an almshouse" would have. WSC to Lady Randolph, March 22, 1898, CV1/2-895.

90 Reviewers made note of the sloppy copyediting. MEL, p. 153.

90   without cringing with embarrassment. Jenkins, p. 32.

91   made nearly £400. Manchester, *Visions of Glory*, p. 262.

Chapter 7: The River War

93   "each capable of firing six hundred rounds a minute". Shonfield.

93   "ansars, or servants of Allah . . . ". Shonfield.

94   Sudanese had never given much thought to religion. Churchill, *The River War*, p. 20.

94   "in the name of Christianity". D'Este, p. 87.

94   naturally eager to join the enterprise. MEL, p. 160.

95   this glory seeker and self-promoter. MEL, p. 161.

95   only soldiers with at least four years' service. Lady Randolph to WSC, January 13, 1898, CV1/2-867.

95   urged his mother to exert her influence in all quarters. WSC to Lady Randolph, February 2, 1898, CV1/2-874.

95   wonderful to be back in London. WSC to Lady Randolph, June 1, 1898, CV1/2-942.

95   up to his neck in applications. MEL, p. 162.

96   "Get out my way, you drunken swabs!" Hastings, p. 310.

96   aware of Churchill's quest for glory. Best, p. 17.

96   launched a major charm offensive on all fronts. MEL, p. 162.

96   Salisbury greeted Churchill with a salute. MEL, pp. 162–163.

96   he had learned more from the book. MEL, p. 163.

97   if there was anything he could do to help. MEL, p. 163.

97   He wanted to be a witness to history. D'Este, pp. 92–93.

97   Not even Sir Evelyn Wood . . . could persuade Kitchener. Sir Evelyn Wood to Sir Herbert Kitchener, July 10, 1898, CV1/2-949.

97   The prime minister could do no more. Lord Salisbury to WSC, July 19, 1898, CV1/2-951.

97   temporarily attached to the Lancers. MEL, p. 166.

97   "Hope you will take Churchill". Gilbert, *Churchill: A Life*, p. 90.

98   if he died, he would send . . . message. MEL, p. 166.

98   Churchill caught the 11:00 train. MEL, p. 166.

98   He was attached to "A" Squadron. WSC to Lady Randolph, August 5, 1898, CV1/2-956.

98   a journey made by rail and paddle steamers. MEL, p. 167.

98   an exercise in organized chaos. *Morning Post*, August 31, 1898.

99   four miles an hour against a six-knot current. WSC to Lady Randolph, August 5, 1898, CV1/2-956.

99   the campaign would be a luxury. WSC to Lady Randolph, August 5, 1898, CVI/2-957.

99   This struck Churchill as overkill. WSC to Lady Randolph, August 5, 1898, CVI/2-957.

99   forced upon him was the food. *Morning Post*, August 31, 1898.

99   "shades of red and orange". Churchill, *The River War*, p. 3.

99   a realm of make believe. WSC to Lady Randolph, August 5, 1898, CVI/2-957.

100   imagine "awestruck worshippers". *Morning Post*, August 31, 1898.

100   asked the man if he had explored the temple. *Morning Post*, August 31, 1898.

100   "One idea grows steadily . . . ". *Morning Post*, August 31, 1898.

100   "It is the great waterway of Africa". *Morning Post*, August 31, 1898.

100   a fear he found impossible to shake. MEL, p. 167.

101   the general shrugged it off. MEL, p. 169.

101   "stretched their limbs". *Morning Post*, August 31, 1898.

101   could not fathom why any sane individual. *Morning Post*, August 31, 1898.

101   several "fresh steamers". *Morning Post*, August 31, 1898.

101   The ruins of the temple of Philae. *Morning Post*, August 31, 1898.

101–102 "the past looked down on the present . . . ". *Morning Post*, August 31, 1898.

102   begged those on board for alms. *Morning Post*, August 31, 1898.

102   people could live with so little. *Morning Post*, August 31, 1898.

102   "to hear about war and bloodshed". *Morning Post*, August 31, 1898.

102   Atbara, the army's railway staging point. MEL, p. 167.

102   until you see the campfires. *Morning Post*, September 27, 1898.

103   passed with no such sighting. *Morning Post*, September 27, 1898.

104   settled down for the night. *Morning Post*, September 27, 1898.

104   predawn hours "along the Nile". *Morning Post*, September 27, 1898.

104   "proclaimed him a man of some self-respect". *Morning Post*, September 27, 1898.

104   "fingers whose dark skin alone . . . ". *Morning Post*, September 27, 1898.

105   a bowl of sweet, dirty milk. *Morning Post*, September 27, 1898.

105   finally catch up with his column. *Morning Post*, September 27, 1898.

105   at a cost of six horses, every day. WSC to Lady Randolph, August 19, 1898, CVI/2-968.

105   far different from anything he had experienced. *Morning Post*, October 3, 1898.

105   any sign of the enemy. *Morning Post*, October 3, 1898.

106   the birds had gathered in anticipation. *Morning Post*, October 4, 1898.

106   "Khartoum in sight". *Morning Post*, October 4, 1898.

106   "an Englishman could have said that with truth". *Morning Post*, October 4, 1898.

106   a "shrewd and energetic man". Moorehead, p. 307.

106   "a retinue of eunuchs". Moorehead, p. 307.

106   "a straggling mud village". *Morning Post*, October 4, 1898.

107   what it was: the Dervish army. *Morning Post*, October 4, 1898.

107   believed to be the long line of zareba. *Morning Post*, October 4, 1898.

107   "other immense masses". *Morning Post*, October 4, 1898.

107   Churchill guessed the enemy horde. *Morning Post*, October 4, 1898.

107   single-shot Martini-Henry rifles. D'Este, p. 101.

107   "British and Egyptian army was advancing . . . ". Quoted in Jackson, pp. 66–67.

108   The enemy, Churchill explained. MEL, pp. 175–176.

108   Wingate . . . approached with an invitation. MEL, p. 177.

109   "a barbaric *fue-de-joie*". *Morning Post*, October 4, 1898.

109   "one man wounded and one horse killed". *Morning Post*, October 4, 1898.

109   blew the top of the dome to pieces. *Morning Post*, October 4, 1898.

110   tossed a large bottle of champagne. MEL, p. 179.

Chapter 8: Last Charge at Omdurman

111   signaling the day of battle. "The Battle of Omdurman," *Morning Post*, September 29, 1898.

111   "with an eager desire . . . ". Burleigh, p. 143.

111   breakfast of sausage, biscuits, porridge, and bully beef. "The Battle of Omdurman," *Morning Post*, September 29, 1898.

111   "Everything was in readiness . . . ". Burleigh, p. 144.

112   "melted away into the deserts". "The Battle of Omdurman," *Morning Post*, September 29, 1898.

112   "It was quarter to six". "The Battle of Omdurman," *Morning Post*, September 29, 1898.

112   like the sound of the sea. "The Battle of Omdurman," *Morning Post*, September 29, 1898.

112   "Allah el Allah!" Burleigh, p. 148.

112   he suddenly felt very insignificant. WSC to Ian Hamilton, September 16, 1898, CVɪ/2-977.

112   army "was drawn up in line". "The Battle of Omdurman," *Morning Post*, September 29, 1898.

113   fired blindly down the slope. WSC to Ian Hamilton, September 16, 1898, CVɪ/2-977.

113   took shelter among some large rocks. "The Battle of Omdurman," *Morning Post*, September 29, 1898.

113   Kitchener's artillery had unleashed a deadly salvo. "The Battle of Omdurman," *Morning Post*, September 29, 1898.

113   twenty shells fell among the enemy ranks. "The Battle of Omdurman," *Morning Post*, September 29, 1898.

114   willing "to die for Allah's sacred cause". "The Battle of Omdurman," *Morning Post*, September 29, 1898.

114   listened to the roar of artillery. WSC to Ian Hamilton, September 16, 1898, CVɪ/2-977.

114   "attended only by a small retinue". D'Este, p. 103.

114   a "suicidal frontal attack". D'Este, p. 104.

114   headlong into nearly three full infantry divisions. MEL, p. 184.

114   "ranged two deep in front . . . ". Burleigh, p. 141.

114   "Whatever happens we have got". D'Este, p. 104.

115   burst "into flame and smoke". Churchill, *The River War*, p. 273.

115   "They came very fast . . . ". D'Este, p. 103.

115   the men prepped their weapons. WSC to Ian Hamilton, September 16, 1898, CVɪ/2-977.

115   Churchill saw flame flicker from countless muzzles. WSC to Ian Hamilton, September 16, 1898, CVɪ/2-978.

115   in their blue robes and clouds of white smoke. MEL, p. 188.

116   a "long, dense white mass of men". "The Battle of Omdurman," *Morning Post*, September 29, 1898.

116   "The Dervishes stood their ground manfully". "The Battle of Omdurman," *Morning Post*, September 29, 1898.

117   clad in tarnished chain-mail armor. MEL, p. 190.

117   "bent double and remained thus". "The Battle of Omdurman," *Morning Post*, September 29, 1898.

117   "through a savage crowd". "The Battle of Omdurman," *Morning Post*, September 29, 1898.

117   "carried him through the Dervishes . . . ". "The Battle of Omdurman," *Morning Post*, September 29, 1898.

117 The man's face had been stripped. "The Battle of Omdurman," *Morning Post*, September 29, 1898.

117 "streaming with blood". *Morning Post*, October 11, 1898.

118 Dervishes falling back into line. WSC to Ian Hamilton, September 16, 1898, CV1/2-978.

118 whipped his horse into a gallop. WSC to Ian Hamilton, September 16, 1898, CV1/2-977.

118 Horses without riders ran aimlessly. "The Battle of Omdurman," *Morning Post*, September 29, 1898.

118 Lancers had lost 71 men. "The Battle of Omdurman," *Morning Post*, September 29, 1898.

118 ordered them to prepare for another charge. WSC to Ian Hamilton, September 16, 1898, CV1/2-979.

118 "prepared with constancy and courage for another shock". "The Battle of Omdurman," *Morning Post*, September 29, 1898.

119 as if someone had scattered large mounds of trash. "The Battle of Omdurman," *Morning Post*, September 29, 1898.

119 "bundles of dead grass". "The Battle of Omdurman," *Morning Post*, September 29, 1898.

119 "In the foreground lay a group of dead horses . . . ". "The Battle of Omdurman," *Morning Post*, September 29, 1898.

119 he could not recall any sound. *Morning Post*, September 29, 1898.

119 "of great personal charm and high courage". "The Battle of Omdurman," *Morning Post*, September 29, 1898.

119 a "dirty, shoddy business . . . ". "The Battle of Omdurman," *Morning Post*, September 29, 1898.

120 it was only half past nine in the morning. "The Entry into Omdurman," *Morning Post*, September 29, 1898.

120 felt little compulsion to show mercy. "The Entry into Omdurman," *Morning Post*, September 29, 1898.

120 would these "savages" have shown. "The Entry into Omdurman," *Morning Post*, September 29, 1898.

120 twenty thousand Dervish warriors consequently escaped. "The Entry into Omdurman," *Morning Post*, September 29, 1898.

121 "The scene . . . is a strange one". "The Entry into Omdurman," *Morning Post*, September 29, 1898.

121 crowded at the water's edge. "The Entry into Omdurman," *Morning Post*, September 29, 1898.

122 "The city presented some horrible sights". *Colonist*, October 21, 1898.

122 the dead had already begun to bloat. Churchill, *The River War*, p. 305.

122 presenting the general with keys. "The Entry into Omdurman," *Morning Post*, September 29, 1898.

122 Men, women, and children staggered from their homes. "The Entry into Omdurman," *Morning Post*, September 29, 1898.

123 "on a broad front". "The Entry into Omdurman," *Morning Post*, September 29, 1898.

123 learned of Howard's death. "The Entry into Omdurman," *Morning Post*, September 29, 1898.

124 "He behaved there so courageously . . . ". Quoted in "Dr. Neufeld," *Appletons' Popular Science Monthly* 54 (November 1898–April 1899): 140.

124 "I could just lift the shackle with one hand". *Morning Post*, October 6, 1898.

124 "make the fitting acknowledgements to Providence". *Morning Post*, October 6, 1898.

124 Kitchener's army buried its dead. *Morning Post*, October 6, 1898.

125 "Representatives of the Reuter Telegraph Company . . . ". *New York Times*, September 9, 1898.

125 "All right—Winston". Telegram from WSC to Lady Randolph, September 3, 1898, CV1/2-973.

125 "I raised my voice and helmet . . . ". *Morning Post*, October 6, 1898.

125 "Khartoum and be damned to it". WSC to Lady Randolph, September 4, 1898, CV1/2-973–974.

125 The whole thing . . . seemed almost unreal. WSC to Lady Randolph, September 4, 1898, CV1/2-973–974.

125 impossible to convey the horror and misery. *Morning Post*, October 6, 1898.

126 "the murderous tornado . . . ". Burleigh, p. 162.

126 bodies had bloated to grotesque proportions. *Morning Post*, October 6, 1898.

126 It was an exceedingly unpleasant thought. *Morning Post*, October 6, 1898.

126 underscored the futility of war. *Morning Post*, October 6, 1898.

127 "many scattered about the plain". *Morning Post*, October 6, 1898.

127 three horrific days for the Dervish wounded. *Morning Post*, October 6, 1898.

127 "Would you be further sickened . . .". *Morning Post*, October 6, 1898.

127 As pitiful as such displays were. *Morning Post*, October 6, 1898.

128 "he had drunk his drink first". *Morning Post*, October 6, 1898.

128 "Spare the conquered and confront . . . ". Gilbert, *Churchill: The Power of Words*, p. 400.

128 "There they lie . . . ". *Morning Post*, October 6, 1898.

128 The luster of war had dulled somewhat. *Morning Post*, October 6, 1898.

129 "officers and men of the 21st Lancers . . . ". *Morning Post*, October 7, 1898.

129 "did not greatly influence the fortunes . . . ". *Morning Post*, October 7, 1898.

129 "From the study of the men . . . ". *Morning Post*, October 7, 1898.

130 "destroyed and profaned" by British artillery. *Morning Post*, October 8, 1898.

130 One rumor he found particularly disturbing. *Morning Post*, October 8, 1898.

130 considered a "false" religion. *Morning Post*, October 6, 1898.

130 He had taken readers on a voyage. *Morning Post*, October 13, 1898.

131 "in these letters I have only tried . . . ". *Morning Post*, October 13, 1898.

Chapter 9: Literary Pursuits

133 what it felt like to be flayed alive. MEL, p. 194.

133 the doctor had a nice patch of skin. MEL, pp. 194–195.

134 would keep the coffers full. MEL, p. 196.

134 boat rocked violently for most of the voyage. WSC to Jack, December 6, 1898, CV1/2-994.

134 It remained his primary focus. WSC to Lady Randolph, December 22, 1898, CV1/2-995–996.

135 Churchill's dislike for Kitchener gradually revealed itself. WSC to Lady Randolph, December 23, 1898, CV1/2-997.

135 "General Officer" expressed umbrage. Letter to the Editor, *Army and Navy Gazette*, December 17, 1898, CV1/2-999.

135 Nowhere in his "daily life". WSC to the Editor, *Army and Navy Gazette*, February 11, 1899 (written January 8, 1899), CV1/2-1001.

136 "equally unworthy of a brave soldier . . . ". WSC to the Editor, *Army and Navy Gazette*, February 11, 1899 (written January 8, 1899), CV1/2-1001.

136 "Solitary trees, if they grow at all . . . ". Quoted in Woods, *Artillery of Words*, p. 40.

136 he fell down a flight of stairs. WSC to Lady Randolph, February 9, 1899, CVi/2-1007.

136 bells sounding the end of the match. MEL, p. 207.

136 involved vast quantities of wine. MEL, p. 207.

136 completed his discharge papers. WSC to Frances, Duchess of Marlborough, March 26, 1899, CVi/2-1015.

137 stayed at the Savoy hotel. WSC to Lady Randolph, March 30, 1899, CVi/2-1016–1017.

137 found the hotel's pens "horrid". WSC to Lady Randolph, April 3, 1899, CVi/2-1021.

137 He urged Churchill not to cater to popular opinion. WSC to Lady Randolph, March 30, 1899, CVi/2-1017.

137 a history of the Sudanese drama. MEL, p. 208.

137 spent his days revising proofs. WSC to Lady Randolph, August 16, 1899, CVi/2-1043.

138 "the Mahdi's head in a kerosene-can as a trophy". *New York Times*, April 3, 2007.

138 a "strongly cotton-dominated borough . . . ". Jenkins, p. 47.

138 why should a sore throat cost him. RSC, p. 446.

138 better care for the poor. Gilbert, *Churchill: A Life*, p. 104.

138 "through the withholding of public house licenses". Gilbert, *Churchill: A Life*, p. 104.

138 came in third with 11,477 votes. Gilbert, *Churchill: A Life*, p. 105.

138 "12,976 and 12,770 votes respectively". Gilbert, *Churchill: A Life*, p. 105.

138 "looked upon the process of counting with amusement". Gilbert, *Churchill: A Life*, p. 105.

138 *Daily Mail* wished to send Churchill to South Africa. RSC, p. 451.

139 Having . . . established the Republics. Thomson, p. 52.

139 "single biggest gold producer in the world". "The Second Anglo-Boer War."

139 "eventually topple Britain from its position". "The Second Anglo-Boer War."

139 countered with extremely generous terms. RSC, p. 451.

139 he put them in for repairs. Receipt printed in CVi/2-1052.

139 placed an order for 6 bottles of champagne. Receipt printed in CVi/2-1052.

Chapter 10: Churchill Restrained

141 an eternity in Churchill's opinion. Churchill, *The Boer War*, p. 1.

141 but incredibly boring. WSC to Lady Randolph, October 17, 1899, CV1/2-1055.

141–142 The Australians roared their approval. Churchill, *The Boer War*, p. 3.

142 clattering across the Great Karoo. *Morning Post*, November 27, 1899.

143 doing little to hide their disdain. *Morning Post*, November 27, 1899.

143 hoped Buller's arrival would soon turn British fortunes around. *Morning Post*, November 27, 1899.

143 "Even the rattle of the train". *Morning Post*, November 27, 1899.

143 with ten thousand corpses or more. WSC to Lady Randolph, November 3, 1899, CV1/2-1058.

143 confined Churchill to his cabin. *Morning Post*, December 6, 1899.

145 he found it boring. *Morning Post*, December 6, 1899.

145 Estcourt was not so much a town. *Morning Post*, December 7, 1899.

145 correspondents set up a small tent city. WSC to Sir Evelyn Wood, November 10, 1899, CV1/2-1058.

145 "a very puny specimen". *Morning Post*, December 7, 1899.

146 "a silent, desolate village". *Morning Post*, December 7, 1899.

146 several buildings that had been burned. *Morning Post*, December 7, 1899.

146 The soldiers seemed to relax. *Morning Post*, December 7, 1899.

146 clung to a ridge of low hills. *Morning Post*, January 23, 1900.

147 "They've had heavy fighting this morning". *Morning Post*, January 23, 1900.

147 Nearly every clash . . . proved an embarrassment. *Morning Post*, January 23, 1900.

147 waging war, "but an institution". Pemberton, p. 26.

147 tactics no longer suited for modern combat. Pemberton, pp. 26–28.

147 "since the muzzle-loading era". Pemberton, p. 27

147 "It is astonishing how we have underrated these people". Quoted in Gilbert, *Churchill: A Life*, p. 108.

148 a detachment of sailors from the HMS *Tartar*. Report by Captain Aylmer Haldane, CV1/2-1065.

148 withdraw at once to Frere Station. Report by Captain Aylmer Haldane, CV1/2-1065.

149 the Boers had let loose. *Morning Post*, January 1, 1900.

149 The collision was violent. *Morning Post*, January 1, 1900.

149   Churchill pulled himself up and climbed. *Morning Post*, January 1, 1900.

150   "What do they think they're paying me for". Paraphrased in *Morning Post*, January 1, 1900.

150   oversee the effort to clear the tracks. *Morning Post*, January 1, 1900.

150   "The working of the engine itself . . . ". "Whitehall, June 13, 1910," *The London Gazette*, June 14, 1910.

150   "Nothing was so thrilling as this". *Morning Post*, January 1, 1900.

150   "Churchill is a splendid fellow". Quoted in Gilbert, *Churchill: A Life*, p. 111.

151   "I would point out that while engaged . . . ". Quoted in Holmes, p. 63.

151   Haldane ordered his men to load . . . wounded. *Morning Post*, January 1, 1900.

151   "hold out there while the engine went for assistance". *Morning Post*, January 1, 1900.

151   yelled at them to keep fighting. Report by Captain Aylmer Haldane, CV1/2-1067.

152   "I can't leave those poor beggars to their fate". Sandys, *Churchill: Wanted Dead or Alive*, p. 53.

152   alone in a shallow ditch. *Morning Post*, January 1, 1900.

152   "When one is alone and unarmed . . . ". Quoted in Sandys, *Churchill: Wanted Dead or Alive*, p. 54.

153   "fifty-six unwounded or slightly wounded men". *Morning Post*, January 1, 1900.

153   "between thirty-five and forty". *Morning Post*, January 1, 1900.

154   loudly proclaimed his role as a journalist. *Morning Post*, January 1, 1900.

154   they caught the son of a lord. *Morning Post*, January 1, 1900.

154   "corrugated iron shed near the station". *Morning Post*, January 1, 1900.

154   struck down during the fight. *Morning Post*, January 1, 1900.

155   set off in a dirty and disheveled line. Churchill, *The Boer War*, p. 53.

155   observation balloon floating above the besieged town. Churchill, *The Boer War*, p. 53.

155   tent remained under constant guard. Churchill, *The Boer War*, p. 55.

155   playing with the breech bolts as if sending. Churchill, *The Boer War*, p. 55.

156 "[Mr. Churchill] set to work heroically . . . ". *The Guardian*, Thursday November 16, 1899.

156 "The railway men who accompanied . . . ". *Pall Mall Gazette*, Friday, November 17, 1899.

156 "Young Churchill, a newspaper correspondent . . . ". Packwood, p. 20.

157 "into a garden of chrysanthemums . . . ". Martin, p. 463.

157 "casts and orchestras". Martin, p. 463.

157 "accompanied by an escort of the Life Guards . . . ". Martin, p. 463.

157 "Lady Randolph Churchill looked in . . . ". Quoted in Martin, p. 464.

157 his injured hand succumbing to infection. Churchill, *The Boer War*, p. 57.

157 Churchill—ravenous with hunger. Churchill, *The Boer War*, p. 57.

157 captives leapt on the feast. Churchill, *The Boer War*, p. 57.

158 the fully loaded breech of his rifle. Churchill, *The Boer War*, p. 62.

158 decided patience would be the wisest course. Churchill, *The Boer War*, p. 62.

158 "ugly women with bright parasols . . . ". Quoted in Sandys, *Churchill: Wanted Dead or Alive*, p. 79.

158 he loathed the enemy. Churchill, *The Boer War*, p. 65.

158 to the State Model School. Churchill, *The Boer War*, pp. 66–67.

159 placed along the wall at fifty-yard intervals. *Morning Post*, January 24, 1900.

159 bought a dark-colored tweed suit. Churchill, *The Boer War*, p. 67.

159 Churchill was miserable. Churchill, *The Boer War*, p. 69.

159 Freedom haunted his every thought. Churchill, *The Boer War*, p. 70.

160 that Churchill "be guarded and watched . . . ". Quoted in Gilbert, *Churchill: A Life*, p. 113.

160 "Churchill is one of the most dangerous . . . ". Quoted in Paterson, p. 152.

160 to the border of Portuguese Mozambique. Gilbert, *Churchill: A Life*, p. 115.

160 Haldane decided on . . . Monday, December 11. Captain Aylmer Haldane's diary, December 11, 1899, CVi/2-1087.

160 "Churchill is in a great state of excitement . . . ". Quoted in Gilbert, *Churchill: A Life*, p. 115.

160 a state of "positive terror". *Morning Post*, January 24, 1900.

160 he . . . tossed the book aside. *Morning Post*, January 24, 1900.

161   Haldane told Brockie to go and see for himself. Captain Aylmer Haldane's diary, December 12, 1899, CVi/2-1088.

161   "it was full of people". *Morning Post*, January 24, 1900.

161   Fear . . . gripped Churchill. *Morning Post*, January 24, 1900.

162   wondering where Brockie and Haldane could be. *Morning Post*, January 24, 1900.

162   Churchill coughed into his hand. *Morning Post*, January 24, 1900.

162   "We can't get out . . . ". *Morning Post*, January 24, 1900.

162   "Mr Winston Churchill's publication . . . ". Quoted in Toye, p. 72.

162   Climbing back over the fence. WSC memorandum on escape, May 20, 1912, CVi/2-1096.

163   "only possessed the moral courage . . . ". Quoted in Toye, p. 71.

163   "I shall go on alone". *Morning Post*, January 24, 1900.

163   Churchill emerged from the bushes. *Morning Post*, January 24, 1900.

164   A wild surge of excitement washed over him. *Morning Post*, January 24, 1900.

164   "signal lights of a station". *Morning Post*, January 24, 1900.

164   He burrowed down among them. *Morning Post*, January 24, 1900.

165   got up slowly, shaken and bruised. *Morning Post*, January 24, 1900.

165   A massive vulture. *Morning Post*, January 24, 1900.

165   Details of Churchill's hiding place. *Morning Post*, January 24, 1900.

165   He dwelled on the futility. *Morning Post*, January 24, 1900.

Chapter 11: Dead or Alive

167   he left a steaming cup of coffee. Sandys, *Churchill: Wanted Dead or Alive*, p. 99.

167   "I have the honor to inform you . . . ". Churchill, *The Boer War*, pp. 78–79.

168   into the courtyard for roll call. Sandys, *Churchill: Wanted Dead or Alive*, p. 100.

168   fell on the commandant to inform de Souza. R. W. L. Opperman to L. de Souza, December 13, 1899, CVi/2-1088.

169   "Englishman 25 years old . . . ". Quoted in Manchester, *Visions of Glory*, p. 309.

169   make a "wide circuit". *Morning Post*, January 24, 1900.

170   spied soft yellow light. *Morning Post*, January 24, 1900.

170   He approached a railroad station. MEL, pp. 275–276.

170   the indignity of being unloaded with the goods. MEL, p. 276.

170 fires soon caught his eye. MEL, pp. 276–277.

170 Churchill dropped to the cold earth. MEL, p. 277.

170 to a psychic premonition. MEL, p. 277.

170 retreating back to the railway line. MEL, p. 278.

171 inquired who was there. MEL, p. 278.

171 he'd been in an accident and needed help. MEL, p. 278.

171 fell off a train. MEL, p. 279.

171 made a point of displaying the revolver. MEL, p. 279.

171 believed his . . . guest to be a Boer spy. John Howard's reminiscences, *Johannesburg Star*, December 11, 1923, CVI/2-1125.

172 opted for the latter. MEL, p. 279.

172 Howard . . . offered to help. MEL, p. 280.

172 led . . . to the entrance of a mine shaft. MEL, p. 282.

173 his triumphant return to British lines. MEL, p. 282.

173 would Churchill be safe from recapture. MEL, p. 284.

173 wake up to something tugging at his pillow. MEL, p. 284.

174 lit a cigar, and enjoyed a smoke. John Howard's reminiscences, *Johannesburg Star*, December 11, 1923, CVI/2-1126.

174 convince them the mine was not haunted. John Howard's reminiscences, *Johannesburg Star*, December 11, 1923, CVI/2-1126.

174 bales of wool would be loaded. MEL, p. 286.

174 He had come to take his freedom for granted. MEL, p. 286.

175 The sound of gunfire late that night. MEL, p. 288.

175 face-to-face with the terrified youth. John Howard's reminiscences, *Johannesburg Star*, December 11, 1923, CVI/2-1126–1127.

175 bribing him with a new set of clothes. John Howard's reminiscences, *Johannesburg Star*, December 11, 1923, CVI/2-1127.

175 left him a revolver, some bread. MEL, p. 290.

176 the inevitable frontier checkpoint loomed large. MEL, p. 291.

176 awoke the next morning to the train's gentle rocking. MEL, p. 291.

176 buried himself deeper beneath the sacks. *Morning Post*, January 24, 1900.

176 fired his revolver three times. MEL, p. 291.

176 Burnham had traveled with the train. Burnham's reminiscences, *Johannesburg Star*, December 22, 1923, CVI/2-1129–1130.

177 arrested Burnham for loitering. Burnham's reminiscences, *Johannesburg Star*, December 22, 1923, CVI/2-1131.

177 covered in coal dust. Burnham's reminiscences, *Johannesburg Star*, December 22, 1923, CVI/2-1131.

177 Churchill threw a fit. RSC, p. 505.

177   every accommodation was made for his comfort. MEL, p. 293.

177   "Goods arrived safely". Sandys, *Churchill: Wanted Dead or Alive*, p. 131.

177   "to dinner with a real table cloth . . . ". *Morning Post*, January 24, 1900.

177   cost the British nearly twelve hundred men. Pakenham, p. 250.

178   dispatched Field Marshal Lord Roberts. Sandys, *Churchill: Wanted Dead or Alive*, p. 136.

178   "Am now writing 'How I Escaped From the Boers' . . . ". Davitt, p. 244.

178   "The 'Standard and Diggers' News' has been honored . . . ". Davitt, pp. 244–245.

Chapter 12: Back in the Fray

181   He promised . . . to reveal the full details. *Morning Post*, January 24, 1900.

181   "With the determination of a great Empire . . . ". Quoted in Sandys, *Churchill: Wanted Dead or Alive*, pp. 137–138.

182   "an hour of turmoil . . . ". *Morning Post*, January 27, 1900.

182   he visited a local hospital. *Morning Post*, January 27, 1900.

182   "Winston Churchill turned up here . . . ". Quoted in Gilbert, *Churchill: A Life*, p. 121.

182   It now lay in British hands. *Morning Post*, January 27, 1900.

182   "has stood two months' siege and bombardment". *Morning Post*, January 27, 1900.

183   Churchill pondered the horrific scenes. *Morning Post*, January 27, 1900.

183   "The desire of murder . . . ". *Morning Post*, January 27, 1900.

184   "roast beef, plumb pudding . . . ". *Morning Post*, February 5, 1900.

184   eased the boredom of camp life. *Morning Post*, February 5, 1900.

184   lay in his tent listening. *Morning Post*, February 6, 1900.

184   Speculation in the camp . . . ran wild. *Morning Post*, February 6, 1900.

185   artillery began blasting the enemy's front. *Morning Post*, February 6, 1900.

185   diversionary tactic had done the trick. *Morning Post*, February 6, 1900.

185   reached a favorable conclusion. WSC to Lady Randolph, January 6, 1900, CVi/2-1143.

185 "satisfactory—though there is . . . ". WSC to Lady Randolph, January 6, 1900, CV1/2-1143.

186 opposing beams of light. *Morning Post*, February 6, 1900.

186 "Battles now-a-days are fought . . . ". *Morning Post*, February 6, 1900.

186 "body-snatchers," as the soldiers. *Morning Post*, February 13, 1900.

187 "at the price of killing him on the fourth". *Morning Post*, February 13, 1900.

187 "19,000 infantry, 8,000 cavalry, and 60 guns". *Morning Post*, February 13, 1900.

187 "Buller started out full of determination . . . ". Quoted in Manchester, *Visions of Glory*, p. 317.

187 only one man suitable for the job. WSC to Pamela Plowden, January 10, 1900, CV1/2-1144.

187 Buller's present plan called for one-third. Sandys, *Churchill: Wanted Dead or Alive*, pp. 149–150; Raugh, pp. 308–309.

188 the cavalry retired strong in the belief. "The Passage of the Tugela," *Morning Post*, February 17, 1900.

188 gun crews claimed to have caused . . . considerable grief. "Five Days' Action at Spion Kop," *Morning Post*, February 17, 1900.

188 would entail unnecessary risk and horrendous losses. "Five Days' Action at Spion Kop," *Morning Post*, February 17, 1900.

188 constitute "a moral defeat". "Five Days Action at Spion Kop," *Morning Post*, February 17, 1900.

188 "to attack Spion Kop by night . . . ". "Five Days' Action at Spion Kop," *Morning Post*, February 17, 1900.

188 an attack force composed of. "Five Days' Action at Spion Kop," *Morning Post*, February 17, 1900.

189 Realizing the hilltop's strategic importance. "Five Days' Action at Spion Kop," *Morning Post*, February 17, 1900.

189 "We should have had the whole hill". Quoted in Pemberton, pp. 175–176.

189 "No words in these days . . . ". "Five Days' Action at Spion Kop," *Morning Post*, February 17, 1900.

190 Boer guns hammering the summit. MEL, p. 308.

190 took off for Spion Kop to assess the situation. "Five Days' Action at Spion Kop," *Morning Post*, February 17, 1900.

190 on his way up the slope. "Five Days' Action at Spion Kop," *Morning Post*, February 17, 1900.

190   "The dead and injured, smashed . . . ". "Five Days' Action at Spion Kop," *Morning Post*, February 17, 1900.

191   present a full report to Warren. MEL, p. 309.

191   Churchill returned to Spion Kop. "Five Days' Action at Spion Kop," *Morning Post*, February 17, 1900.

191   "had fought for him like lions . . . ". "Five Days' Action at Spion Kop," *Morning Post*, February 17, 1900.

191–192   "Better six good battalions . . . ". "Five Days' Action at Spion Kop," *Morning Post*, February 17, 1900.

192   shadowy figures moving among some scorched trees. MEL, p. 310.

192   Thorneycroft to second-guess his decision. MEL, p. 310.

192   maintained an outwardly calm demeanor. MEL, p. 310.

192   "We have approached, tested, and assailed . . . ". "Five Days' Action at Spion Kop," *Morning Post*, February 17, 1900.

192   "It redounds to the honor of the soldiers . . . " "Five Days' Action at Spion Kop," *Morning Post*, February 17, 1900.

193   "All baggage to move east . . . ". *Morning Post*, March 5, 1900.

193   The horrendous sacrifice . . . had been for nothing. *Morning Post*, March 5, 1900.

193   the Boers had considered the battle lost. Sandys, *Churchill: Wanted Dead or Alive*, p. 164.

193   "would not, could not suffer . . . ". Sandys, *Churchill: Wanted Dead or Alive*, p. 165.

193   slow-moving targets for the nearby Boer guns. *Morning Post*, March 5, 1900.

193   five days . . . spent under continual fire. WSC to Pamela Plowden, January 28, 1900, CV1/2-1146.

194   one of the most awful things. WSC to Pamela Plowden, January 28, 1900, CV1/2-1147.

194   as one might enjoy a pleasure cruise. MEL, p. 317.

194   named the . . . gun in her honor. MEL, p. 317.

194   "the Boers had fortified by four tiers . . . ". *Morning Post*, March 10, 1900.

194   lobbing shells along the army's artillery line. *Morning Post*, March 10, 1900.

195   "seven officers and . . . ". *Morning Post*, March 10, 1900.

195   "had retired before the attack . . . ". *Morning Post*, March 10, 1900.

195   share a blanket with his regiment's colonel. MEL, p. 314.

195   hauling their big guns up and down hills. *Morning Post*, March 10, 1900.

196   all . . . had ended in rout and ruin. *Morning Post*, March 10, 1900.

196   as enjoyable as his time on the North-West Frontier. MEL, p. 315.

196   "One lived in the present . . . ". Quoted in Jackson, p. 82.

196   Vital to the Boer's strong hold. Forbes, Henty, and Griffiths, pp. 240–241.

196   "rocky, scrub-covered hill". *Morning Post*, March 19, 1900.

196–197   three hundred rifles blazed from above. MEL, p. 316.

197   before men started falling from their saddles. *Morning Post*, March 19, 1900.

197   Boer shots were falling short. *Morning Post*, March 19, 1900.

197   a savage melee if not for the considerable distance. *Morning Post*, March 19, 1900.

197   lasted no more than ten minutes. WSC to Lady Randolph, February 13, 1900, CV1/2-1149.

197   "It is a coincidence . . . ". Quoted in Manchester, *Visions of Glory*, p. 320.

198   ponder war's random selection. *Morning Post*, March 19, 1900.

198   seizure of Hlangwani depended on capturing. MEL, pp. 318.

198   "all rock, high grass, and dense thickets". *Morning Post*, March 27, 1900.

198   struggled to navigate. *Morning Post*, March 27, 1900.

198   reached the base of Cingolo. *Morning Post*, March 27, 1900.

199   "but famous to the uttermost ends of the earth". *Morning Post*, March 27, 1900.

Chapter 13: Blood and Fury

201   "the restless sleep of men who had done great things". Danes, p. 691.

201   Two miles of Boer fortifications. Danes, p. 691.

201   "So it came to pass". Danes, p. 692.

202   thought the move a monumental blunder. MEL, p. 320.

202   "I am to be of use". WSC to Pamela Plowden, February 21, 1900, CV1/2-1151.

202   having claimed a series of summits. Sandys, *Churchill: Wanted Dead or Alive*, p. 173.

203   clatter "of a tremendous fusillade". *Morning Post*, April 7, 1900.

203   Wynne Hill and Horseshoe Hill. Sandys, *Churchill: Wanted Dead or Alive*, p. 173.

203 "Push for Ladysmith today . . . ". *Morning Post*, April 7, 1900.

203 "Each man was forced to run . . . ". Romer and Mainwaring, p. 63.

203 Stretcher-bearers worked frantically. *Morning Post*, April 7, 1900.

203 "the Dublin Fusiliers, the Inniskilling Fusiliers . . . ". *Morning Post*, April 7, 1900.

204 "crowned with sangers and entrenchments . . . ". *Morning Post*, April 10, 1900.

204 they fell like dominoes. *Morning Post*, April 10, 1900.

204 "In the gathering darkness the Boer . . . ". Romer and Mainwaring, p. 65.

204 "a frantic scene of blood and fury". *Morning Post*, April 10, 1900.

205 Two colonels, three majors, and twenty officers. *Morning Post*, April 10, 1900.

205 six hundred were killed or wounded. *Morning Post*, April 10, 1900.

205 a shrapnel shell detonated overhead. *Morning Post*, April 10, 1900.

206 fell short of their targets obliterated the wounded. Romer and Mainwaring, p. 66.

206 "We have advanced, crossed the Tugela . . . ". WSC to Pamela Plowden, February 21, 1900, CVi/2-1151.

206 his nerves remained steady. WSC to Pamela Plowden, February 21, 1900, CVi/2-1152.

206–207 "despoil the dead and wounded . . . ". *Morning Post*, April 10, 1900.

207 "a ceaseless rifle-duel". Romer and Mainwaring, p. 68.

207 more disturbing by the raw, gaping wounds. *Morning Post*, April 10, 1900.

207 three survivors were found among eighty twisted corpses. Pakenham, p. 379.

207 Two miles downstream, to the right of the Boer positions. Sandys, *Churchill: Wanted Dead or Alive*, p. 174.

207 this would be the last chance. *Morning Post*, April 10, 1900.

207 "long-range rifle fire" if necessary. *Morning Post*, April 11, 1900.

208 "We soon had a capital loud noise . . . ". *Morning Post*, April 11, 1900.

208 "like a stage scene . . . ". *Morning Post*, April 11, 1900.

208 "it looked like one long line . . . ". Stott.

208 taken in fierce hand-to-hand fighting. MEL, p. 322.

208 The decision rankled Churchill. MEL, p. 322.

208 "loafers round a public house". *Morning Post*, April 11, 1900.

209 "Waggons were crowded together . . . ". Pearse, p. 235.

209   "I beat the enemy thoroughly yesterday . . . ". Pearse, p. 235.

210   "they gave 'em 'ell, sir". Quoted in *Morning Post*, April 12, 1900.

210   "Most of these poor creatures". *Morning Post*, April 12, 1900.

210   led him to a "bloke . . . without a head". *Morning Post*, April 12, 1900.

210   left the soldier "mightily disappointed". *Morning Post*, April 12, 1900.

210   The ride exhilarated Churchill. *Morning Post*, April 12, 1900.

211   "The voices of strong men break . . . ". Pearse, p. 238.

211   not long before "a horseman . . . ". Pearse, p. 240.

211   Someone started singing "God Save the Queen". Pearse, p. 238.

211   Churchill dined with Sir George White. MEL, p. 322.

211   no more than four days' worth of rations left. Pearse, p. 243.

211   reveled in being part of a momentous occasion. *Morning Post*, April 12, 1900.

211   difficult to discern the caregivers from the sick. *Morning Post*, April 16, 1900.

212   "Sun, stink, and sickness . . . ". *Morning Post*, April 16, 1900.

212   British had lost more than five thousand. *Morning Post*, April 16, 1900.

212   allowed a professional to handle such deals. A. P. Watt to WSC, February 16, 1900, CV1/2-1157.

212   "It will not add to the reputation . . . ". Quoted in Woods, *Artillery of Words*, p. 59.

212   had earned him £1,500 in royalties. Manchester, *Visions of Glory*, p. 321.

213   Churchill considered writing a play about the war. WSC to Pamela Plowden, March 22, 1900, CV1/2-1159.

213   "Winston Churchill is the one exception to the lot". Quoted in Gilbert, *Churchill: A Life*, p. 124.

213   "the garrison reverted to a full . . . ". *Morning Post*, April 16, 1900.

213   struggled to keep his emotions in check. *Morning Post*, April 16, 1900.

213   The men looked worn and battered. *Morning Post*, April 16, 1900.

213   "It was . . . a procession of lions". *Morning Post*, April 16, 1900.

213   Churchill railed against such attitudes. *Morning Post*, March 31, 1900.

213   "an eye for an eye and a tooth for a tooth". *Morning Post*, March 31, 1900.

213   for the ensuing peace to bear the ugly stain of racial hatred. *Morning Post*, March 31, 1900.

214   "I have always urged fighting wars . . . ". Quoted in Langworth, p. 195.

214   The message did not go down well in England. MEL, p. 327.

214   an outraged public. Sandys, *Churchill: Wanted Dead or Alive*, p. 185.

214   "From the military point of view . . .". *Morning Post*, March 31, 1900.

215   only reward them for their treachery. J. Cumming to WSC, March 31, 1900, CVI/2-1165.

215   Many feared the Boers would simply keep fighting. Jack to Lady Randolph, April 3, 1900, CVI/2-1165–1166.

215   "Those who can win a war well . . . ". Quoted in Langworth, p. 29.

215   Churchill set his sights on joining. MEL, p. 325.

215   ("the heart of the Boer territory"). RSC, p. 522.

215–216   Churchill realized he knew every undulation. *Morning Post*, May 14, 1900.

216   "all the luxuries of a first-class . . . ". *Morning Post*, May 21, 1900.

216   Lord Roberts and Churchill's father. MEL, p. 324.

216   war correspondents enjoyed a certain status. MEL, p. 329.

216   the obstacle to his plans was. MEL, p. 329.

216   Roberts had taken issue with a dispatch. MEL, pp. 329–330.

216   hands "of a village practitioner?" *Morning Post*, March 5, 1900.

217   care more about converting savages. *Morning Post*, March 5, 1900.

217   "Lord Roberts desires me to say . . . ". Quoted in Sandys, *Churchill: Wanted Dead or Alive*, p. 188.

217   He had every right as a journalist. WSC to Lady Randolph, May 1, 1900, CVI/2-1171–1172.

Chapter 14: Adventures and Escapes

219   "a town of brick and tin". *Morning Post*, May 17, 1900.

219   "crowded with officers and soldiers . . . ". *Morning Post*, May 17, 1900.

219   men from every regiment. *Morning Post*, May 17, 1900.

219   "One cannot see any gaps . . . ". *Morning Post*, May 17, 1900.

219–220   gray-haired man of diminutive stature. *Morning Post*, May 17, 1900.

220   Roberts walked past. MEL, p. 331.

220 not waste time worrying about it. MEL, p. 331.

220 "All right . . . you may try". *Morning Post*, May 28, 1900.

220 "We'll give you a show". *Morning Post*, May 28, 1900.

220 Churchill had promised the scouts. *Morning Post*, May 28, 1900.

221 turned and ran for his life. *Morning Post*, May 28, 1900.

221 was "a disabling wound". *Morning Post*, May 28, 1900.

221 "Death in Revelations, but life to me". *Morning Post*, May 28, 1900.

221 trooper Clement Roberts. RSC, p. 526.

221 "They won't hit you". *Morning Post*, May 28, 1900.

221 "But their hour will come". *Morning Post*, May 28, 1900.

221 "had thrown double-sixes again". *Morning Post*, May 28, 1900.

222 "but it's the horse I'm thinking about". *Morning Post*, May 28, 1900.

222 "Whether I am to see the White Cliffs . . . ". *Morning Post*, May 28, 1900.

222 "I acquit myself of all desire . . . ". *Morning Post*, May 28, 1900.

222 "I had another disagreeable adventure . . . ". Quoted in D'Este, p. 159.

222 hidden compartment beneath the floorboards. MEL, p. 342.

222 fanned the flames in . . . seconds. Churchill, *The Boer War*, p. 312.

223 "I have had so many adventures . . . ". Quoted in Gilbert, *Churchill: A Life*, pp. 127–128.

223 eager to ascertain public sentiment. WSC to Lady Randolph, May 1, 1900, CV1/2-1172.

223 Lindley . . . fell . . . on May 18. Pakenham, p. 448.

223 a bottle of shampoo to a piano. Churchill, *The Boer War*, p. 313.

223 thrilled by the British Army's arrival. Churchill, *The Boer War*, p. 314.

223 spread terrible lies about British barbarity. Churchill, *The Boer War*, p. 314.

224 men who had welcomed the British as liberating heroes. Churchill, *The Boer War*, p. 316.

224 The *Times* man wasted not a moment. Churchill, *The Boer War*, p. 316.

224 "History . . . does not record . . . ". Churchill, *The Boer War*, p. 316.

224 his stomach twisted by nerves. *Morning Post*, July 3, 1900.

224 set the tall grass on the slopes on fire. *Morning Post*, July 3, 1900.

225 "might have, at least, thrown themselves down". Danes, p. 1171.

225 fifty yards shy of the Boers' firing line. Danes, p. 1171.

225 "shouting as only Highlanders can shout . . . ". Danes, p. 1171.

225 came within yards of the retreating enemy. MEL, p. 342.

226 "the chill and silence of the night . . . ". *Morning Post*, July 3, 1900.

226 "Men of the Gordons, officers . . . ". Pakenham, p. 450.

226 the bodies of eighteen Gordon Highlanders. Churchill, *The Boer War*, p. 340.

226 fought solely for control of South Africa's gold mines. Churchill, *The Boer War*, p. 340.

226 had taken part in the attack on the armored train. Churchill, *The Boer War*, p. 342.

226 better to be taken prisoner at the end of a war. Churchill, *The Boer War*, p. 342.

227 Surely a Dutchman wouldn't notice. Churchill, *The Boer War*, p. 344.

227 entered Johannesburg, a dead city. Churchill, *The Boer War*, pp. 344–345.

227 put him in front of a firing squad. MEL, p. 344.

227 The horseman had an unpleasant look about him. Churchill, *The Boer War*, p. 345.

228 Roberts flashed an approving smile. Churchill, *The Boer War*, p. 348.

228 Johannesburg officially surrendered. Pakenham, p. 453.

228 "the most serious strategic mistake . . . ". Pakenham, p. 453.

228 "extend the fighting by nearly two years . . . ". Pakenham, p. 453.

228 numbered some 200,000 men. RSC, p. 528.

229 "a long tin building surrounded . . . ". *Morning Post*, July 17, 1900.

229 "Presently, at about half-past eight . . . ". Reproduced in Churchill, *The Boer War*, p. 387.

229 and wearing red staff tabs. MEL, p. 347.

229 going so far as to give a receipt. MEL, p. 347.

230 into a "wire cage". *Morning Post*, July 17, 1900.

230 "The victorious army then began . . . ". *Morning Post*, July 17, 1900.

230 *From London to Ladysmith* . . . had arrived in stores. RSC, p. 532.

230 "I am 25 today". Quoted in Gilbert, *Churchill: A Life*, p. 115.

230 "along a high line of steep . . . ". *Morning Post*, July 20, 1900.

230 the "Diamond Hill plateau". *Morning Post*, July 20, 1900.

231 "the country round Pretoria . . . ". *Morning Post*, July 20, 1900

231 1944, when Ian Hamilton published his memoirs. RSC, p. 530.

231 "Men and kings must be judged . . . ". Langworth, p. 14.

231 "The key to the battlefield". Hamilton, p. 248.

231 "He climbed this mountain as our scouts were trained . . . ". Hamilton, p. 248.

232 having lost 180 men. Jones, p. 121.

232 "the turning point of the war". Hamilton, p. 249.

232 his friend's "initiative and daring". Hamilton, p. 249.

232 only a "press correspondent". Hamilton, p. 249.

232 until they faded from view. *Morning Post*, July 25, 1900.

232–233 "May they all come safely home". *Morning Post*, July 25, 1900.

233 "a suitable meal of sardines, pickles, and whisky". *Morning Post*, July 25, 1900.

233 didn't have much luck when it came to trains. *Morning Post*, July 25, 1900.

233 "two dark horsemen" fleeing the scene. *Morning Post*, July 25, 1900.

233 "sightseers" who had disembarked. *Morning Post*, July 25, 1900.

233 came scurrying back. *Morning Post*, July 25, 1900.

234 the protection of its five-inch gun. *Morning Post*, July 25, 1900.

234 "was shunted several times during the night". *Morning Post*, July 25, 1900.

234 frost-covered ground crunched. *Morning Post*, July 25, 1900.

234 large bonfire feeding off a junked railway carriage. *Morning Post*, July 25, 1900.

234 "A loud monotonous chant". *Morning Post*, July 25, 1900.

235 "with the most extraordinary earnestness and conviction". *Morning Post*, July 25, 1900.

235 had so far sold eleven thousand copies. WSC to Jack, July 1900, CVı/2-1183.

235 "the highest sum yet paid to a journalist . . . ". Gilbert, *Churchill: A Life*, p. 131.

235 "I have about £4,000 altogether". Sandys, *Churchill: Wanted Dead or Alive*, p. 209.

235 "I make my bow to the reader . . . ". *Morning Post*, July 25, 1900.

235 "under a waggon, in the shadow of a rock . . . ". *Morning Post*, July 25, 1900.

Epilogue: Into History

237 only two weeks older than Churchill. Gilbert, *Churchill: A Life*, p. 133.

237 "bronzed and healthy . . . ". *Morning Post*, July 23, 1900.

237 "was continually broken by the arrival . . . ". *Morning Post*, July 23, 1900.

237 "the great operations are over". *Morning Post*, July 23, 1900.

237–238 "He is essentially a cavalryman". *Morning Post*, July 23, 1900.

238 "fight until they are either killed . . . ". *Morning Post*, July 23, 1900.

238 "eleven Conservative constituencies". Manchester, *Visions of Glory*, p. 329.

238 More than ten thousand people crowded the streets. Gilbert, *Churchill: A Life*, p. 133.

238 "the people of England will never . . . ". *Morning Post*, July 26, 1900.

238 "His wife's in the gallery". Gilbert, *Churchill: A Life*, p. 133.

238 Great Britain would face . . . invasion. *Morning Post*, August 18, 1900.

239 harbored any moral reservations about invading another nation. *Morning Post*, August 18, 1900.

239 "with a further 1,500 copies in the United States". Gilbert, *Churchill: A Life*, p. 136.

239 arrived in New York City on December 8. *New York Evening Journal*, December 8, 1900, CV1/2-1220.

240 "Mr. Clemens, introducing the speaker . . . ". *New York Times*, December 13, 1900.

240 "Mr. Churchill by his father is . . . ". Gilbert, *Churchill and America*, p. 37.

240 "he showed nervousness at first". *New York Times*, December 13, 1900.

240 "I have never liked Winston Churchill". Quoted in Jenkins, p. 69.

240 he and Churchill "were so alike". Quoted in Jenkins, p. 70.

241 he stayed over Christmas at Government House. RSC, p. 544.

241 Pamela was the only woman. RSC, p. 544.

241 would soon become Lady Lytton. Manchester, *Visions of Glory*, p. 366.

241 in which his greatest concern was. RSC, pp. 545–546.

241 "was to be spent before the public eye". Gilbert, *Churchill: A Life*, p. 139.

241 Churchill took his seat in Parliament. Jenkins, p. 71.

242 who sat in the Ladies' Gallery. Jenkins, p. 72; Gilbert, *Churchill: A Life*, p. 139.

242 how they handled "native races". "The Maiden Speech."

242 "If the Boers remain deaf . . . ". "The Maiden Speech."

242 "held a crowded House spellbound". Quoted in Manchester, *Visions of Glory*, p. 344.

242 "forcibly recalled his father". Quoted in Jenkins, p. 73.

244 "won 37 percent of the poll . . . ". Gilbert, *Churchill: A Life*, p. 508.

244 "What part does Churchill play?" Gilbert, *Churchill: A Life*, p. 508.

245 "My good friends, for the second time in our history . . . ". Manchester, *Visions of Glory*, p. 360.

245 "Do not suppose this is the end". Manchester, *Visions of Glory*, p. 371.

246 "You ask, what is our policy?" *Hansard Parliamentary Debates*, p. 1502.

Index